financial industry. It is my sincere hope that this book provides the catharsis and serenity she sought, and that for the remainder of her life, she never again encounters anyone even remotely connected to murder.

Don Lasseter
2010

Murdered at Home

As soon as Joe Matise entered the dark house, he immediately had to control the reflexive urge to throw up. An overpowering stench of rotting flesh left him breathless. Before two full minutes had passed, he staggered back outside, with an agitated expression twisting his face. "Don't go in the house." Choking back his own emotions, Joe added, "Your parents are dead!"

Paramedics located the bodies of Brian and Jeannie Legg, who had died in a sitting position on a love seat, shot to death, and covered with blankets. Their remains, decomposing in the smothering heat, had been there at least five or six days.

The killer had shot the woman three times, once above the right ear, another at the hairline, and the final blast above her eyebrow. Two lethal bullets had entered the male victim's head, one in the forehead and the second near his temple.

"They were sitting side by side," Joe Matise later said. "I wonder now, did they know they were going to die? Did they know who was going to kill them?"

Also by Don Lasseter

Cold Storage

Honeymoon with a Killer

You'll Never Find My Body

Meet Me for Murder

Die for Me

If I Can't Have You, No One Can

DEADLY DECEIT

1

Visit from a Killer

Nothing in their imaginations, or nightmares, could have been more horrific to Jeannie and Brian Legg. They recoiled in disbelieving shock, eyes wide and mouths open, stunned and bewildered by the assailant who waved a .22-caliber semiautomatic handgun in their faces.

Seated side by side on a blue-and-red–plaid love seat in the family room of their spacious home, the couple, ages fifty-six and fifty-two, had been enjoying a warm spring evening watching television. Casually dressed, Jeannie wore a navy blue short-sleeved blouse and red-plaid shorts, which resembled the upholstery's color scheme. Brian, leaning gently against her left shoulder, also attired himself for the June weather of Phoenix, Arizona, in tan Bermuda shorts and a coral-beige–plaid sport shirt. Tired after a day of shopping and a family dinner, both had slipped off their

shoes and had left them lying on the floor close to their bare feet.

Neither Brian nor Jeannie could have conceived the possibility of being violated in this manner. Nor did they grasp the reality of a life-threatening crisis. The overt signals of intention to murder them made no sense at all.

Without any hint of mercy, though, the gun wielder aimed the muzzle toward the right side of Jeannie Legg's head, at nearly point-blank range, and pulled the trigger twice.

Horrified and outraged, Brian started to lunge upward, when he heard another blast from the semi-automatic. A bullet glanced off a magazine lying on a glass-topped end table next to him, tore through a potted plant, and disappeared into the wall. Still in the split-second process of rising, Brian didn't make it, because the pistol struck him hard on the right temple and thudded against his forehead, just above the left eye. Dazed, he sank back onto the couch in a sitting position. A fourth detonation ended Brian's life with a bullet into his temple.

Just to make certain that neither of the victims would survive, the killer delivered coup de grace shots into both of their heads.

Then the plunder began. An expensive, sparkling solitaire-diamond ring, along with a gold wedding band, was pulled from the limp third finger of Jeannie's left hand. With the speed of a hungry scavenger, greedy claws emptied Brian's pockets, taking his wallet and credit cards. Ransacking drawers in other rooms, the thief snatched checkbooks and more credit cards.

Returning to the pair of dead victims, the killer chose for some reason to cover the gruesome work with blankets

dragged from an adjacent master bedroom. First a blue-and-pink-flowered comforter was stretched over their legs and laps; then a thick quilt concealed their upper bodies. As blood seeped through the two layers, a gray-striped white blanket was settled over the victims' heads. Two yards of hemp twine was peeled from a roll and used to lash down the improvised shrouds. In addition, the cold-blooded assassin used great care in closing windows, drapes, shutters, and switching off every light inside the house.

Jeannie and Brian Legg would repose in the hot, silent, dark room for almost six days before finally being discovered.

2

Did They Know
They Were Going to Die?

Tightening knots of tension twisted inside George Price's (pseudonym) stomach like a hangman's noose as he tried, for what seemed like the hundredth time, to telephone his mother and stepfather. Usually, the former U.S. Air Force captain, now an executive in a technology firm, had no trouble reaching them on a weekly basis, and he had last connected by telephone on Saturday morning, June 8, 1996. It had been a fun chat. A friend of Price's, planning to celebrate his seventy-fifth birthday, had asked George and his wife if they could teach him to do the cha-cha. They had laughed and said they didn't know that dance, but perhaps George's stepfather, Brian, did.

"Sure," Brian had said, with his usual boisterous laugh. "I'll be glad to show you when we get together next weekend for Father's Day."

Now, with the date rapidly approaching, George wanted to arrange details of the family gathering. He had called Brian and Jeannie Legg's residential line repeatedly, beginning on Tuesday, but reached no one. Several more attempts to make contact through their home business number at least allowed him to leave messages on an answering machine. But they had not responded. Never before had his mom or stepfather failed to return telephone calls; usually, they got back within a matter of hours. And any planned trips were always preceded by advance notification to the offspring.

It did nothing to soothe his anxiety when George called a few hotels his parents might patronize, only to hit more dead ends. Inquiries to other relatives met equally disappointing failure.

Separated from them by about 115 miles, the distance between his Tucson home and the Phoenix suburb where Brian and Jeannie lived, Price thought about making the trip just to satisfy himself that nothing disastrous had happened. First, though, he decided to telephone a cousin, Joe Matise, who lived in a neighborhood not far from the Leggs' upscale home.

"Joe," George said, trying to hide the deep concern in his voice, "I can't reach Mom and Dad. Could you do me a big favor and drive over there to see if they are okay?" Matise readily agreed to see what he could find out. In less than two hours, he called back to say he had gone over to the house on 14th Street, rang the bell, knocked loudly, and walked all around it. But no one appeared to be home.

For two more days, George continued attempts to contact his parents, still without success. At last, on Saturday, June 15, Price, with his wife Diana (pseudonym),

drove northwest on Interstate 10 for nearly two hours. Strained with anxiety, he steered into a tract of expensive homes, custom built in the preceding two years. The modern development covered a low slope of dry, rocky desert terrain set against a backdrop of rugged mountains, ten miles outside of Phoenix. Called Ahwatukee, probably from an ancient Native American name meaning "land on the other side of the hill," the community included a string of real estate developments. Each cluster of houses bore picturesque names, such as Desert View, Paradise Valley, and Camelback, which described a humpback mountain near the Gila River Indian Community (GRIC).

On that June afternoon, with the clear sky scorched by desert sun, George and his wife still held out hope their trip would have a happy ending. After turning into the short cul-de-sac of 14th Street at 1:30 P.M., George parked in the driveway situated on an expansive corner lot. He and Diana had been there many times, and they thought Brian and Jeannie had chosen well when they bought the place in the previous year. The tract featured spacious lots and gorgeous homes, many with swimming pools. Xerophilous landscaping, with dry, rocky ground cover and desert plants, would need little watering or maintenance. The backdrop of ragged, boulder-strewn, purple hills fit perfectly with the ancient geographic ambience of Arizona, marred only by several distant communications towers on top of the ridge.

Emerging from the car, George and his wife looked for some signs of life, but they found only eerie, empty silence. Nothing about the two-story, Spanish-style sandy beige structure indicated catastrophic

events. No broken windows. No signs of forced entry. Oddly, though, the bulb was illuminated in a lamp fixture on the garage exterior. Brian would never allow that to happen in the daytime.

A sense of doom hovered over the worried couple.

Repeating the same steps taken by Matise on Thursday, George and Diana walked under the towering entry arch, knocked, rang the doorbell several times, and yelled his parents' names. Price considered using the spare house key he had brought along, but some deep, fearful intuition blocked him from doing so. Attempts to peer through giant arched windows proved futile, since interior drapes and blinds obscured any possible view. This alarmed George, as he knew the Leggs preferred plenty of light and ventilation.

Using his key to a gate next to the garage, George and Diana entered the backyard. They turned near a sparkling swimming pool and skirted the barbecue pit Brian and Jeannie had built. Under a roofed patio, they cupped hands at the sides of their foreheads in futile attempts to peer through windows. Only one glass pane at the back offered the slightest of views inside, and Diana could barely see blankets on a love seat. She told George that it looked like someone might be asleep under the comforter. That only heightened their fear.

Back at the front entry, George used his cell phone to call Joe Matise and asked him to come over. Later explaining it, George said, "I had a suspicion something had happened, and I wanted Joe there. I contemplated calling the police, but I wanted him there first." Since Matise already had made the inspection on Thursday, Price reasoned, "we wanted to make sure

that things looked as they did when he walked around the house."

While they waited for Joe's arrival, events of the past skipped through George's mind in a montage, like in a music video. His mother, Palma Jean, better known as "Jeannie," had given birth to three children with her first husband. A divorce ended that union. Not long after George's seventh birthday, Jeannie married Brian Legg, an officer in the U.S. Air Force. She delivered a fourth child, David, giving Brian a son of his own. Home, at that time, had been several places in Illinois and in Michigan. After the three older kids matured into independent adults, and young David started high school, Brian retired from the military. He, Jeannie, and David relocated to San Ramon, California, then to a country club home near Danville, in the San Francisco Bay Area. Both parents had dabbled with entrepreneurial efforts. David had met a young woman with whom he worked, and taken her as his bride.

By 1995, Brian and Jeannie decided to move from California to the dry, warm Arizona environment. Brian had tackled a part-time second career as head of the family planning division at the Gila River Indian Health Services (IHS). Jeannie turned one room of the new home into an office, where she ran a physician's recruitment service.

Other more troubling images blighted George's mental movie. While the marriage of Brian and Jeannie Legg provided them with apparent happiness, they had struggled with financial security. Several other family problems had created a certain amount of strain. David had found multiple ways to embarrass

his parents with strange behavior before marrying his girlfriend, Alicia LaFlesh, and joining the army. Shortly after George's young half brother had left for basic training, Brian Legg had suffered a heart attack and had undergone triple coronary bypass surgery.

Still, as the eldest male sibling, George always enjoyed the close relationship with his mother and her husband. He seldom let more than a few days pass without speaking to them, either by telephone or with a personal visit. Relationships with his sisters had been sporadic, with one of them choosing to have little contact with her family. He hadn't seen his younger half brother, David, since Thanksgiving the previous year, during a celebration of the holiday and David's birthday.

Joe Matise's arrival put an end to George's reverie. The cousin skidded to a halt at the curb and joined his relatives. After a short discussion, he said, "Give me the key. I'll go in and check it out."

As soon as Joe entered the dark house, he immediately had to control the reflexive urge to throw up. An overpowering stench of rotting flesh left him breathless. Before two full minutes had passed, he staggered back outside, with an agitated expression twisting his face. The odor also reached George's nostrils. Even Diana, out in the driveway, could detect it. Tears filled the eyes of all three people. Matise implored George and Diana, "Don't go in the house." Choking back his own emotions, Joe added, "Your parents are dead!"

A few minutes of overwhelming emotion wracked the trio. George finally used his cell phone to call 911. The sequence of people arriving amazed him. He later spoke of it: "Well, I remember the first thing was

the newspeople showed up. Following that was the fire people. Then, after that, were the police."

Fire department personnel entered the house before anyone else. Neither George, nor Joe, nor Diana went inside with them. Paramedics, who are trained to cope with the odor of human decay, located the bodies of Brian and Jeannie Legg, who had died in a sitting position on a love seat, shot to death, and covered with blankets. Their remains, decomposing in the smothering heat, had been there at least five or six days.

Phoenix police officers arrived soon afterward. Sheriff's coroners showed up to perform a cursory examination of the deceased couple and make the official pronouncement of death.

One of the coroner's technicians peeled back the gray-striped white blanket to reveal the victims' heads. The killer had shot the woman three times, once above the right ear, another at the hairline, and the final blast above her eyebrow. Two lethal bullets had entered the male victim's head, one in the forehead and the second near his temple.

George Price controlled his emotions enough to identify the couple as his mother and stepfather.

No doubt remained that they had met their savage deaths at the hands of someone else. It had not been a murder-suicide. So the attending officers and specialists left everything intact, pending the arrival of detectives.

Later speaking of the horror, Joe Matise said, "When I first walked in, I thought it was a suicide. There was no sign of a struggle." He would later change his opinion after learning of the multiple gunshot wounds. Pondering the horror, he turned philosophical. "They

were sitting side by side. . . . I wonder now, did they know they were going to die? Did they know who was going to kill them?"

The crime scene remained under investigation through the night into the next day, Sunday, the sixteenth day of June. Happy Father's Day.

3

Trail of Greed

Detective Ronald Jones arrived at the murder scene Saturday afternoon, at about four o'clock, along with Detectives Bob Mills and Ken Hansen. Jones had been an integral part of the three-man team, members of the Phoenix Police Department's (PPD) Homicide Unit, for nearly three years. When called out to crime scenes, the trio rotated duty as "case agent," meaning taking on responsibility for overseeing most aspects of the investigation. He later explained, "One time you'll get the case, one time you'll do the scene, and one time you'll fill in, based on the complexity of the case." They divided the work equitably, including witness interviews, searching for evidence, keeping records, or tagging along with the case agent to assist him. For this double killing, it would be Bob Mills's turn to be the case agent.

Tall and lean, Ron Jones brought to mind cowboy

actors from old movies in which Gary Cooper or
Randolph Scott tracked the bad guys and brought
them to justice. His deep-set, intense brown eyes, confident expression, and calm demeanor fit this image
perfectly. When he was deep in thought, creases appeared on Jones's forehead, and the dimple in his
chin seemed even more pronounced. Graying, neatly
trimmed hair, middle-parted and combed back, gave
him an aura of respectable maturity.

A twenty-one-year veteran of the department, Jones
had joined the force in 1975. He had excelled in the
fourteen-week academy and graduated with honors.
The first field assignment as a uniformed patrolman
took him to the Squaw Peak Precinct, where he
roamed the eastern-central portion of the city for two
years. Superior performance led to an assignment as
a training officer, showing new recruits the ropes,
from 1978 to 1980, in the west side of town, called the
Maryvale Precinct. The next eight years, Jones mo-
tored throughout the region as a solo traffic officer.
He often found himself conducting security measures
at special events, protecting dignitaries, or pulling
over speeders and DUI offenders. In 1988, Jones shed
the uniform to become a plainclothes detective. For
several years, he investigated missing persons, assaults,
and domestic violence. In 1993, he reached his goal
to join the homicide squad.

When Jones arrived at the Leggs' home, a pair of
patrol cars occupied space at the curbs near the driveway. Yellow crime-scene tape stretched all the way
across the concrete pavement and the front yard.
Jones parked his unmarked vehicle, climbed out, and
admired the awesome two-story structure, with red-
tiled roof, several gables, and three giant arches at the

front. The peaceful atmosphere seemed inconsistent with what Jones knew waited inside for him.

A lieutenant already at the scene briefed the three detectives, repeating details provided by the uniformed officer who had originally responded. As the trio entered the house, they passed a staircase to their left, walked through a hallway toward the back, and glanced at another short passage leading to a master bedroom. Just before they entered the family room, the detectives noticed a mirror mounted on the back wall over a fireplace. Its grisly reflection enabled them to see the bodies of Brian and Jeannie Legg still seated in deathly repose on the love seat, covered by blankets. Someone had peeled back a portion of the gray-striped shroud to reveal only their heads. The room reeked with the odor of decomposition, and each of the detectives struggled to control gagging impulses.

Inside the family room, an officer pointed out lengths of twine someone had looped and knotted to hold the covers in place. An astonishing amount of blood had seeped through all three blankets. With the heavily stained shrouds removed, Jones and a criminalist took on the gruesome task of examining clothing on the bodies and looking for identification papers.

To experienced sleuths, small details can reveal important information. Jones and Hansen made copious notes recording the fact that the deceased male sat with his hips at the very front of the love seat, his feet drawn back underneath in contact with fabric. This indicated the victim's probable attempt to rise and stand, perhaps to battle the killer or to protect the woman, just before bullets took his life away. The

female's more relaxed posture, with her hips farther back in the seat and her knees at a greater than ninety-degree angle, indicated no attempt to stand up, fight, or flee. She most likely had died first.

George Price had said the victims were his mother and stepfather, but detectives needed concrete proof. The search, though, yielded no supporting documents. Later describing it in his typical laconic cop-speak, Jones said, "I became aware that identification of the two victims was missing, and that brought up a need for additional follow-up investigation." The inside-out back pockets of the male victim's walking shorts made it clear that someone had taken his wallet. The woman's purse had obviously been emptied of valuables. No driver's licenses, credit cards, or other personal documents could be found. This turn of events suggested a possible scenario—perhaps a burglary turned violent and culminating in tragic murder. For Jones, the missing documents left a big question mark. Commenting on the crucial need for these items, he related them to the tried-and-true methodology employed by homicide detectives across the nation. "Adults leave history. It's a tool of an investigator. People create a history of themselves through financial records and personal records." This history can often illuminate a path leading to valuable clues in identifying the killer.

While Ken Hansen took dozens of crime scene photographs, case agent Bob Mills conducted interviews of George Price, his wife, and his cousin Joe Matise. Price told Mills of two second-story rooms used by Brian and Jeannie as their offices. Jeannie had started a business called Physician Placement

Incorporated and conducted operations from her office. Brian used his room to work part-time for the IHS.

Hoping they might find other cards—either debit, credit, membership—or any plastic belonging to the dead couple, Jones and Hansen climbed the stairs to continue searching. As the designated crime scene processor, Hansen looked through files and drawers, while Jones, as helper, drew rough sketches of their observations and began a numerical list of everything collected. They located a variety of receipts containing credit card numbers, jotted down the information, and placed each item into an evidence bag. From this data, the team would be able to contact the issuing banks to see if any of the cards had been used within the past few days.

On the lower floor, crime scene technicians scoured the house for clues. Fingerprint expert Joseph Silva and trainee Nancy Ferrera dusted multiple surfaces with black powder and began lifting latent prints. She bagged an empty Pepsi can for more extensive scrutiny in the crime lab. On tile floors in hallways and the kitchen, they used an electrostatic dust print lifter. Hansen later described it. "It's called an EDPL. They place a piece of Mylar plastic on the floor and then electro-charge it. It is an attempt to pick up any foot or shoe print impressions."

The searchers found broken candle holders, shattered glass, a cracked vase, and a spool of binding twine on the bottom shelf of an entertainment center. In a hallway dirty-clothes hamper, one of the investigators discovered latex rubber kitchen gloves, with possible bloodstains on them. One officer searched the kitchen and even opened the dishwasher, where

he saw water glasses, silverware, cooking utensils, and four plates, all clean—nothing unusual.

George Price had mentioned to Mills that his mother usually wore an expensive diamond ring, more than three carats, given to her by Brian as a present for their twenty-fifth wedding anniversary. A quick check of her hands revealed that the ring and a wedding band were missing! When Jones and Hansen heard this, they made a point of searching throughout the house for the jewelry. The killer had evidently wrenched both rings from her dead hand and counted them among the loot taken.

While detectives and crime scene personnel initially labored at the Legg home, another man who would play a key role in the unfolding drama sat at home watching television with his wife. Glenn McCormick had been with the Maricopa County Attorney's Office for six years. The former professional football player still looked like he could strap on pads and line up with any team. Standing six-five and weighing in at nearly 250 muscular pounds, with thick dark hair and brown eyes, McCormick wore glasses that gave him the perfect image of Clark Kent. Some would later think he bore a close resemblance to actor Brandon Routh, who would play the dual role of Kent and the "Man of Steel" in the 2006 film *Superman Returns*.

Retrospectively discussing the case, McCormick said, "At that time, our homicide bureau had a rotation system. Whenever a homicide occurred, the DCA (deputy county attorney) would be called out to the

scene by the investigating agency." From the nine available prosecutors, it was McCormick's turn to stand by on weekend duty. He received the call from the Phoenix Police Department late Saturday afternoon, along with directions to the Legg home in Ahwatukee. "When I arrived there, I went into the PPD mobile command center, essentially a recreational vehicle shell containing an emergency office setup. Detectives briefed me on what had been discovered, after which I was given a tour of the scene inside the home."

McCormick didn't know it yet, but he had begun a project that would extend over the next four years.

As soon as the dinner hour had passed, Detective Ron Jones walked outside and began knocking on doors to canvass neighbors. He wanted to find out what friends or acquaintances might know about the Leggs, or if anything suspicious had been noticed within the last week. Jones's two hours of inquiries produced nothing useful, and he returned to the home's interior.

By this time, George Price had composed himself enough to answer more questions from Detective Bob Mills. Among other queries, Mills asked Price the names, addresses, and phone numbers of other family members. (This is an automatic element in murder probes. Key pieces of the puzzle are often discovered by interviewing as many people from the family tree as possible, as well as their close friends and business colleagues.) The distraught son gave the names of his two sisters, and his half brother, David. One of the sisters, he said, lived in Tennessee, and the other was

an officer in the air force. But he couldn't pin down
David Legg's current address. The youngest sibling
had left to serve in the U.S. Army shortly after being
married in February 1992. Since then, there had
been limited communication between Price and his
half brother, and their last time together had been
the previous Thanksgiving. George said he thought
David had been recently assigned to Fort Bliss, Texas.

Curious, Detective Jones recalled, "A family member's
whereabouts were unknown. We were told this
person was potentially in Fort Bliss, a U.S. Army post
in Texas. . . . I started following that."

Using a phone in the mobile command vehicle
parked in the driveway, Jones began a series of inquiries. First he decided to see if he could find out
more concerning the whereabouts of David Legg.
Making contact with the military provost, Jones
learned some basic information. "I verified the actual
name, date of birth, Social Security number of [Spe-
cialist David Legg], the person I was looking for. They
knew he was supposed to be on the base, but could
not find him."

Putting that issue on a back burner, Jones continued his probes by telephone, even though the midnight hour had passed. "I made numerous calls
throughout the credit card system. At the American
Express headquarters, I spoke with a supervisor, explained the reason for my calls, and was given information as to the use of two cards. I was told that cards
had been used on June tenth and June eleventh. One
of the charges had been made in Hawaii." Jones
noted a possibility that the killer had either fled across

the Pacific, or the card had been mailed to a confederate on the Islands.

No different from what ordinary citizens experience when trying to get information from large corporations, Jones found himself in a maze of bureaucracy. Still, as a law enforcement officer, he managed a few shortcuts. Having connected with a supervisor at American Express, he learned more about charges made to Brian's credit card. "It had been used for three major purchases, one being from Delta Airlines on June tenth. A second expenditure turned up with Dollar Rent A Car in Hawaii, and one more with a gift shop in Hawaii."

Another call to the airline company would have to wait for regular business hours. Jones considered trying some other numbers, where the charges had been made, but decided to wait. "I did not want to call Hawaii, because I didn't want to alert anyone on that side as to the cards being used. We had no information as to who was using them." Such calls, Jones indicated, might have the undesired result of tipping off the person making these expenditures, which could cause the hot trail to grow cold.

Back inside the home, Jones joined Hansen to explore every room. He studied numerous photos, many of them displayed on walls. With the help of George Price, the detective made entries in his notebook, spelling out identification of people in the pictures, including Brian and Jeannie, George, his two sisters, and David Legg, pictured with a young woman.

In addition to the calls made from their mobile command vehicle, Jones picked up telephones on Brian and Jeannie's desks. "I did last-number redials

for each one of the house phones, which captures the last outgoing calls. I also collected the answering-machine tapes." Most of the recorded incoming calls had been from George Price, trying to find out if his mother and stepfather were okay.

Coroner's technicians waited until case agent Mills concluded searching for clues around the bodies, then placed the deceased couple on gurneys to be loaded into a waiting van. They would be transported to a facility for autopsies, with special emphasis on re-covering all or part of the lethal bullets.

After removal of Brian and Jeannie's bodies, the detectives continued searching for any clues inside the Leggs' home. Ken Hansen later spoke of it. "A bullet fragment was found on the family room floor, behind the love seat that the victims were seated on." The location suggested it had possibly pierced one of the victims' heads. "And then there was also a bullet found underneath the carpeting in the master bedroom, which is immediately adjacent to the west side of the family room. It had passed through a wall and embedded itself in the carpet."

In an attempt to trace the path of the slug found in the bedroom, Jones and Hansen went into the family room and examined the stem of a potted plant that had been pierced. A hole in the Sheetrock wall next to it indicated the bullet's flight. By inserting a long, slim wooden rod through both holes, they determined the path of a bullet, which appeared to have glanced off a magazine lying on a glass-topped end table near Brian's body. Like an arrow, the rod pointed directly to the stray bullet, which wound up in the bedroom

carpet. Hansen aimed his camera at the reconstruction of an errant shot from the murder weapon.

Other evidence collected by Mills, Hansen, and Jones amounted to very little. They bagged and tagged a roll of twine, latex rubber gloves, the shroud blankets, some photos, and a stack of documents. No revealing forensic clues turned up. All three men realized that a long and difficult road of investigation lay ahead.

4

This Diamond Ring

Five days before the horrific discovery of two bodies in an Ahwatukee neighborhood, a transaction took place just a few miles away.

Monday, June 10, dawned bright, clear, and warm in the Phoenix area. A clean-cut young man, wearing a polo shirt and shorts, glanced at a page he had torn from a Yellow Pages directory and walked into a shop on 48th Street. By his side, an attractive, dark-haired young woman stayed close.

The proprietor, Warren Williams, greeted them and asked how he could be of assistance. The youth asked if Williams was interested in buying a nice diamond. "Of course," Williams replied. "That's our business."

Reaching into his pocket, the customer extracted a ring, on which was mounted an obviously expensive solitary gem, and handed it over.

Williams scrutinized the diamond and said, "Well, normally a stone this size, I've got to pull it out of the mounting because if I have to do the grading on it, it's the most accurate way. If I don't remove it, then, obviously, if there's any leeway as far as the quality goes, I'm going to make it in my favor. So it's in your best interest to have me pull it out."

The young man nodded and replied with a simple "Okay."

While the client waited, Williams stepped behind another counter to a repair bench, still in full sight of the young couple. He picked up a prong puller and carefully lifted the stone from its setting. Williams weighed the 3.3-carat gem, examined it with a jeweler's monocular, ten-power magnifying glass, called a loupe, and used his long experience to grade it.

Back at the counter, he said, "Well, you know, a stone like this—I'm going to offer anywhere from sixty-five hundred to seventy-five hundred." While speaking, Williams continued to examine the diamond from various angles, then said, "You know, I'll give you seven thousand dollars for this."

Keeping a poker face, the customer replied, "I'd really like to get seventy-two hundred for it."

"No, no," Williams shot back. "When I come up with an offer, that is really the offer, and there are no more negotiations involved with it." He glanced at the female, who had wandered up toward the store's front to gaze at other jewelry and talk with a saleslady. Williams made a mental note that she appeared to be of Hispanic heritage.

The young man, seemingly in deep thought about whether or not to accept the offered price, turned to

DEADLY DECEIT

25

the girl and asked, "You know, the offer is seven thousand. Should I take it?"

With a sweet smile, she murmured, "Yeah."

He asked Williams, "Could I at least have the mounting back that the stone was in?"

"Yeah, I guess so," the proprietor replied. "There really isn't much value to it. Is there any particular reason for wanting the band?"

"Just for sentimental reasons," the customer mumbled.

Later recalling these events, Williams said, "I kind of make it a habit when somebody comes in and tries to sell me something, to get a little background behind it. This was a three-plus–carat diamond and a young guy. More than likely, he didn't go out and buy it himself, so I asked him where he got it. He said that his aunt had passed away and left it to him. And I distinctly remember him saying that his brothers got the houses and the cars, and all he got was this diamond. And I said, 'You know, that's not too shabby. Normally, the story is your grandmother left it to you.' I meant it all as kind of a joke, and chuckled when I said it. But he didn't seem to think it was very funny. He just kind of stared at me."

By law, the transaction required documents to be filled out, and for the person selling the gemstone to produce photo identification. Williams explained this necessity, and the young man pulled out an Arizona driver's license from his wallet. Reading from it, Williams wrote on his forms the name "Daren Maloy," along with the license number, an address on 48th Street, and a telephone number. With the paperwork completed, Williams reached for a checkbook, exclusively set up to draw from a personal credit line,

and started to write. Frowning, Maloy asked, "Why
don't you write me a company check?"

A little startled, Williams courteously explained, "I
don't always keep that kind of money in a checking
account. But don't worry, this is my credit line. It's
good. I'll call the bank for you and tell them you're
on your way up there. If you want to go over there,
you can go ahead and cash it right away. That should
be okay."

"Where should I cash it?"

Williams gave directions to a nearby Bank of America branch, where he kept the credit line. With Maloy's
assent, he completed making out the check and then
called the bank. The shrewd dealer realized he had
made a pretty good deal, mentally estimating the diamond's resale value at maybe $15,000 or $16,000.

During this exchange, Williams noticed that Maloy's
female companion had stopped to admire a particular ring in a display case. He overheard Maloy discour-
aging her from buying it, and before walking out with
her, he said, "We'll just get something in Hawaii."

5

A Tangled Maze
of Paper and Plastic

On the second day of the investigation, June 16, Father's Day, Detective Ron Jones rose early, sat down at his home desk, and resumed work on the murder case. Neither the date of celebration for dads, nor the fact that it occurred on Sunday, would be an obstacle to Jones in meeting his job responsibilities.

Using his written notes and mental recollections, Jones began working on a timetable of the Leggs' last day of life. Later discussing it, he said, "By noting documents on their desks, records around the desks, and notes around telephones, we were given a fairly clear picture of the last activities in the home. Calendars turned to June seventh—notes of incoming calls, outgoing calls, all gave the impression that their last workday was June seventh, which was a Friday. Additional information found on a notepad in the kitchen—

specifically lottery numbers [that] came from June eighth—would indicate someone wrote these on or after that date. Receipts we found in the bedroom reflected purchases on June ninth. Those were the final dates in their lives we can account for."

From all appearances, it could be concluded that the couple had probably been shot to death on the evening or night of Sunday, June 9.

The last receipt from that date had been for a purchase at a JCPenney department store. Jones scribbled in his notebook a reminder to visit the well-known shopping establishment and see if a security video might have captured the purchase by Brian or Jeannie.

Jones next tackled the issue of airline tickets paid for with Brian Legg's American Express credit card. After learning about the transaction by a call to American Express on Saturday, the detective had been unable to reach a knowledgeable manager at Delta Airlines. He tried again, but he still failed to connect with anyone who could help. Persistent, Jones called the police desk at the Phoenix International Airport, known as Sky Harbor. He asked an officer to go over to the Delta counter and get a supervisor to call him back. This gambit produced immediate results. Within a few minutes, the on-duty Delta supervisor, Dan Barczak called Jones.

Jones requested a check to determine if Brian Legg's credit card had recently been used to purchase airline tickets. Barczak put him on hold for a short time, then came back with an answer. Yes, someone had paid for two round-trip passages to Hawaii, with a charge of $1,948. The tickets had been issued on June 10 for Brian Legg and Kimberly Miller.

Jones entered the development in his growing notebook. The murder victim, Brian Legg, had evidently died sometime late on June 9, so he certainly had not used his card on June 10 for anything—much less airline tickets. Several possibilities ran through the detective's mind. First, and most likely, the killer had used the card while pretending to be Brian, backed up by Brian's driver's license as identification. Or maybe the shooter had given the card to an accomplice or associate. Another remote possibility also existed. Brian's wallet, with cash removed but still containing the card and driver's license, might have been thrown away and found by someone completely disassociated with the murders.

Information given by Delta supervisor Barczak needed to be pursued. Later speaking of it, Jones said, "He gave me the information and I recall the ticket numbers ending in two-four-nine and two-fifty. He also mentioned that one of the tickets had been changed to a number ending in one-oh-six. As he checked into it, he indicated that it looked like the female name had been changed from Kimberly Miller to Kimberly Maloy. The alteration had been made in Los Angeles."

The conversation with Barczak ended at about ten o'clock Sunday morning, after which Jones left home and headed for his office downtown.

Before diving headlong into the continuing investigation, Ron Jones, Ken Hansen, and Bob Mills huddled with their supervisor. It was obvious to all of them that this case would take some concerted effort over an undetermined time span, which might cause some problems, with Mills acting as case agent. Jones

explained, "It was going to be a complex investigation. But Bob Mills was due to retire soon, and we realized this was going to be a little more involved. So we came to an agreement that I would take over as case agent. I was changed from assisting Ken Hansen, and would take over Bob Mills's role."

Shouldering the new responsibility, Jones resumed his probe of the credit card angle. From gathered receipts, he discovered expenditures charged to a Visa card issued to Brian Legg by the U.S. Pentagon. Legg had probably obtained the card while still in the air force. On the telephone again, Jones soon learned of additional purchases made in Hawaii with a second American Express card, up through June 14, no more than forty-eight hours earlier.

The previous day, Jones had found evidence of a transaction with Dollar Rent A Car at Honolulu International Airport. A call to one of the firm's supervisors in Hawaii resulted in a promise to fax a copy of the rental agreement later that day. It arrived at three o'clock, Sunday afternoon.

Eagerly, Jones pulled it from the fax machine and examined every detail. He saw a familiar name entered on the contract. It had been issued to "Legg, David Brian." But the signature at the bottom read, "Brian Legg." It made sense that someone who stole credit cards from Brian Legg would use his name for illicit purchases. But the name of Brian's son, David, on the contract suggested his presence in Hawaii. Could it be that the killer-thief knew David and stole his identity as well? Or was David somehow involved?

Two other details jumped out at the detective. The home address for the car renter did not match the crime scene address, 14th Street. Instead, a 48th Street

address in Phoenix had been entered. Also, the renter's home telephone number did not match either the residential number at the home of Brian and Jeannie Legg, nor the Physician Placement service operated by Jeannie. Jones entered these facts in his notebook, and made plans to check out the 48th Street location.

Recognizing that the Legg family had lived in California before moving to Phoenix, Jones put in a request to the California Department of Motor Vehicles (DMV) and the Arizona Department of Transportation (DOT), Motor Vehicle Division (MVD), to obtain copies of driver's licenses issued to the two victims and to David Legg. He also underlined at the top of his priority list a notation to find David Legg.

Checking again with Delta Airlines, Jones's blood pressure shot up a couple of notches when he learned that whoever bought the two round-trip tickets to Hawaii, in the name of Brian Legg and Kimberly Maloy, had booked a flight from Honolulu to Los Angeles on this very day, Sunday, June 16. At this hour, in the late afternoon, they could be somewhere over the Pacific Ocean, or nearly ready to land in California. Jones grabbed the phone and made immediate contact with the police station at Honolulu International Airport. He asked for an expedited inquiry with Delta. Had anyone named Brian Legg, David Legg, Kimberly Miller, or Kimberly Maloy, boarded the flight to LAX? Jones drummed his fingers on the desk and waited anxiously for the reply. It came within minutes. No. No one by those names had embarked on the flight. The unused tickets remained valid for the purchaser to reschedule a flight.

At home that night, the detective couldn't stop

thinking about the case, especially the complexities of obtaining and sifting through financial transactions with the stolen credit cards. He realized that someone with expertise on such matters could be extremely helpful, and he knew exactly the right person to ask.

On Monday morning, Jones approached a detective assigned to another unit, Brian McIndoo.

A twenty-year veteran of the force, McIndoo had spent five years with the Document Crimes and Forgery Unit. If Hollywood chose to portray him in a movie, they might cast John Travolta in the role.

McIndoo later described the request made of him: "Detective Jones came over to the squad where I was working and said he had an investigation [that] involved a lot of document materials in it. Since I had just come from the Forgery Unit, he asked me if I could help out, since I had quite a bit more experience in that specialty than other members of his squad. So he basically gave me an outline of what had occurred, what documents they already had, and banking accounts they were aware of. He asked me to contact the banks and follow up on all aspects of documentation and paper trails and forgeries or anything related to that matter."

Without hesitation, McIndoo agreed to lend a hand. His cooperation led to becoming an indispensable part of the investigation team.

On that same Tuesday, he started by seeking credit ratings for Brian and Jeannie Legg, along with a list of all credit cards in their names. It amazed him to learn that Brian had twenty-five outstanding accounts, including American Express, Visa, Discover, MasterCard, and others. And he used them prodigiously, as seen by twenty pages of open debt listed with his credit scores,

in the 700 range. Whoever was using the cards had a virtual gold mine available, and apparently planned to draw generously from it. McIndoo decided to start with plastic from Visa and American Express.

"When I contacted First USA Visa, and gave them some dates, I asked for information about any transactions that had occurred on recent dates." Within a short time, his fax machine signaled incoming reports, which sent McIndoo to the telephone for long conversations with several representatives of banks that issued the cards.

Meanwhile, Detective Ken Hansen, who had completed collecting, cataloging, and storing the sparse evidence found at the crime scene, drew one of the most unpleasant duties of a homicide investigator. Having been with the Phoenix PD for eighteen years, ten of them as a detective, the solidly built Hansen knew his way around the intricacies of murder scenes. If Ron Jones was the tall, slim Western hero image, Hansen was the thoughtful, calm James Garner type. The veteran cop's hair had remained dark brown, even though it had receded considerably. His oval face, somewhat large, sleepy eyes, framed by tortoise-shell glasses, and tight lips often reflected a quizzical or even skeptical expression.

Hansen didn't relish attending the final but necessary violation of the victims' bodies, but he accepted the assignment with his usual stoic demeanor. Observation of this gruesome procedure by a member of the investigative team is essential. The detectives want to know the cause of death and the path of bullets when a gun has been used. If whole bullets or slug fragments remain in the body, the detective needs to recover them for forensic examination. Also, if other

injuries are present on the victims, information about these can help the investigator build a scenario of what happened within the time frame of death.

It took Hansen less than five minutes to walk from his office on West Washington Street to the Forensic Science Center on West Jefferson Street. Inside, he met Dr. Philip Keen, the chief medical examiner (ME), who had occupied that job since June 1992. Deputy County Attorney Glenn McCormick also showed up to observe the autopsy. Keen escorted Hansen and McCormick into the laboratory to meet Dr. Udelle Zivot, the medical examiner who would conduct the procedure.

Hansen, McCormick, and Dr. Zivot were intimately familiar with the whole process, since Keen's organization processed about three thousand cases a year, which included roughly three hundred homicides.

Dr. Keen knew the autopsies of Brian and Jeannie Legg would be made more difficult by decomposition, which had ravaged the bodies for five or six days inside the sweltering house before they had been discovered. Keen later explained, "Indoors, with a temperature in the order of ninety degrees, the corpses will decompose. The process will accelerate if they are covered with any kind of fabric material, blankets, sheets, anything to decrease the air circulation. Within a day and a half, a lot of swelling and discoloration will occur."

The first step of postmortem examination is to cleanse the corpses, then measure and weigh them. Even though the after-death swelling made each body appear heavier than it was, both Brian and Jeannie had been overweight. He had stood five feet eight inches tall and weighed 225 pounds. Her full height

had been five-four, at a chubby 171 pounds. The doctor removed a gold wedding band from the ring finger of Brian's left hand. Hansen examined it with care, made mental notations, and had it packaged for use as evidence.

Jeannie Legg, Keen later said, had died of multiple gunshot wounds to the head. Three bullets had "entered the head on the right side, from the temple to the parietal area, from the forehead back to behind the ear. Each, a penetrating wound, meaning they entered and did not exit the skull, causing internal damage to the brain."

From his years of experience, Hansen knew that whole bullets are seldom found inside corpses. Instead, fragments are usually retrieved. He had learned long ago that slugs are fragmented from striking any bony structure within the body, especially the skull.

Aware that Detective Hansen needed all the information he could get about the angles and trajectory of the bullets, Dr. Zivot explained, "Because there was no perforating defect, we don't have a second hole to line up trajectory. We can only analyze the characteristic of skin injury, which is a little bit distorted." Trying to be as helpful as possible, the doctor offered her opinions: "Two of the wounds, right to left, appear to be consistent with contact-type wounds, slightly downward and from front to back. There is an irregularity in the opening . . . an elliptical abrasion cuff where the outer layer of the skin is removed and scraped away from the spinning bullet as it strikes the epidermis, and the asymmetry of that cuff shows a direction from which the bullet is traveling."

She also defined the term "contact" wounds. "That

is consistent with the barrel of the gun actually touching the skin at the time of the shooting."

Further observations regarding Jeannie Legg's body helped confirm an assertion by her son George Price that an expensive diamond ring she had worn was missing. "There is evidence that she normally wore a ring or rings on the third finger of her left hand, as seen in the change and intensity of the pigment and in contour indentation. At times, a person's hand tends to swell a little bit, and the ring is essentially a tourniquet around the finger, so it impairs some of the blood circulation . . . causing the indentation."

Turning to the remains of Brian Legg, Dr. Zivot noted the cause of death as multiple gunshot wounds to the head. "There were two penetrating wounds, which entered the skull. Only one exited, in the left forehead. The other one entered in the right frontal forehead, temple area."

No part of an autopsy is easy to observe, but perhaps the most unnerving is the use of a Stryker saw to cut away the skullcap and lift it off, exposing the brain. Dr. Zivot pointed out the bullet paths, as seen from inside the head. "The chipping pattern of the bone is indicative of the bullet's path of direction. When you put a bullet through the skull bone, it essentially produces a dissipation of energy in a conical, expanding kind of field, so that, in general, the entrance wound will be smaller than the exit wound. The bullet that went all the way through took a path right to left, slightly downward."

Other abrasive injuries to Brian Legg's head, said the doctor, had been made within seconds before he died, probably from being struck with a blunt object, such as the gun.

Always glad when this part of his job came to a conclusion, Detective Hansen, along with DCA Mc-Cormick, left with very little information that might help catch or convict the killer. Three bullet fragments recovered from Jeannie's head and one from Brian's during the procedure would be of negligible value other than noting the ammunition's caliber.

Nothing, so far, pointed with any certainty to a solid suspect. The old "48 hours" axiom stated that if a possible killer is not identified within two days, the chances of solving the case drop precipitously. In the previous year, 1995, nearly seventeen thousand homicides had occurred in the United States. Not quite two-thirds of them had been solved.

Hansen vowed that the murders of David and Jeannie Legg would not fall into the category of unsolved mysteries.

6

Don't Name It After Me

Often described by his family and acquaintances as a friendly, easygoing, jolly jokester, Brian Edmond Legg kept the other side of his personality a secret. The bitter, angry "Mr. Hyde" part of him was known by very few people. Some attributed these dark features to his soul-searing experiences in Vietnam.

A native of New York, Legg was born on January 24, 1944, at the pinnacle of a World War raging in Europe and the Pacific. Legg spent much of his childhood in the region, then later in Michigan. He reached his full height of five-eight while still in high school. His kid brother, Mahlon, six years younger, idolized Brian as a role model.

In 1966, with a war escalating in Southeast Asia, Brian enlisted in the air force. He completed U.S. Air Force Officer Training School (OTS) and soon found himself serving as a young lieutenant in Vietnam.

Brian's military specialty, as an intelligence expert, repeatedly exposed him to life-threatening circumstances on covert missions, each one more traumatic than anything he had previously experienced. He would later speak of the "intense fear" engulfing him during those mind-bending months "in country." Regarding it as nothing short of miraculous that countless flying bullets and hurling shrapnel never struck him, Brian survived the tour of duty with no physical wounds.

The existence of psychological damage would remain unmeasured.

At about the same time Brian faced the rigors of jungle combat on another continent, Palma Jean, mother of three young children in Illinois, confronted her own life-changing crisis. Her marriage had floundered, so she at last made the decision to go through a divorce. She took her young son, George, along with her daughters, Barbara and Gail (pseudonyms), to start a new life.

When Brian Legg returned to the United States, he was stationed in Illinois. He met the divorcee and fell in love. Jeannie had been born on Christmas Day, 1940, making her four years older than the handsome, if slightly overweight, air force captain who charmed her. Neither the age difference nor the presence of three kids in the relationship fazed him. Brian lavished affection on Gail, age eight, George, age seven, and Barbara, age six. The couple took marriage vows in 1970. Typical of military family life, they moved frequently to various postings, including San Antonio, Texas, but mostly in Michigan and Illinois. On November 12, 1971, Jeannie presented Brian with a son of his own. They named him David Brian Legg.

With Jeannie taking care of her three children,

plus the new baby, she no longer produced income from a job. They lived on Brian's military salary. Family photos would later reveal that Jeannie, an excellent seamstress, often made clothing for all four of her children. A family member recalled, "All of their clothes matched, cute little plaid dresses and boy's shirts in the same patterned material. They supplemented Brian's wages with food stamps, so spending money on clothing for the kids, who grew out of them in a matter of months, was not even an option."

An extremely attractive child, David soon developed some unusual characteristics. Jeannie told people close to her that the little boy could not stand to be dirty. According to her, if David played outdoors, he would find it necessary to come inside four or five times a day to wash up or take a bath. He kept his room spotless, and made up his own bed every morning. He brushed his teeth regularly with no coaxing or prodding. His older half siblings got along well with the family newcomer, and they spoiled him with loving treatment.

Being the youngest child, and one who seemed to be a perfect little boy, David received special treatment from his parents. If he erred, they would rationalize it. Through kindergarten and elementary school, if David found any type of trouble, or cut classes, Brian would make excuses and protect his son from any punishment. But, according to later reports, breaking the rules at home met with much harsher discipline.

David would later allege that his father delivered harsh penalties to him for infraction of rules during his childhood. He stated that he suffered rough treatment, up to the age of twelve. If Brian caught him

misbehaving or heard of any misconduct, he would order David into his room, force him to drop his pants, and bend over the bed. Using a leather belt, Brian lashed David's back and buttocks until they reddened with livid welts.

This corporal punishment was relatively infrequent, said David. Friends and relatives of the Legg family held the boy in high regard. He performed well in Little League baseball. And it impressed everyone when he became a Cub Scout, then graduated to the next level as an active member of the Boy Scouts of America. Eventually David would reach the pinnacle in the program, an Eagle Scout. This achievement placed his name in a pantheon of luminaries, such as astronaut and first man on the moon Neil Armstrong, Rhodes Scholar/NBA star/U.S. senator Bill Bradley, Supreme Court justice Stephen Breyer, electronic television inventor Philo Farnsworth, U.S. president Gerald Ford, human sexuality scientist Dr. Alfred Kinsey, film director Steven Spielberg, and hundreds of other famed men in a myriad of professions.

Brian Legg didn't try to conceal his delight at David's accomplishment, showing the face that most of his acquaintances were accustomed to seeing. As a general rule, people thought of Brian as gregarious, friendly, and humorous. On the other hand, he reportedly could be angry, explosive, and domineering. His two stepdaughters would one day describe him as "manic-depressive."

The pride Brian exhibited at David's achievement with the Scouts sometimes took a backseat to expressed scorn.

A story later circulated that Brian had used his car in an attempt to run over David. A member of the

family recalled, "David was out late, or was somewhere
he wasn't supposed to be. When Brian found out, he
went after David in the car. Some kind of a collision
took place between the car and David's bicycle. David
claimed his father had tried to run over him. But in
the parents' version, David threw his bike at the car
and it got run over."

Family insiders recalled that Brian sometimes
spoke in derogatory terms of his son and often criti-
cized him. David would one day indicate that treatment from his father had been "cold, intrusive, and
rejecting." In his recollection of childhood years,
David said his father set very specific rules to follow.
For example, when the family took a trip by car, they
had to get out of bed before dawn on the first day and
drive at least one hundred miles before they could
have breakfast. Then the next meal had to wait until
another three hundred miles had been covered. The
worst part, he said, involved bathroom breaks. There
weren't any. If one of the children had to go, Brian
would refuse a rest stop break, complaining that they
should have thought of it before leaving home. This
sometimes resulted in embarrassing accidents inside
the car, and the offending child would have to clean
it up when they finally did stop for gas or a meal.

At other times, Brian seemed to treat David as his
young buddy, chatting with him about many subjects,
including sex. David asserted that his father owned a
collection of pornographic tapes, which the curious
son surreptitiously viewed on occasion. He didn't
know whether or not his mother had ever seen them
or was aware of their existence. The frankness of his
father on these matters gave David the feeling that he
could take any problem to his dad for discussion. At

the age of thirteen, David revealed to Brian that he had experienced sex with a girlfriend. Instead of offering paternal counsel, according to David's recollection, Brian simply laughed and said, "Be careful. And don't name it after me."

An ever-increasing interest in sex and relations with young females would become a major preoccupation with David Legg. He would one day be diagnosed as "hypersexual." Not long after the frank father-son discussion, Brian discovered that David had made a staggering number of calls to "900 number" sex lines, incurring a telephone bill exceeding $2,000. For minor transgressions in household rules, Brian had reportedly lashed David with a belt. But for extravagant expenditures on sex calls, Brian apparently saw no need for punishment. Perhaps he believed that all boys go through a period of erotic curiosity and shouldn't be criticized or punished for it.

Interest in his father's Vietnam experiences also lodged in David's mind. In subsequent discussion of the subject, he recalled times in which Brian confided in him about the horrors of jungle warfare. He quoted Brian's description of the intense fear, saying that he "felt so scared you would just point your M16 and blow the whole magazine." David swelled with a sense of pride from Brian's claims of skill with firearms. "He always told me that whatever he tried to hit, he hit. He did what he had to do." To the impressionable lad, this invoked images of killing people.

In these accounts of combat, Brian told David that much of his wartime experience involved secret intelligence activities, which required a great deal of training and experience. As an example, he told of learning how to steal the identity of a total stranger.

In considerable detail, Brian explained to David how
easy it was to meet someone in a bar, befriend them,
and gradually gain access to the victim's Social Security number, driver's license, and other personal information. With that data, it would be easy to become
that individual for any purpose, including financial
transactions.

As an air force officer, Brian took advantage of the
opportunity for international travel at reduced costs
for himself, Jeannie, and the boy. David had the privilege of visiting Berlin, Amsterdam, Paris, and villages
in the Alps. Brian often expressed his opinion that exposing children to other cultures and new ideas
would help round out their personalities and expand
their ways of thinking.

Despite the perks of travel and other privileges,
Brian's career as an officer in the air force evidently
failed to satisfy him. His performance may have left
his superiors with negative impressions as well. After
serving twenty-two years, he had advanced no further
than the rank of captain. Acquaintances spoke of "in-
terpersonal" problems with military peers creating ir-
reparable friction. To friends, he had expressed
anticipation of promotion to major, but instead, he
suffered a setback. In 1986, orders came down reliev-
ing him from an important post as a military hospital
administrator, and reassigning him to a recruiting
office in Chicago. He retained his rank, but the message was clear: no promotion waited on the horizon.
This appeared to depress Brian profoundly, and he
decided to retire from the service that same year.

By this time, the three older siblings had long since
left the household. Eventually George and Barbara
joined the air force and advanced to the rank of captain,

just as their stepfather had. The younger sister, Gail, also an air force officer, had separated from the Legg home years earlier, and eventually she moved to another state.

If Brian had expected to find lucrative employment to supplement his pension after leaving the military, things didn't go as well as he hoped. For a while, he labored in temporary, lower-level jobs, including packing baby food, but he stayed with none of them very long. Taking another direction, he and Jeannie decided to give entrepreneurial efforts a try, establishing their own business. At first, they dabbled in importing jewelry to be sold in hotel concession booths. For the most part, this effort provided little more than an opportunity for extensive world travel to shop the wholesale markets. A few other business trials also failed to create any substantial income.

During his military career, Brian had been known to create the impression of wealth, which he really didn't have. He reportedly fell into a pattern of escalating debt, keeping at least eighteen active credit cards, and often paying off one by shifting the outstanding balance to another. According to David, this pattern continued into civilian life, eventually putting him on the brink of bankruptcy. Instead of making serious attempts to reconcile financial difficulties, Brian kept spending, buying expensive tools and equipment. He also increased the frequency of moving the family from place to place, to Michigan, Illinois, and eventually California.

These constant relocations created scholastic problems for David. His innate intelligence allowed him to make high grades, but the moves undermined any chance of lasting social connections. Rather than make friends, David occupied himself at home with learning

to play drums, and he achieved almost-professional skill. He listened incessantly to earsplitting popular broadcasts. Mötley Crüe, a hard-rock band, enthralled David, and he spent a good portion of his time concentrating on their music. He paid particular attention to the work of drummer Tommy Lee. Their albums, especially 1989's *Dr. Feelgood,* seemed to give him a sense of purpose. Alternately, David worked to imitate his other idol, drummer Lars Ulrich, of the heavy-metal band Metallica. Hits by either of these groups could elevate David to euphoric heights. But when his moods shifted, he would hit extreme lows. At times, he appeared enthusiastic and happy, but he would sink inexplicably into silent, deep depression. His emotional pattern appeared to emulate that of his father.

As a father, Brian Legg may have erred more than once. But he made efforts to please his son, if not always in the best of taste. In 1987, he took fifteen-year-old David to a Mötley Crüe MTV taping of their big hit, "Girls, Girls, Girls." They sat in the fifth row and watched as the band entered the stage on chopper-type motorcycles, roared the engines, then launched a performance of the earsplitting music. Scantily clad, gyrating young women performed sexually suggestive moves in ambient foggy red lighting. The song's lyrics refer to strip clubs, girls being best when they are "off their feet," and make mention of a ménage à trois. According to a relative's memory, David bought a copy of the tape and watched it repeatedly, thrilled by a short segment where the camera captured people in the audience leaping to their feet, dancing, reaching for the sky. For a fleeting moment, Brian and David could be seen, and in David's words, "rockin' out." He loved playing the tape and pausing it at that spot.

Between 1986 and 1991, residential moves forced David to change schools at least six times. At South Haven High School in Michigan, he started in September 1986 and left in December. He stayed considerably longer at Naperville Central High School in Illinois. In 1990, another move took David back to Michigan's South Haven High School in February, but he attended only four weeks before leaving again.

The last two relocations were precipitated by problems in the Legg family life.

During David's tenure at Naperville Central High School in Illinois, he befriended a fellow student named Dawn (pseudonym). From the age of thirteen, when he lost his virginity, David knew that girls found him sexually attractive. Dawn was no exception. They sought ways to be alone and acted out their fantasies. This time, he didn't tell his father about it. Especially when Dawn told David she was pregnant.

Maybe the shock of being a father at sixteen unbalanced David's logic. He handled the problem by stealing his parents' credit cards, and spending hundreds of dollars on maternity clothing, supplies for the coming baby, and furniture. And as he shopped, he incurred charges of $2,000 by treating himself to a set of drums.

If the young couple hoped for a future together, it soon dissolved, like most dreams. They argued and broke up. David, distraught and torn, salved his feelings by writing an $8,000 check to buy a 1985 Mustang. It bounced, and authorities arrested him.

Instead of losing his temper, Brian came to his son's rescue. He happened to know the judge who would preside over a court hearing on the matter. It amazed the prosecutor when the judge ruled that

David would avoid charges of grand theft. And the benevolent magistrate gave David a choice. He could either go to jail for a few months, or he could undergo psychiatric examination at an appropriate facility, to be determined by a mental-health specialist.

On March 10, 1990, a psychiatrist concluded that David "was impulse-ridden, self-destructive, and showed signs of sadness and depression." The boy also demonstrated possible bipolar disorder. In a written report, the doctor noted: *Before this he is described as an ideal, model child who was never late, accepted parental limit setting . . . and did well in school. Everything about his personality deteriorated.* Due to David's mood swings and attention-deficit/hyperactivity disorder (ADHD), the doctor recommended hospitalization.

Three weeks later, Brian and Jeannie took their son to Forest Park, Illinois, and handed him over to administrators of Riveredge Hospital. It would later be alleged that a physical examination revealed lateral scars on the youth's lower back and buttocks, for which David had no explanation. The psychiatrist had recommended a stay of six weeks, but his health insurance covered only seventeen days, so he was discharged on April 20. Doctors reportedly begged the insurer to grant additional coverage, but the company refused.

During the hospital stay, David received several medications, including Prozac, which is often prescribed to treat major depression and obsessive-compulsive disorder. Back in the Legg home, but still under outpatient care by the same psychiatrist, David continued to take Prozac for the next six months, and he appeared to be stabilized. Assuming their son

was cured, Brian and Jeannie saw no need to continue the medication.

To Brian, it seemed like the right time to leave all of these problems behind and make another move. He took his wife and son to San Ramon, California.

7

Cruising in Paradise

Friday, June 14, 1996, turned out to be an interesting day for someone named Hansen, no relation to Detective Ken Hansen. This person worked not in the dry, arid desert of Phoenix, but in the trade winds–cooled tourist Mecca of Honolulu, Hawaii. Kathleen "Kit" Hansen didn't care too much for the term "travel agent." She preferred "cruise consultant," because her specialty involved booking travelers on cruises around the Islands. Of Pacific Island heritage, she had lived in Hawaii her entire life and worked the preceding three and a half years for an agency in the Ala Moana Center mall, between Kapiolani and Ala Moana Boulevards.

At about midday, Kit Hansen received a phone call from a man who identified himself as Daren Maloy. He said he was interested in booking a trip the next day with the American-Hawaii Line. Kit explained that it

was a seven-day cruise starting from the Honolulu port, visiting four islands, and ending back in Honolulu. She asked how many people would be traveling and for their names; then she said she would check the availability and call him back for credit card information.

Maloy said just he and his wife would be going. Also, he didn't have a credit card and would pay in cash. In that case, Hansen explained, they would have to come to the office to finalize arrangements. She wrote down the names Daren and Cecilia Maloy. In less than a half hour, a casually dressed young couple entered Kit's office and introduced themselves as the Maloys.

Later recalling it, Hansen stated, "I would say he was probably in his midtwenties. Nice-looking gentleman. Average build. He wasn't, you know, overweight or anything. Just a nice-looking young man. The woman that he said was his wife looked very young. She appeared to be about fifteen or sixteen, to me. But she was of Spanish ancestry, and, you know, we have the same kind of blood, and we all look a little younger than we are, usually."

Kit greeted them with a friendly hello. Daren spoke a courteous "hi," but Cecilia only smiled, and said nothing during the entire meeting. Seeming a little nervous, she seated herself several feet away at the front of the office, while Daren took a chair next to Hansen's desk.

Employing her usual gregarious manner, Kit said she had managed to secure a cabin for them, but she wondered why they hadn't booked the cruise in advance. Maloy replied that it had been a spur-of-the

moment decision, since they were in Hawaii on their honeymoon. The agent smiled her understanding.

In order to arrange for transportation the next morning, Kit asked the name of the couple's hotel. Maloy said they were staying at the Turtle Bay Hilton, which is on the far north point of Oahu, about forty miles from the Ala Moana Center. Kit explained that transportation to the ship terminal would be available from the Ala Moana Hotel. Perhaps they would like to move from Turtle Bay so they wouldn't have to travel all the way across Oahu on Saturday morning. Maloy agreed, so Hansen called the hotel and arranged for the relocation.

In a conversational manner, Hansen asked questions necessary to fill out required forms, and booked the couple in one of the better (called Category B) accommodations, in cabin 296. She told Daren Maloy the total cost would be $2,315. He reached into the front pocket of his jeans and pulled out a startlingly thick wad of greenbacks.

Raising her eyebrows and flashing a good-natured grin, Hansen "scolded" him for being so careless and failing to keep so much money in a secure billfold. Maloy understood her humor and laughed. He counted out the correct amount, handed it to her, and waited for the receipt and tickets. Boarding passes would be available at the ship's terminal.

The transaction took somewhere between forty-five minutes and one hour, after which Maloy thanked Kit Hansen and left with his bride.

The couple did some shopping at the Ala Moana mall on Saturday morning and made some purchases before boarding the cruise ship *Independence*. At the terminal, they showed their photo identifications,

with names to match their tickets, received boarding passes, and settled into cabin 296 for seven days of leisurely fun.

Earlier in the trip, Maloy began recording their fun with a camcorder, while laughing and teasing each other. Acting as videographer, he aimed the lens at his young wife. In a mirthful voice, he instructed her, "Say 'hi,' honey. Hi. Don't turn away from the camera. I am recording this, you know." As she danced away, giggling and flipping her skirt up, he asked, "Are you scared of the camera?" In the next few days, with the camcorder running, they exchanged ongoing banter and expressions of love. He commented, "We should come to Hawaii more often." At one point, he asked if they had been having too much sex, mentioned making an X-rated tape, and told her to stick her tongue in the camera. During another sequence, she commented, "I made the Tasmanian Devil." She referred to a handmade stuffed toy resembling a Warner Brothers animated cartoon character. When they boarded the ship for a seven-day cruise, he continued recording the carefree adventures.

By all appearances, this young couple had no cares or worries. They were simply enjoying their honeymoon.

8

Three Missing People

Still pursuing credit card information on Monday, June 17, Detective Ron Jones heard from a local Bank of America manager who said he had located a security camera videotape of an older man at a bank drive-through window, using Mr. Legg's card. Jones hoped this development might be a new lead. But it turned out to be Brian Legg in the vehicle on Saturday, June 8. The investigators had estimated that Brian and his wife had been killed on Sunday evening, June 9, just a little more than twenty-four hours after Brian had visited the bank's drive-through window at the bank.

Another piece of information needed to be explored. The Dollar Rent A Car contract in Hawaii had shown the customer's Phoenix address as being on 48th Street. Jones contacted Detective Ken Hansen, who had left the autopsy lab, and asked him to drive over to 48th to see who had been living there. Within

the hour, Hansen called back and announced that the address was a large apartment complex. "There's no one by the name of Legg living here," he said.

Jones replied, "Can you check to see if there is anyone by the name of Kimberly Miller, Kimberly Maloy, or any other combination of Miller and Maloy?"

A short time later, Hansen called again. Someone named Daren and Kimberly Maloy lived in one of the apartments, he said, but no one answered the door. Since it was almost six o'clock, Jones agreed to meet Hansen there the following day, Tuesday, to see what more they could learn with the use of a search warrant.

Six o'clock in a Phoenix evening is still early afternoon in Honolulu, with the time difference. Reversing his previous decision not to arouse the suspect's suspicion by contacting merchants in Hawaii, Jones stayed on the job to make a series of telephone calls. He spoke to several salesclerks, but he learned little about whoever was using Brian Legg's credit cards.

With a search warrant in hand on Tuesday morning, June 18, Detective Ken Hansen drove to the Ahwatukee suburb and parked in the apartment complex on 48th Street. A uniformed officer met him there to assist. The manager provided a passkey.

Hansen later spoke of the search. "The apartment was clean and orderly, with the bed made. No dirty dishes or anything. Miniblinds covered all of the windows." The two cops looked first for a computer, which has the potential of providing a wealth of useful information. They found only an empty computer hutch. But it appeared, from an assortment of wires and a disconnected printer, that a computer had been there not long ago.

A drawer of the hutch stood partially open, and

Hansen spotted two boxes containing checkbooks. With care to avoid spoiling any possible fingerprints, he lifted them from the drawer, opened them, and examined the imprinted name. The blank checks belonged to Brian E. Legg.

In another drawer, the detective found a box full of business-style checks in the names of Brian and Palma Legg, along with a few credit cards for the businesses Brian and Jeannie had started. Yet another box contained information for a bank account owned by Daren Maloy.

Sifting through various papers, Hansen picked up something else he thought might be important. Several military record documents were in the name of Daren Maloy, including a U.S. Army pay voucher. Something seemed odd about the forms, though. Hansen collected them and made a note to do a more intensive examination, perhaps with the help of document expert Brian McIndoo, to find out if Maloy was still in the army.

Even more credit cards issued to Brian and Jeannie Legg turned up in the next drawer, along with a statement and matching invoice from a firm called Audio Express. It reflected installation of car stereo equipment.

One of the officers noticed an instruction manual for a video camera, but he found no camera. Nearby lay a key ring, with several keys attached. Along with the checks and manual, they photographed each item, then bagged and tagged them for identification and follow-up investigation.

On a tabletop, Hansen discovered monthly statements for credit cards issued to Brian and Palma Legg. They also found documents indicating Daren

Maloy had worked a short period of time for a local branch of Terminix, an insect extermination business.

In the bedroom, an open closet door caught Hansen's attention, mostly because of the stuffed animals placed at eye level. Most of them were Mickey Mouse figures in various sizes. Others looked like characters from Warner Brothers animated cartoons. The detective immediately recognized the Tasmanian Devil. When he moved it, he spotted something else far more important. He switched on his camera again and pointed the lens toward a plastic container holding twenty-seven live .22-caliber long-rifle Mini-Mag rounds of ammunition. The slugs found in the bodies at autopsy, and a spent bullet at the crime scene, were all the same caliber. Also inside the box were several empty bullet casings.

His curiosity piqued by the Mickey Mouse toys, Hansen wondered if a child perhaps had been living in the apartment. He looked around for more indicators of a youngster's presence. Inside the walk-in closet, he saw a few army uniforms hanging up, and then glanced at the surface of a small dresser. On it lay several doll-like figurines, no more than two inches tall. Even more of the miniatures decorated a shelf above the bed. It took the detective a few minutes to realize what they were. It finally popped into his mind that he was looking at an assortment of toys that accompany McDonald's Happy Meals for children.

Hansen continued looking around, and picked up a couple of diary covers imprinted with Mickey Mouse images. These all could have been the possession of a child, or perhaps a prepubescent juvenile.

Also in the same bedroom, Hansen found a small brown leather purse, the size that might be carried by

a teenage girl. From inside it, he examined several receipts, one from a store called Incredible Universe, showing a purchase of an entertainment center for $1,358.06. Hansen looked even closer. Someone had made the transaction a little more than one month earlier, April 29.

The officer with Hansen opened a laundry hamper in the bathroom and summoned the detective. From underneath other soiled garments, they pulled out a pair of tan shorts with an elastic waistband. On the right side of the crotch, they noted a reddish, rust-colored smear, and another similar stain on the outside of the left leg. After snapping a few pictures, Hansen had the garment bagged in a biosafe container for future lab analysis.

Elsewhere, corollary matters kept Detective Ron Jones busy all of Tuesday morning and much of the afternoon. He decided to seek more help in Hawaii, hoping the law enforcement agencies there might be as powerful and effective as the fictional *Hawaii Five-O* team depicted in the television series. Original episodes of the police drama usually wound up with its star, Jack Lord, telling James MacArthur, as Officer Danny Williams, "Book 'em, Danno." Nothing would have made Jones happier than to give the same order after arresting whoever had killed Jeannie and Brian Legg. Jones recalled, "I made phone contact with the Homicide Unit of the Honolulu Police Department and gave them information based upon the names we had, and the activities, asking them to query their data, or any sources they had available, related to the

names, the rental car information, or any other activity that might aid in the location of these people."

Several more queries to the U.S. Army, at Fort Bliss, Texas, and Fort Sill, Oklahoma, revealed only that military officials had lost track of one of their soldiers, Specialist David B. Legg. They would not confirm that he was absent without leave (AWOL), but they said they would continue attempts to locate him. Possibly, said a provost officer, he had been reassigned, and was on leave before reporting to his new post.

Frustrated, Jones then checked in with Detective Brian McIndoo to see if any more information had been developed about the use of credit cards stolen from the Leggs. Additional expenditures had shown up, as recently as June 15, mostly in Hawaii. The thieves had visited several ATM machines to withdraw cash. Unfortunately, they had managed to hide their faces from security cameras.

A few earlier charges, though, said McIndoo, had been made locally. For some reason, Daren Maloy had paid for a hotel room on Monday, June 10. This would necessitate investigation to determine if Maloy had occupied the room rather than staying in the apartment he leased with Kimberly Maloy. Another local transaction had occurred that same Monday morning. Brian Legg's oil company card had been used to pay for gasoline in the Ahwatukee area, just a few blocks from the apartment complex. Purchases had been made midday at a Macy's, and at a Sears outlet on the afternoon of June 10. That was the same day airline tickets had been charged to another card. So the thief had apparently checked into the hotel sometime late Sunday or perhaps in the wee hours of Monday morning, gassed up a car, drove to the mall

to buy some last-minute necessities for the trip, then headed to the airport. The ticket reservations were for a 4:00 P.M. flight to Hawaii on that Monday.

After June 10, all use of the credit card usage in the Phoenix area had abruptly halted. Then it had started in Hawaii, and ended again within a few days. "It appeared that all credit card activity seemed to stop on June fifteenth." Had the perpetrator somehow realized that police were onto the hot trail left by expenditures using plastic stolen from the murder victims? Would he, or they, change identities and vanish into a void?

Jones recruited another detective to check with the hotel and planned to later visit Macy's and Sears himself. Meanwhile, based on a receipt found in the Leggs' home, dated June 9, he stopped at a JCPenney store. A manager for the large chain handed over a security camera videotape of shoppers making purchases that Sunday.

From JCPenney, Jones headed to 48th Street in the Ahwatukee suburb, and joined Ken Hansen at the apartment complex a little after five o'clock.

At the detectives' request, the apartment manager produced the original lease application, made a photocopy, and brought it into the apartment. Scanning the information, Jones saw that it had been signed by Daren and Kimberly Maloy. They had listed a car to be parked in the allotted spaces: a recent-model Ford Escort, with a Hawaii license plate.

The Hawaii connection grew larger. And the military uniforms, plus documents found in the apartment, indicated Maloy either had been a soldier, or perhaps was still a member of the army. Jones wondered if Maloy had lived in the Islands or had been stationed there.

While Hansen and his helper wrapped up the search, Jones made a series of telephone calls: one to a police agency, one to Terminix, one to a pizza restaurant, and one to an auto stereo business. First he reached the Sky Harbor Airport police. With information that Maloy had registered a green Ford Escort for parking at the apartment, Jones wanted to know if it might have been left at the airport prior to the Hawaii trip. Later discussing the investigation, he said, "Based on the fact that an airline ticket had been purchased on June tenth, I asked them to check for a green Ford Escort that may have been in the airport property since that Monday. I also gave them the Hawaii license number."

On the Terminix call, he spoke to service manager Lance McMahon, who confirmed that Daren Maloy had worked for him as a new trainee, beginning in late May. McMahon recalled that Maloy had twice needed to leave early, before the end of the shift, during his short tenure, which lasted only one week. When he had abandoned the job, it had been necessary for a manager to recover the company truck Maloy drove. Daren had mailed the keys to him. Jones thanked McMahon and arranged for a future interview.

The third call by Jones went to the store dealing in automobile stereo equipment. A manager there confirmed that Daren Maloy had brought in a Ford Escort for installation of sound equipment.

A pizza take-out manager, on the fourth call, stated that Daren Maloy had placed an order on Thursday evening, June 6, and the pizza had been delivered to an apartment in the complex on 48th Street.

Since documents in the apartment indicated that the renter, Daren Maloy, might be in the army, Jones made

one more call to inquire, and heard confirmation that a specialist named Daren Maloy was indeed a soldier. But the officials, who couldn't seem to find David Legg, also seemed to have trouble locating Maloy.

Just as Jones and Hansen were wrapping up to leave at about seven, the phone rang. Sky Harbor police announced to Jones that they had found the dark green Ford Escort, with a Hawaii license plate.

Homicide detectives' hours on the job, including overtime, frequently depend on breaks in the cases, necessitating drastic departures from routine day shifts worked by most people. Ron Jones understood this and adapted to it with ease. While civilians enjoyed going home for dinner and relaxing afterward in front of the television, Jones rushed to the sprawling airport known as Sky Harbor. In a multistory parking structure for terminal number three, he followed a police officer to the Ford Escort. It amazed him that whoever had parked the car had chosen the more expensive short-term area rather than taking advantage of better rates at the long-term area about one mile away. The majority of travelers whose trips lasted more than a few days preferred the cheaper outlying lot, with shuttle bus service. Daren Maloy seemed extremely indulgent with the money that had belonged to Brian and Jeannie Legg.

Since no immediate emergency existed, Jones didn't need to break into the locked vehicle. Instead, he arranged for it to be towed downtown. At the Police and Public Safety Building, on West Washington Street, it would be secured in the basement. Prior to opening the vehicle for a search, Jones had to arrange for a warrant to be issued.

Before ending his day, Jones made one more call. "I

contacted the security director at Honolulu International Airport, a Mr. Morrison, giving him the information about two open tickets, two people with a combinations of names—Daren Maloy, Brian Legg, Kimberly Miller, Kimberly Maloy, or David Legg—and asked if he could distribute the information to all of the air carriers that might have a flight leaving Honolulu, to see if anyone using a combination of those names had made reservations or boarded. I requested him to let me know if anything came up."

9

Molestation and Madness

If Brian and Jeannie Legg experienced rocky times after she gave birth to David, their troubles paled in comparison with the nightmare existence of a girl who would one day become David's wife.

Alicia LaFlesh had blanked out many painful memories of her childhood, but what remained in her mind was still heartbreaking. Born in Groton, Connecticut, November 1969, she was the first of three children delivered by her mother, Carol (pseudonym). Her father, Joe (pseudonym), a U.S. Navy submariner stationed at the giant New London base a few miles up the Thames River from Groton, often spent months at sea. These long absences left the mother completely on her own. When at home, according to what Alicia's relatives told her, Joe spent a considerable amount of time in local bars.

An uncle openly expressed his hatred of Joe, from

the time he met him. Alicia recalled, "My mom's younger brother called my father nothing but a street punk who tried to emulate the classic James Dean look, with a much nastier attitude."

To make matters worse, according to Alicia, her mother sometimes seemed to withdraw from reality and refused to face problems.

The young parents' pattern of behavior continued when the navy reassigned Joe to Hawaii in 1972. His wife and daughter accompanied him to Oahu to live in Ewa Beach, just west of Pearl Harbor. A year after their arrival, following Alicia's fourth birthday, her mother delivered another little girl and called her Heather (pseudonym).

Alicia recalled occupying a "huge" yellow house, with a squeaky front screen door, and that a lady living across the street made "authentic" Hawaiian pillows for both Alicia and her baby sister. But these few fleeting pleasant thoughts were like a small umbrella in a monsoon. Mental images of other events and conditions brought tears to her eyes. "I've been told that my mom had several emotional breakdowns before we left Hawaii." As the problems increased, the amount of money for adequate food, rent, and decent clothing dwindled.

When his current hitch in the navy ended, Joe left the military. He took his family back to Connecticut, where he earned a sparse living as a house painter. In 1978, a third child arrived, a little boy they named Christopher. By borrowing money from Joe's relatives, Alicia's parents acquired a dilapidated Victorian house, not far from her paternal grandmother's home. Joe started a project of restoring it, doing most of the work himself. But the progress was often delayed by debilitating hangovers.

Alicia dreaded each day during that period of her life, but the poverty, difficulties with her parents, hunger, and social rejection were almost routine. Other memories, however, brought the most pain.

"The sexual molestation started when I was eight or nine. With my mother busy taking care of my little sister and infant brother, and no privacy in the house, a male relative would take me 'fishing.' We would go out on a little boat, a tin dinghy, or on an old twenty-five-foot cabin boat that needed a lot of work. I had to stay with him all day Saturday and Sunday. I always hated going fishing, hated that boat, and hated being alone with him."

Looking back in time, Alicia still struggled with her emotions when speaking of the sexual abuse. "One of the ways he would start it was to have me 'rub his head' or walk on his back. He would moan disgustingly. Sometimes he would lie on a couch with his head in my lap and make me rub his gross, thick, ugly forehead, with the reek of alcohol emanating from every pore. Other times, he would make me strip to my underwear, while he did the same thing, and start with the horrible head-rubbing routine."

Painful recollections of those events and a multitude of other family issues sometimes kept Alicia awake, even now. "My father was cruel to my mother. I watched him punch her in the face, throw her backward over a clothes basket, and almost cause her to fall off the second story of our old house. I remember being terrified that he was going to throw her out the upper-floor window and screaming at him to stop hurting her."

Alicia blamed Joe for an incident that nearly killed her little brother. "My father was very irresponsible

around the house. One day in his sporadic attempts to bring the old Victorian back to its former glory, he had been stripping paint off the doors and shutters, and left a brush in an open can of paint thinner on the far side of the yard. My mother was trying to do some gardening, and wasn't paying much attention to my little brother, about ten months old. He was scooting around in his walker and made it all the way to the other side of the lot. He grabbed the brush handle and pulled it out of the can. It was just dripping with old paint and thinner. I guess he thought it looked tasty and immediately pushed the wet bristles into his mouth. Terrified, I screamed at my mom that he was eating paint. She rushed him into the bathroom, put his head under a faucet, faceup, and turned the water on full force. I was yelling my head off and thought she was going to drown him, or that he was going to die from ingesting the paint thinner. He survived, but still has permanent scarring in his lungs and esophagus that show up clearly on X-rays. Thanks, Mom and Dad."

Yet another relocation in 1980 took Joe, his wife, and three kids to Spring, Texas. The small town is located just north of Houston, adjacent to Interstate 45. Alicia had no idea why they made the move, but she remembered that it was "terrible" as their lives descended into more poverty and misery.

Alicia's little sister, now six, had asthma, which required emergency clinic visits almost every week. They lived in a shabby, run-down apartment building her mother managed. It embarrassed Alicia when she heard other kids call her mother "the Dumpster lady," inspired by her mom's habit of rummaging through the large trash bins in search of valuables. The old

cliché that "other people's trash is someone else's treasure" still grates on Alicia. "I thought it was gross, and it really humiliated me to go around the complex with her. She also used to go to construction sites to find wood and materials."

The only source of solace for the young girl came from music. Dredging the ruins of her past, she came up with one cherished memory of her parents. "I came home from school on the first day of the fifth grade and told my mother I had signed up for band and needed a flute by the following Monday. They went out and bought me a brand-new Gemeinhardt flute, open-holed, the kind used by adult professionals." Alicia learned to play it, and spent as much time as she could in practicing and perfecting her skill as a flautist.

Once again, Joe and Carol turned to relatives—this time the wife's parents—to borrow money. They used it for a down payment on a house in Humble, another small town, located about ten miles away on Highway 59, a little closer to Houston. Alicia thought that moving into it would be a fresh start for a normal life. Their chaotic existence and the relocations had made it impossible for the three children to form friendships, perform well in school, or establish any lasting roots.

Instead of a new, better life, conditions grew even worse for Alicia and her two siblings. Her parents, she thought, didn't manage their meager income very well. In seemingly endless violent arguments, they screamed and cursed, terrifying the three kids. Lonely and unhappy, Alicia experienced few bright moments in her daily existence. But one came via a gift from her father's half sister. "I received a jade turtle pendant from my aunt and I wore it all the time." The

traditional mythology that turtles represent long life and stability gave her some degree of comfort.

When Alicia completed the sixth grade, her parents sent her to live with her maternal grandparents for the summer. She felt relief to be away from the turmoil temporarily, but she worried about the welfare of Heather and Chris. In September, Alicia returned to the same horrible routine. One month later, another crisis erupted.

"It was the fight of all fights between my mother and father. He punched her a few times and then went on a rampage in the house. He punched holes in the walls, even right through mirrors. He literally tore the cabinet doors off their hinges, broke windows, and basically totaled the house with his bare hands. He took all of my mother's belongings and threw them out onto the driveway, even an antique jewelry box, which had been a gift from my grandfather to my grandmother. It was smashed to bits, and I remember trying so hard to gather up the jewelry scattered all over the lawn, my tears so big and heavy I could hardly see. My father then decided to get the car and run over everything he had thrown out of the house.

"The three of us kids had to stay with some neighbors, while my mom got things together for us. The next morning, she told us to pack some of our favorite possessions and we drove away in an old wood-paneled Ford station wagon, speeding away, locking the doors, watching my father run after us in a rage. We took everything we could fit into that wagon, all the way to Orinda, California, to live with my mom's parents, my grandmother and grandfather."

In this turmoil of indigence, traumatic personal degradation, and flight, it came to the young girl as a

relief that her parents had finally split up. She hoped that moving to California might also end the repugnant sexual molestation, and could be the beginning of something far better.

In Orinda, on the east side of San Francisco Bay, Alicia, her two siblings, and her mother lived beside the grandparents' home in a fifth-wheel trailer house. It had no heating, so they shivered under blankets each night. To minimize financial burden on their hosts, the kids were allowed to bathe only once each week, and they ate the cheapest food available.

Despite all the hardships, Alicia still felt a sense of relief to be separated from her father. But he came back to haunt her again in California. Joe followed them to Orinda and, she later heard, secretly stalked all three of his offspring. "None of us knew it or saw him at the time. He eventually revealed that he would sit in his car, near our school, and watch us walking, trying to come up with a plan to take us away from my mother."

One evening, Joe showed up at the grandparents' home. After the children had gone to bed, Alicia woke up and saw him in the room. When she screamed, her grandfather rushed in, wielding a shotgun, chased him off the property, and called the police. Joe fled, but he still hadn't capitulated. He filed with the courts for legal custody.

His wife fought back. In her deposition, she asserted: *[I took] our children due to the [alcohol] use and physical violence of my husband. On October 22, 1981 he came to my parents' home in Orinda, where I am living and became totally irrational and uncontrollable. He attacked both me and my father and attempted to take our children in the car with him. He said "I am taking the . . . kids and if you stand in the way I am going to kill you." He has called several times*

but on Monday, December 28, he advised me that he was
going to California. I feel he is still [dangerous] and will
become violent when he sees me again.

With no mention of her own failings, Alicia's
mother gained legal custody of her three children by
court order.

At Orinda Intermediate School, Alicia felt like an
outcast. "It was hard for me to adjust. I was the newcomer, not 'cool' in any sense of the word. Other kids
teased me endlessly—so bad, in fact, that I spent a lot
of time alone in the bathroom, crying, when I should
have been in class." She had only one friend, a girl
who still holds a place in Alicia's heart. Correen De-
Berry, from a large Mormon family, treated her with
warmth and compassion. "She was so kind, would talk
to me, and was never mean. I will never forget her."

Alicia's mother met and mated with a new man.
When school ended in June, she took her children
to live with him in Concord, a few miles northeast
of Orinda. They all crowded into a cheap, tiny, two-
bedroom apartment. In September, her mother
tapped the life savings of her parents to borrow
money for a down payment on a small house in Pittsburg, on the south side of the Sacramento River, east
of Concord. Alicia enrolled in Central Junior High
School and took band classes. She depended on her
mother to pick her up each evening after practice
sessions and Girl Scout meetings.

Even this simple parental responsibility failed. "My
mom had some friends she used to play cards with,
while also drinking and smoking. There were at least
three occasions where she just completely forgot to
come pick me up from band practice. One evening,
I sat in front of the school from six o'clock until

almost midnight. A teacher, who was working quite late, saw me waiting and offered to drive me home. I remember the look on my mother's face when I walked in on my own, fifteen minutes after midnight. They were having the best time, laughing, playing, drinking, chain-smoking—completely unaware that she even had a daughter. She tried to apologize, but I couldn't even look at her. I felt totally alone."

While they still lived in the same river town, Alicia graduated from the eighth grade and began attending Pittsburg High School. She found a niche of self-esteem as a flute-playing member of the marching band, resplendent in their black-and-orange uniforms and performing with their Pirates sports teams. The experience provided the welcome opportunity for traveling with the group, and feeling as if she finally belonged somewhere.

Unfortunately, Alicia's life couldn't break free from a negative pattern. For everything good, something bad would happen. While Alicia was in the ninth grade, her maternal grandmother was diagnosed with breast cancer and passed away.

Financial difficulties for her mother forced another move. They found a house in a neighboring community, known first as Shore Acres, then Bella Vista, and later changed to Bay Point. Its reputation for rowdy residents inspired some to call it "Gun Point."

It broke Alicia's heart to leave the school and the band, but she had no choice. In the fall, she entered Mt. Diablo High School, and had to catch a bus at six fifteen each morning to arrive on time for classes. At last, though, she had made her final school change. She stayed at Mt. Diablo, until graduating in 1987.

Staying in the same "run-down" house for three

years did not make Alicia's life easier. Her mother had taken a new husband, a man only ten years older than Alicia. He didn't exactly impress her as a father figure. Another former U.S. Navy seaman, his service had ended with a discharge for bad conduct. The new stepfather pressed all three children to take his name, but Alicia refused. And, like her real dad, this replacement also drank prodigious amounts of alcohol.

Living conditions grew worse daily, especially for the kids. "For almost a year, when we first lived on Canal Drive, there was never enough to eat. For example, one time we ran completely out of food. All three of us were *soooo* hungry. My mother had put her wedding cake in the freezer as a keepsake. Well, with nothing else to eat, we decided, after they went to sleep, that we would just have to take our chances on enraging them. I could not believe how good an old frozen wedding cake could taste."

The stepfather also found a way to make Alicia uncomfortable and suspicious of his intentions. Later speaking of it, she said, "He tried very hard to get me to talk about intimate matters with him on many, many occasions. He would take me out to practice driving and would try to have discussions about personal things that embarrassed me. "

Soon after completing high school, Alicia started dating and found joy in having a boyfriend. But not for long. "My mother and her husband alienated him and we broke up. Not long after that, we lost our house to foreclosure, and then moved into an even shadier neighborhood and a smaller shack."

As her family sank ever deeper into debt and poverty, most of the money went for things other than life's necessities. Alicia tried to attend community college,

while working full-time at a fast-food restaurant and part-time at a convenience store, but she had to drop the classes due to exhaustion. Still, in order to help support her siblings, she found another part-time job at an ice-skating rink. There, she also found a new boyfriend.

Another crisis came when her mother lost her job. The distressed woman started pressuring Alicia to pay more rent. Recalling it, Alicia said, "Now, I had pretty much been providing for my family at that point for almost a year. I had managed to save almost nine hundred dollars, and thought about buying a car. Mother demanded that I hand it all over to her. I refused, and for the first time in my life, at age eighteen, stood up to her. She literally and physically shoved me out the door and told me I was kicked out. If I wouldn't give her the money, I was no use to the household. I had to call the police to get my belongings."

Alicia moved into an apartment with her boyfriend. The arrangement seemed fun and exciting at first, but after a few months, she felt the onset of disillusionment again. Feeling sorry for her little sister and brother, she invited them to live with her for a while, but it didn't work out very well. "There were so many emotional, mental, and social problems. I just could not handle being their parent. Now I felt doubly guilty for not being able to continue to care for them. They ended up in foster homes for a few years. Eventually they went back to live with my mom, but my contact with her became almost nonexistent."

Weighed down by guilt and stress, Alicia's relationship with her live-in boyfriend deteriorated. She thought she loved him, but they quarreled, and gradually all of the magic vanished, like fog retreating

back to the Golden Gate Bridge. "It just wasn't the right fit," she later said. "There were a lot of issues and it became dysfunctional. After living with him for three years, I moved out in 1991 and rented a room from a family in Pittsburg."

She registered with a temp agency, which sent her to a company that built electronic fish finders used by commercial fishermen and party boat operators. It paid well enough, and Alicia felt a sense of satisfaction at the assembly-line work, where she "installed the screens, corrected the pixels, and tested the completed units."

At the age of twenty-one, she also relished her newly found independence. Alicia had grown not only in her philosophical outlook, but also as an attractive young woman. Her sweet smile, piercing hazel eyes, shining dark brown hair worn below shoulder length, and a luminous vulnerability in her expression, along with a buxom figure, made an appealing combination.

That spring, another temporary employee caught her eye, and she enjoyed his flirtation. "We were immediately attracted to each other."

10

A Convenient Law

So far, the murder investigation had been disappointing to Ron Jones and Ken Hansen. While the apparently fraudulent use of credit cards belonging to the victims had created a trail of thievery, which might or might not be connected to the killings, no forensic evidence had turned up to point directly at the person, or persons, who had slain Jeannie and Brian Legg.

Cutting-edge technology, called EDPL, had been utilized at the crime scene in an attempt to lift fingerprints or shoe prints on a tile floor; it failed to produce anything usable. Hansen would say, "There were a number of smudged impressions, but nothing that would lead to any type of reconstruction."

A ball of twine had been used to lash a blanket over the bodies, but it also led to a dead end.

Bullet fragments had been taken from the bodies, and a partial slug, which had pierced a wall, were col-

lected and analyzed, but since no weapon had been found, the technicians could make no comparisons other than with a handgun of the same caliber. No shell casings had been seen near the bodies. This would indicate one of two possibilities. Either a revolver had been used, in which the casings would remain in the cylinder; or if it had been a semiautomatic pistol, which ejects the casing, the killer had carefully picked them up.

No fibers, hair, or blood belonging to anyone other than the victims had been found. Rubber gloves pulled from a clothes hamper had produced tiny traces of blood, but not enough to provide usable evidence. Thus, DNA would not lead to the killer. A sense of frustration gnawed at the detectives.

Ken Hansen drew the duty of searching the Ford Escort, which had been impounded at Sky Harbor International Airport and towed to the police storage lot on West Washington in downtown Phoenix.

After a technician had picked the locked door and opened it, Hansen meticulously examined the interior. A ticket on the console first caught his attention. Hansen recognized it as a parking receipt, the type a motorist retrieves by pushing a button at the entry and waiting for the gate arm to raise before driving into the lot. He tried to read stamped data on the lower left corner, but part of it was illegible. Hansen could barely discern enough to see that the driver had apparently entered the building at 1509 hours, or 3:09 P.M., but the date was blurred beyond recognition. In all probability, the detective figured, it was June 10, since the airline tickets had been purchased from Delta for a 4:00 P.M. flight on June 10.

In the glove compartment, Hansen spotted a gold ring, which he thought looked like a wedding band.

It looked so familiar to him, and it took a while for his mind to make the connection. The ring was a duplicate of one taken from Brian Legg's third finger, left hand, during the autopsy. Hansen wondered if this one had been on Jeannie's finger, along with the twenty-fifth-anniversary diamond.

Another piece of paper Hansen discovered in the car's trunk had been ripped from a Yellow Pages phone directory. Handling it carefully to preserve any possible fingerprints, Hansen saw that the page listed numerous jewelry pawnshops in the Phoenix area.

A third slip of paper Hansen found turned out to be a receipt dated June 10 from a Sears store for purchase of some luggage. So the car's driver had apparently been in a hurry that Monday morning to buy some suitcases and Delta tickets, just a short time before departing on an air trip to Hawaii. The pattern possibly suggested a hasty, last-minute decision to travel.

One more thing in the car caught Hansen's attention, and rang a mental bell of recollection. He noticed that dashboard-mounted stereo equipment, including a compact disc (CD) player, looked quite new and bore a Kenwood label. He flashed back to two receipts he had found in the apartment on 48th Street: one reflecting $500 for the purchase of a Kenwood stereo player and another one for installing the equipment.

While Detective Hansen completed his hunt for evidence inside the Ford Escort, Detective Ron Jones followed up on another possible clue. He took the ring of keys Hansen had found in the 48th Street apartment and drove to the Leggs' home. George Price, Jeannie's first son, had stayed in town to follow the investigation, and agreed to meet Jones at the Legg home. With Price watching, the detective attempted to

insert three of the keys into the front door's lock, without success. But the fourth one slipped in easily and turned the tumblers with little effort.

One of the keys appeared to be for an automobile ignition, so both men went into the garage. Again, with Price witnessing, Jones easily slipped the key into a door lock of an older Lincoln Continental, and then into the ignition slot. This experiment added one more piece to the puzzle, linking the occupants of the apartment to crimes against Brian and Jeannie Legg.

The key ring, Jones concluded, very likely belonged to the dead victim Brian Legg. But several documents located in the apartment had shown some connection to David Legg, Brian and Jeannie's son. So possibly the key could have been his. Certainly, it would not have been unusual for the son to have keys to his parents' home or to their car.

Jones had a list of questions he wanted to ask David Legg and hoped the U.S. Army people, with whom he had left several messages, would respond soon to notify him of the missing soldier's location. Of course, with his long experience, Jones had not excluded David from some level of culpability in the crime. The degree of his involvement remained to be seen.

Jones's desire to interview two soldiers—Specialist David Legg and Specialist Daren Maloy—climbed higher on his priority list each day.

Regarding Maloy, Jones explained the urgency of finding him. "Information we found in the apartment during the search made it imperative to find him and his wife, Kimberly Maloy. There were military records in there and uniforms. Some of the uniforms were marked with David Legg's name. Most of the military records were to a Daren Maloy, with a few to Legg. The pay voucher we

found was in Maloy's name. The odd thing about those documents was they looked like they had been altered somehow, and we needed to look into that."

Once more, Jones tried to obtain information from the U.S. Army by telephone. He asked if they could tell him where he might find Specialist Daren Maloy. Just as it had with inquiries about David Legg, the response didn't provide what Jones needed. The officials with whom he spoke said they would notify the detective as soon as possible.

The next day, Thursday, June 20, a new development led the detectives on a more promising path. Jones turned his attention to the diamond ring taken from Jeannie Legg's finger.

Arizona State Law, title 44-1602, provides law enforcement a valuable resource. Called the "Requirements of Dealers of Precious Items," the statute bylaws are:

A. *Each dealer shall keep for six months from the date of purchase of a precious item and make available on request of a peace officer:*

1. *The name, current address, date of birth and signature of the person from whom the item was purchased.*
2. *A description of the person, including height, weight, race, complexion and hair color.*
3. *Identification card serial number as required under subsection B.*
4. *A list pursuant to subsection C describing the items purchased from that person.*

B. *Before making a purchase, a dealer shall require the person from whom he is purchasing to identify*

*himself with a valid motor vehicle operator's
license, valid motor vehicle non-operating identification license, valid armed forces identification
card or other valid photo identification sufficient
to verify the information required pursuant to
subsection A of this section.*

C. *Each dealer shall, at least once each week in which
he makes a purchase, make out and deliver to the
local law enforcement agency a true, complete and
legible list of all items purchased during the period
since the last report. The dealer shall use local law
enforcement agency forms to meet the requirements
of this subsection if such forms are issued by the
local law enforcement agency. The list shall include:*

1. *The brand name and serial number, if
any.*
2. *An accurate description of each item sufficient to enable the local law enforcement
agency to identify the item.*
3. *The date and time when the item was received.*
4. *The amount paid for each item.*

On June 20, Ron Jones ran a computer inquiry to
a data bank required by title 44-1602. He entered a
description of the missing diamond ring, along with
the names Kimberly Miller, Kimberly Maloy, Daren
Maloy, and David Legg.

The feedback came shortly, listing a shop at which
a transaction had been made with Daren Maloy on
Monday, June 10. Using the necessary protocol, Jones

keyed in a few more entries, which led him to the shop's name and address.

Later asked if he had called the business, Jones's face creased with a knowing smile. He replied, "My experience as an investigator is, you do not inquire over the telephone to pawnshops. You go there and do business face-to-face." Pausing thoughtfully, he added, "The item you are looking for might not be there via a phone call."

Instead, Jones drove to the address, only to find that the business had moved. Another inquiry gave him the new address, a short distance away, and he hurried to that location. The place surprised Jones. Instead of the usual security-grated windows in the front, and interior shelves jammed by guitars, television sets, tools, golf clubs, and assorted electronic gadgets—or guns and other valuables on display in locked cabinets—the detective found a remarkably impressive business. Describing it, he said, "I'd call it an upper-class jewelry store. It deals primarily with expensive stones and settings, just as if you walked into one of the finer establishments in a mall, not costume jewelry or watches or something like that. Primarily rings, bracelets, those types of items."

Speaking with the shop's owner, Warren Williams, Jones asked to see a copy of the transaction with Daren Maloy on June 10. The cooperative businessman disappeared for a few moments and returned with the requested document, a green pawn slip. In addition, he carried a small gray felt-covered box. When he opened it, the 3.3-carat stone, which had belonged to Jeannie Legg, sparkled under the bright store lights. Williams had put it in a new ring setting.

Scanning information on the pawn slip, Jones

noted that Maloy had entered an Arizona driver's license number. The form also indicated that a check for $7,000, drawn on a Bank of America credit line account, had been given to Maloy. The diamond ring given by Brian Legg to his wife had probably cost at least twice that much. The killer had placed an avaricious price tag on it, deciding the ring was more valuable than Jeannie's life.

Jones had brought a camera with him, and he used it to photograph the ring, the felt box, and the green document. He informed the business owner that the law required him to confiscate the diamond ring; he gave him a receipt for it, plus the gray felt-covered box.

The proprietor, answering a few questions from Jones, remembered that Maloy had been accompanied by a very young, immature-looking woman. He described to the detective what he could recall about the entire transaction.

Back at headquarters on that Thursday evening, Jones returned his attention to the unused return airline tickets Maloy had bought. Hoping for something new to break, he made yet another call to the security director at Honolulu International Airport and asked for current status on airline tickets, from any carrier, in the names of Maloy, Miller, or Legg. At last, something positive showed up. "From the efforts of the director, I learned that one possible return flight may have matched. It was with ATA Charter Airlines, on June twenty-second, only two days away, at approximately five P.M., under the initial *T*, as in Tom, last name Legg. But there was only one ticket listed."

11

We Just Wanted
to Be Together

In the spring of 1990, after David Legg's stay at Riveredge Hospital in Forest Park, Illinois, Brian and Jeannie packed up everything they owned and took their son to California. They found a comfortable home in San Ramon, a modern community located fifteen miles east of San Francisco Bay, along I-680, in a north-south valley flanked by rolling hills. In the early 1980s, large corporations, including Pacific Bell Telephone Company (later absorbed by AT&T) and Chevron Oil Company, had established headquarter buildings on the former cattle ranches. Their presence triggered a rapid growth of industrial and commercial structures. The small towns of San Ramon and Danville morphed into sparkling urban complexes attracting hordes of real estate developers who created bedroom

tracts for people tired of living in the crowded San
Francisco Peninsula and East Bay cities.

David entered California High School, highly respected for academic achievement, with its distinctive
circular library building and sports teams known as the
Grizzlies. But the final change of schools for David somehow didn't fit. He dropped out just a few weeks before
the 1990 graduation class accepted their diplomas.

During the period that Brian, Jeannie, and David
Legg lived in San Ramon, they sometimes found themselves in economic difficulties. They both took jobs
with a financial industry firm in Pleasanton, a twelve-
mile commute south of San Ramon. Jeannie became
a human resources manager overseeing personnel
and payroll issues, while Brian supervised operations.
He also drew a fairly comfortable pension from the air
force. But, according to statements later made by
David, his parents were not good money managers,
and they fell back into the pattern of incurring heavy
debts. He claimed that Brian liked to live beyond their
means and insisted on having the best of everything.
Credit cards were used extensively, he said, and Brian
would run one card up to its maximum, then pay it off
with another card. David claimed they sometimes
teetered on the edge of bankruptcy.

It helped considerably that Brian Legg had post exchange (PX) privileges at Travis Air Force Base (AFB),
an easy forty-mile freeway drive north, across the
Sacramento River, and through Fairfield, on I-80. As
he had done in Indiana, taking his family on frequent
trips to an air force commissary, Brian would drive to
Travis AFB and use his Pentagon-issued credit card
for massive food purchases. Said David, "Who needs
fifteen roasts? Who needs eighty bottles of tomato

sauce? A lot of time we lived on his credit cards. They kept a revolving debt, and they would float checks."

To help his parents, and to compensate them for bailing him out from his extravagant use of their money in Illinois, when he had paid for his girlfriend's maternity clothes and bought an expensive set of drums, David worked at various short-term jobs.

Dissatisfied with the house they had rented, Brian zeroed in on a beautiful new home in a growing community about ten miles north of San Ramon, near Danville. A swanky country club, with two golf courses and peaceful lakes, occupied a gorgeous setting in the hills, close to towering Mt. Diablo. Real estate moguls had gobbled up 4,800 adjacent acres, and laid out eight gated developments of elite custom homes. They named it Blackhawk after a huge ranch that had been there since the early 1900s. A new shopping mall topped it off. Not only did it seem to Brian like the perfect place to live, but it also provided ideal safety from crime. No murder had ever been recorded in Blackhawk.

Somehow, through the miracle of "creative financing," which would undermine the nation's economy a couple of decades into the future, Brian managed to buy one of the new homes at 100 percent financing. He, Jeannie, and David moved into the small-scale mansion in late winter, while a dusting of snow still capped Mt. Diablo, which could be seen from their new residence.

David registered with an employment agency specializing in placement of workers at firms needing temporary help. They sent him about twenty-five miles up the Sacramento River delta to Pittsburg. He took a

job on a production line assembling commercial fish finders.

Not long after he started there, an attractive female coworker caught David's eye. He asked her to join him for lunch and she accepted.

It didn't take long before they ate together every day.

David Legg's physical appearance would probably have attracted any number of young women. Built solidly at five-eight and 158 pounds, he moved with a certain athletic grace. Blessed with smooth facial features, full lips, placid brown eyes, and well-groomed brown hair, he had adopted appealing mannerisms to complement his good looks.

In her recollection, Alicia LaFlesh said, "He was very charming, very gentlemanly, even opening doors for me. He had gorgeous brown hair, brown eyes, and kept himself extremely neat and tidy. I admired his intelligence, too, and couldn't understand why he was working for the same six-fifty an hour that I earned. But I was really, really attracted to him. It amazed me when I realized that he wanted to spend every single second of the day with me. And I loved it, because no one had ever cared for me so much. He completely swept me off my feet."

It didn't matter that David Legg was just five days short of being two years younger than Alicia. After all, his father was four years younger than his mom. He admitted to Alicia that he had dropped out of high school, and had to use most of the money he earned to pay off a pretty big debt to his parents. He drove a battered old car, but that didn't bother Alicia, who rode

her bicycle to and from work. The couple expanded their lunch meetings to dinners and movies, nearly every night. "We just wanted to be together. Sometimes his dad let him use his car, and we made love for the first time in it. Later, we used my rented room." Alicia quickly added that "making love" meant petting, not sex.

Romance always has its downside, and the first aspect of it came within a short time after David and Alicia began dating. The fish finder company's policy prohibited relationships between employees, so they fired both of them. The temporary-employment agency soon placed David with a major utility company as a reprographics technician, which Alicia later characterized as a "fancy name for a copy boy." She found a job as a live-in au pair for a family in Walnut Creek, six miles north of Danville. It provided not only a salary, with room and board, but also full use of a car.

Two months into their relationship, David Legg took Alicia to meet his parents in their beautiful country club home. She fell in love with Brian and Jeannie. They seemed like the perfect all-American couple to her. During her troubled childhood, she had never even imagined being inside such a wonderful residence. It didn't matter to Alicia that the furniture didn't quite live up to the luxurious setting. Jeannie told her they had brought it from their San Ramon house, and they hadn't yet had a chance to buy better things. They had used the same kitchen cookware, pots and pans, for about twenty years. Even their car fell short of the neighborhood's social strata. "They had an older Lincoln Continental, used by both of them, and kept it in immaculate condi-

tion. Their opinion was, why do we need a new car when this one works perfectly fine?"

Certainly, Alicia had no detailed knowledge of the Leggs' financial problems. She thought they chose to be frugal, except in their choice of a lavish home. Also, she noted, "they usually spent their money on going out to dinner, on vacations, and on living an upscale lifestyle. Blackhawk Country Club is an exclusive community, where you have to pay for the prestige. I think even the famous football coach and sportscaster John Madden lived in there."

On that day of the first meeting, the family treated Alicia to an early-afternoon dinner. She would recall, "Brian loved to cook on his barbecue grill. He made a big roast, which he burned, but that's the way he liked it. They were so very welcoming and nice to me. I felt like I belonged there with them."

To Alicia, this was heaven, the way things were supposed to be. Like families she had seen on television— a total contrast to her own fractured life. "I loved the way they cared for their home, their lives, and their kids. It was a real family." Soon after meeting David's parents, she began addressing them as "Mom" and "Dad."

Alicia felt especially comfortable in the family room, and enjoyed watching Brian and Jeannie as they sat on a blue-and-red–plaid love seat to watch television. "They would sit very close together and did little things, like holding hands and winking at each other. Their favorite programs were *Guiding Light, General Hospital,* and *The Young and the Restless.* If they had something else to do during the scheduled programs, they would record the episodes and view them later in the evening. Nearly every night, they

would drink a couple of 'toddies' made of rum and Diet Coke while watching the soaps or late news."

It didn't take long for Alicia to learn not to argue politics with Brian. "Dad was a super Republican and very opinionated. No one ever tried to broach politics or religion with him. He didn't believe in God and would say, 'If God existed, there would be no war or pain or suffering.' I am pretty certain that his experiences in air force intelligence service really opened up his eyes as to what any one human can do to another. It made him question God's existence, even though he might have previously believed in the Almighty."

To Alicia, Jeannie was the perfect mother. "Mom was always much more lighthearted and a far easier conversationalist. A very intelligent woman, and one of the best listeners I have ever met. She loved her children dearly and would do anything for them."

At night, Alicia would gaze heavenward, and give thanks for her blessings. "I was so grateful for being accepted into David's family. At the same time, though, it made me sad, because I realized what should have been there with my own family just wasn't. It was kind of a double-edged sword. I had finally found what I always wanted in my parents, and it made me realize even more what I had missed out on before. But I loved Brian and Jeannie with all my heart, and they treated me like a daughter."

Jeannie had noticed a jade pendant in the shape of a turtle Alicia often wore. After she heard an explanation of how much it meant to Alicia, Jeannie and Brian made it a point to buy turtle symbols for her whenever they spotted one in a gift shop.

As David and Alicia's romance turned even more serious, he told her about something from his past. At

high school in Illinois, he confessed, he had been going out with a girl and she got pregnant. But, said David, "that wasn't my kid. There was a DNA test, and the kid belonged to a guy I caught her in bed with." Alicia felt even closer to him for being so honest about such a troubling and embarrassing situation.

The couple continued dating all summer. David decided he needed better transportation, so with the cosigning help of his father, he traded in his junker on a bare-bones Toyota pickup truck. It came in handy for his favorite recreation, taking Alicia on camping trips. Later speaking of it, she said, "It was a way to be alone, where we could sleep together and be intimate. He and I had camping down to a science and knew we could get away with about thirty-five dollars for food, maybe seventy-five dollars for gas. Since David was still paying his parents back for the cost of a mental institution and legal fees defending him from car theft in Illinois, we didn't have much money. Camping was inexpensive entertainment for us."

Back at home, something began to puzzle Alicia. Frequently, while David was supposed to be working, he visited her, instead, and even admitted lying to his parents about it. It made her feel guilty in the presence of Brian and Alicia to be a part of the subterfuge, keeping the truth from them at David's request. At that point in her life, she simply wanted to avoid "screwing things up," and she didn't realize she was seeing the beginning of a compulsive pattern in the man she loved.

An opportunity for another au pair job came to Alicia much closer to the Legg home, and she accepted it. Her new employer worked for Blackhawk Realty and lived in the community.

By November, when trees on the hillside slopes and in the state park surrounding Mt. Diablo turned amber and gold, David and Alicia spoke of making their relationship permanent. They sealed it with an engagement party at the Leggs' home. Brian and Jeannie celebrated the event with an extravagant two-family dinner. Even though Alicia's contact with her mother had been virtually nonexistent for many months, Alicia called and asked her to attend. She also invited her sister, Heather, and brother, Christopher, to join the festivities. To make it a memorable, special moment, David got down on one knee and proposed to Alicia in front of the entire assembly. Joyous and thrilled, she kissed him and accepted. It all took place on her twenty-second birthday in November, five days after he turned twenty. They set the wedding for February 22, 1992.

To show their delight about the engagement, Brian and Jeannie gave David an additional gift, informing him that with the marriage, they would forgive the debts he had incurred.

Both Alicia and David recognized that neither of their jobs provided any future security. They discussed the issue, and David told her that he had decided to pursue a military career. His father had chosen the air force as a career, and so had David's stepsiblings. It had worked out well for all of them. Even more important, joining the service would make him eligible for benefits, including health insurance, education, and housing. Not only that, it would be a way to show his patriotism as well.

With the idea in David's mind that he would be gone for some time before Alicia could join him at his

military posting, he expressed concern for her welfare. David spoke to his parents, and with their consent, he invited Alicia to move into the Blackhawk house with them. It would be convenient and a big money saver.

At the same time, Alicia's employer asked her to accompany the family to their native country, and she refused, which caused the loss of her job. It didn't take her long to land different employment with an insurance firm.

She recalled, "I moved in with Mom and Dad. They were so nice and welcomed me into their home." With a little laughing blush, she added, "Of course, I wasn't allowed to sleep in David's room. It was not 'appropriate,' but I respected that, because I loved them. I had to sleep on a futon in the loft. We did that for a month."

Shortly after the New Year's holiday, Brian Legg led his son into an air force recruiting station.

David later told Alicia all about it. He said that he had aced two written exams. First, David claimed, his Armed Services Vocational Aptitude Battery (ASVAB) scores were "off the charts." Then he had taken the Air Force Officer Qualifying Test (AFOQT) and passed it with a near-perfect score. The veracity of his story is difficult to verify.

The paper-and-pencil AFOQT exam is not easy. It's a multiple aptitude series of questions used for qualifying applicants who wish to become officers via OTS. It is also a screening process for future pilots. Test scores are combined with educational achievement, college grade-point averages, types of degrees earned,

and previous flying experience. The candidate must also pass rigorous medical and physical examinations.

In his first ten years of school, David earned outstanding grades, and his IQ was probably considerably higher than average. And it is certainly possible that David's father, with twenty-two years of intelligence service in the air force, could have pulled some strings to grease the way, but unlikely. Since David had not even completed high school, his qualifications for these elite levels would have been highly questionable.

According to his explanation to Alicia, the air force had offered David the opportunity to attend Officer Training School and pilot training, but he would have to wait six to eight months for an opening. He said he just couldn't delay his new career that long.

Within a few days, David marched into a recruiting office for the U.S. Army and signed up to start as an enlisted private! He would enter basic training within a few weeks.

Years later, the decision still puzzled Alicia. "David didn't want to wait. He always wanted instant gratification, without regard to consequences in the future. It baffled me. Why would you join the army just because they would take you now, when you could have been a pilot in the air force? I think he wanted in, more than he wanted in for the right reasons."

Even the army enlistment required weeks of waiting before departure to Fort Benning, Georgia, for basic training. Alicia and David used the time to make wedding preparations. Later recalling one of the most pleasant, dreamy periods of her life, Alicia said, "David was extremely involved. It was great to have his help making the decisions, picking out the colors, preparing guest lists, and everything. We literally

spent every single day working on wedding plans. We shopped together for things we needed, but were on a limited budget. It helped that we both lived with his parents, which allowed us to spend both of our paychecks for the coming event. We chose a royal purple and silver color theme, and Mom (Jeannie) offered to make all the dresses for the girls. We all pitched in to buy the material and help Mom with the sewing."

The preparatory tasks turned into an entire family project. "We would all sit around the kitchen table— Mom, Dad, David, and I—working on the invitations and favors, while drinking unsweetened tea and snacking on chocolate."

Neither Alicia nor David had affiliated themselves with any particular religion, and they never attended church. Brian Legg called himself an atheist. For these reasons, and to economize, the family decided to hold the ceremony at home. "Mom and Dad agreed to let us use their beautiful Blackhawk house for the ceremony. We hired a female nondenominational minister."

The eagerly anticipated day dawned dark and gloomy, and it rained all morning. Looking back on it, Alicia said, "Everyone kept telling me that rain on your wedding day was good luck. I was hoping it was true. But it cleared up by lunchtime, and turned into a beautiful sunny February afternoon. My sister Heather was the maid of honor. My brother, Chris, had recently reached his thirteenth birthday, and he looked so handsome in the tux and bow tie he wore as a groomsman. When I was walking down the stairs to meet David at the altar, I was shaking so hard, I could hear my bouquet rustling. It felt like a dream come true. We exchanged our vows

with promises to care, support, and love for the rest of our days."

After the nuptials, all thirty-five of the relatives and guests gathered in the broad backyard for food, music, and dancing. Alicia said, "David's family from back East sent gifts. Boy, did they send gifts! We were overwhelmed at the generosity of everyone. We got almost everything on our list, plus a lot of cash. I remember how fast the day went by, and how thrilled I was to share my excitement with my family and have them see what a great man I had married. I did a lot of crying that day. I cry when I am happy, and I couldn't have been happier than I was at that moment."

The gift money helped pay for their honeymoon. David and Alicia drove to Southern California for visits to Disneyland, the *Queen Mary,* and a nearby display of the famous gigantic wooden aircraft known as the "Spruce Goose," built and flown one time by Howard Hughes. They spent hours strolling along the colorful promenade at Venice Beach. Exhausted and happy, they arrived back at his parents' home a few days before his mandatory departure to Fort Benning, Georgia.

In that first two months of 1992, three major events took place in the life of Brian Legg.

First, he celebrated the twenty-fifth anniversary of his marriage to Jeannie by giving her a choice. He would buy her a new car or a diamond ring. She thought about it for approximately three seconds and chose the ring. They selected a 3.3-carat solitaire stone. Jeannie's face sparkled even brighter than the stunning gem.

Second, he saw his son married to a loving young woman who fit perfectly into the family.

The next event wasn't quite so happy. Two days after David left to begin his army career, Brian Legg came perilously close to death. He had been experiencing some shortness of breath and chest pains. But as men often do, he attributed it to indigestion. At Jeannie's insistence, Brian scheduled a physical examination. He drove to John Muir Medical Center in Walnut Creek, where he underwent the usual electrocardiogram and stress test. Feeling fine, Brian walked out to the parking lot, climbed into his Lincoln, and inserted the ignition key. With no warning, he felt as if a cannonball had slammed into his chest. The sudden pain and a tingling in his left arm signaled a heart attack. Fortunately, someone noticed and called for emergency help. Medics rushed him back inside. The quick treatment saved Brian's life, but he required a week of hospitalization after triple coronary bypass surgery.

Jeannie notified officials at Fort Benning, where her son had barely started boot camp. They, in turn, arranged an emergency leave for Private David Legg. He flew home to be at his father's side during the crisis, along with his stepbrother, George, and one stepsister, Barbara. As it turned out, David's presence gave no support to Brian. Nor was it perfect for Alicia. Instead, it frightened and disillusioned the recent bride.

Looking back in time, Alicia said, "David came home for two weeks. After his father got out of the hospital, David had a blow[up] with his parents over some minor matter. That was the first time I ever saw him angry. He locked himself in the bathroom and kept punching the door with his fists, and wouldn't come

out for nearly two hours. Instead, he sat in there, crying, yelling, screaming, and punching the door. When he finally calmed down and came out, it was like, 'Okay, I'm done.' Just as if nothing had happened. He didn't want to talk about it or deal with it. Brian and Jeannie just pretended like it didn't happen. He had thrown a tantrum, like he was two years old, and then it all just went away. It was very stressful for me, wondering what the heck was going on."

12

Tracking Prints

A slim hope for a breakthrough in evidence rested with a specialist working in the Phoenix PD crime lab.

With fourteen years of experience examining latent prints left at crime scenes, either from fingers, hands, feet, or footwear, Joseph Silva had spent several hours at the crime scene as he looked for evidence. His education in the field included college, an FBI course, and on-the-job training with other experts. In 1984, he had passed a test by the International Association for Identification (IAI) and received certification for conducting latent-print analysis, an honor bestowed on fewer than a thousand people in the entire world. To achieve this, each candidate must submit a case to the certification board containing testimony and enlarged charts, then pass tests of actual fingerprint interpretation and comparison of latent prints.

One of the specialties for which Silva had qualified involved use of the electrostatic dust print lifter. Silva spoke of it. "The EDPL is used in various locations for detection of latent footwear [prints]. One of the things often overlooked in many crime scenes is footwear that may be present on floors, carpets, clothing, and things like that." The technology utilizes a very thin specialized film, black on one side, and a silvery surface on the other side.

The silvery surface, he said, is metallic and will hold an electrical charge. The dark surface, then, will attract dust particles, which can be photographed. "We lay a sheet of this specialized material down with the shiny side up. We attach electrical probes, which look very much like an antenna you might see on a portable radio." The positively charged dust particles under the Mylar film are attracted by and attached to the negatively charged side. Later, it is examined in the lab with strong lighting that will reveal any footwear prints that may have been present on the floor.

Silva took Nancy Ferrera, a trainee, with him to the Legg house on the day the bodies were discovered, and they conferred with the detectives who had already arrived. For several hours, they worked meticulously to see if any latent prints might help lead to someone who wouldn't have ordinarily been in the house.

First Silva performed the EDPL process, and carefully lifted the Mylar sheets into cardboard protectors for transportation back to the lab. Then he supervised and Ferrera applied black powder to dozens of surfaces for the detection of fingerprints. Together, they lifted numerous latents to be entered into computers for electronic searches. The initial comparisons would

be made with known samples of the victims and family members.

Silva said, "We have a computer with the ability to search millions of prints in a matter of minutes. They have not found two individuals in the entire populations to have identical fingerprints."

Samples on file are not necessarily related to criminal activity. Fingerprints are often required by businesses and government agencies. Most states require fingerprints or driver's licenses. So the data bank scans countless innocent people, as well as known felons.

After leaving the crime scene, Silva and Ferrera resumed work on the case in the crime lab. They began by examining a pair of latex rubber kitchen gloves found by technicians in a clothes hamper. Silva recalled, "My particular part of the gloves examination began with visual inspection, after which I used a chemical process method called Superglue method. Then I used a luminescent magnetic powder on them. It is applied in conjunction with a forensic light source."

Silva knew in advance the possibility of finding usable prints was almost nonexistent. He explained, "It is not easy to lift prints from this material. The kitchen-type gloves, commonly called latex gloves, are usually manufactured with a rough surface on the outside. They often have a chevron pattern to give the user better grip on kitchen utensils, especially wet ones. In general, it is extremely difficult to identify latent prints on them."

Finding nothing of evidentiary value on the gloves, Silva turned them over to another expert for analysis

of the tiny reddish spots that looked like possible blood.

The Pepsi can Ferrera had bagged and brought to the lab produced a clear print of what appeared to be a small index finger. But the computer could find no matching sample. Silva noted it and put the can in safe storage for possible future use.

A similar result came when Silva examined a blue checkbook box seized from the 48th Street apartment registered to Daren and Cecilia Maloy. On one corner, he lifted a small thumbprint, but no match could be found for identification of its owner.

One more development produced some reason for optimism. It is not commonly known that fingerprints can be lifted from paper surfaces. But Joseph Silva had long since learned the process. It is accomplished with a chemical called ninhydrin. Application of it reacts to amino acid residue that the ridges on skin might deposit on the paper. It works on something as flimsy as paper used for printing Yellow Pages directories. While searching the Ford Escort after it was towed from a Sky Harbor parking garage, Ken Hansen had recovered a partial page, torn from a Yellow Pages book, advertising pawnshops.

Using the chemical carefully, Silva found a clear fingerprint on the torn page. A computer run, though, failed to match it to any known exemplar.

Serologist Tom Boylan examined the latex gloves in the crime lab, and he noted they were size eight, which would be considered large. He found a small dot on the palm of the left glove that proved to be human blood. Boylan knew that enzymes are present in everyone's blood, called PGM, a designation for

phosphoglucomutase that can be categorized in specific types. The type on the left glove, he concluded, would match approximately 22 percent of the general population. The stain, he said, would be consistent with coming from either Brian or Jeannie Legg. He turned both gloves inside out, and found no stains from the person who had worn them. It appeared the gloves would have negligible value in leading to a killer.

Delivering all of these results to Detective Ron Jones, Silva apologized for not being able to produce anything more definitive. Jones told him not to be concerned. Maybe something would turn up when they finally located David Legg, Daren Maloy, and the young woman calling herself either Kimberly or Cecilia.

13

Hawaiian Hurricane

David's two weeks of emergency leave to be with his ailing father flew by, and in late March, he returned to Fort Benning, where he had to start all over with a fledgling basic training class.

Alicia continued to live with her parents-in-law, while working full-time. Still deliriously happy as a recent bride, she wrote letters to David almost daily. He often replied twice a day. They longed to be together and looked forward to learning where he would be assigned after boot camp and the follow-up mandatory training in a military occupational specialty (MOS) school. The total period apart would be about five months.

The long absence, with David so far way, left a deep hole in Alicia's daily existence, but it gave her the opportunity to know her mother-in-law even better. On Mother's Day, May 10, 1992, Alicia presented Jeannie

with a personal gift expressing her heartfelt devotion and gratitude. She composed a poem, hand stitched every letter on linen, eighteen by twenty inches, then mounted and framed it.

You are the Mother I received the day I wed your son
And I just want to thank you, Mom, for the things
*   that you have done*
You have given me a gracious man with whom I
*   share my life*
You are his lovely mother and I his lucky wife
You used to pat his little head, and now I hold his hand
You raised in love a little boy, then gave to me a man.

Jeannie beamed her gratitude, then held the lovely gift up in a pose for Alicia's camera.

David performed well in the rigorous army disciplines, especially in marksmanship. Perhaps reflecting the intense interest he had shown in his father's tales of firearms skills, David earned "expert" badges with multiple weapons. The extensive training lasted until August. For the graduation ceremonies, he asked his wife and family if they would come to Georgia to attend the pageantry. Alicia drove all the way by herself, while Brian and Jeannie flew.

They watched proudly as David passed by in tight formation with his unit. A military band played rousing John Philip Sousa marches. Brian saluted passing American flags and stood at attention while the commanding general reviewed the troops. Alicia recalled, "Mom and Dad were both crying because they were so proud of him, and happy that he had followed the family military tradition."

Brian might have preferred that his son had chosen

to become an officer in the air force. If so, he managed to conceal his feelings as he posed for a picture with David, their arms across each other's shoulders.

With graduation came orders for David's next assignment. He and Alicia could not have been more delighted. The army assigned him to Schofield Barracks, Oahu, Hawaii, and would cover all relocation expenses, even transportation of his vehicle to the Islands. To prepare for the move, he had been granted a thirty-day leave. So, after his parents boarded a California-bound plane, David and Alicia set off on a sightseeing automobile trip across the country. They headed for South Haven, Michigan, to visit his extended family and friends and to show Alicia where he had spent a large part of his childhood. En route to the West, the contented couple also stopped at Yellowstone National Park and the Grand Canyon.

For the remaining two weeks of his leave they stayed at his parents' Blackhawk home. He told Alicia that in Hawaii they would live in off-post quarters, and he would commute to and from Schofield Barracks each day. It would be no different from having a nine-to-five job.

Alicia could see a subtle change in David's personality. Since coming back from Georgia, he seemed hypersensitive to being told what to do. If suggestions from his mother or father sounded too much like orders, he seemed defensive about it. Alicia worded her requests carefully. She figured that he was fed up with being barked at by drill instructors, noncommissioned officers, and young lieutenants wishing to show their authority over him.

David decided that he would go to Hawaii on a military transport plane, and Alicia could join him a

couple of weeks later. This would enable him to choose a place to live and have it all set up before her arrival. She had hoped to help select their first apartment, but she gave in to his wishes.

On the day before he left, he posed for one more photograph with his parents, just outside the office building where they both worked. Wearing his Class A army uniform, David draped his left arm across his father's back. In a dress shirt, necktie, and dark slacks, Brian stood between David and Jeannie, with both arms over their shoulders. Jeannie wore a blue patterned blouse and slacks. All three of them showed happy, smiling expressions, the parents pleased with their son's immediate future in Hawaii, and David thrilled to be starting his own married life.

Two weeks later, on the last day of August, Alicia boarded an airliner bound for Honolulu. She recalled her early childhood living in Ewa with her parents, and she hoped this time things would be so much better. Everything appeared to be going so well now, in sharp contrast to her first twenty years of life. It seemed too good to be true. They would be living in everyone's dreamland, Hawaii, near one of the most desirable military locations in the world. Surely, this portended a future of bright happiness, living out their vows to care, support, and love one another for the rest of their days.

It wouldn't turn out quite that way.

One of the finest novels ever written about army life may have contained a more accurate prophecy of the future for Alicia and David Legg. James Jones, an ex-soldier, wrote *From Here to Eternity* in 1951. The classic film made from his book, starring Burt Lancaster, Deborah Kerr, Montgomery Clift, and Frank Sinatra,

came out in 1953 and earned eight Academy Awards, including one for Sinatra's work as supporting actor. Jones's riveting story portrays the tragedy of misbegotten love, infidelity, violent death, and the misadventures of a nonconformist soldier at Schofield Barracks. The protagonist, Private Robert E. Lee Prewitt, is a "hard head" who lands in prison and finds it necessary to take the life of another man.

Coincidentally, David's best friend during training at Fort Benning happened to be a young soldier named Robert E. Lee.

Although neither the book nor the movie specifics the army unit portrayed, it is presumably the "Tropic Lightning" 25th Infantry Division, which was originally formed in Hawaii and has occupied Schofield since 1941. *From Here to Eternity* takes place in the final months of that year, climaxing on December 7, when Japanese torpedo planes attacked and devastated the U.S. Naval fleet at Pearl Harbor. Even the inland army base came under withering machine-gun fire from Japanese fighter planes swooping between peaks of Waianae Mountains at Kolekole Pass. So the fictional Private Prewitt must have been a soldier in the 25th, just as Specialist David Legg would be. He would wear the distinctive shoulder patch: a red taro leaf bordered in yellow and emblazoned with a yellow lightning bolt. Taro is a plant commonly grown on Pacific Islands, where the thick roots are considered a food staple.

David met Alicia at Honolulu International Airport and drove to their first home, an oceanfront apartment in Makaha, a small town of fewer than seven thousand residents on Oahu's west coast. The threestory building featured sliding glass doors with panoramic views of the swimming pool, white sand beach,

and blue sea beyond. David had selected a ground-floor unit. Alicia loved it, and inhaled the fragrance of plumeria growing everywhere. The only drawback would be that he had to drive more than thirty miles to Schofield Barracks each day.

David had already adjusted to the island humidity. Alicia would need a few days, but found the trade wind breezes delightful. Coco palms everywhere added to the tropical effect. It truly seemed like a paradise.

It didn't take long, though, before troubling signs began for Alicia. "At first, it was really nice. I was looking for a job and he was getting into the swing of army duties. But David had already started stressing out—especially about being dirty at work, having pain in his feet caused by long marches with full field pack, and everyone telling him what to do every single day."

If the two young haoles (Hawaiian word meaning white person or foreigner) thought these problems were important, they soon experienced an event dwarfing everything else.

On September 11, 1992, Hurricane Iniki hit the Hawaiian Islands with unprecedented force, taking eight lives and causing damage worth nearly $2 billion. The hurricane's eye passed over Kauai, but mighty gales also slammed into western Oahu, on the Waianae coast and the town of Makaha. It raised tides almost three feet and drove enormous waves into coastal buildings. *Iniki,* in the Hawaiian language, means "a strong and piercing wind."

Alicia recalled the stunning horror. "When we got the hurricane warning, we evacuated our complex and went to Schofield Barracks, quite a distance inland, to stay with another couple. They had never been through a hurricane before, either. We slept in

the closet with mattresses around us until the next
day. Outside, we saw an oak tree that had been hit by
lightning and split exactly down the middle. When we
got back to our apartment, there was still about thirty
inches of water inside."

The ocean had moved up, covering the beach,
swimming pool, and the entire landscape around the
apartments with water thirty inches deep. "We saw television sets, tables, chairs, toys, pictures, and countless
furnishings from the lower-floor units floating, much
of it caught in the chain-link fence surrounding the
invisible pool."

The landlord owned an older Waikiki high-rise in
Honolulu, and he arranged living accommodations
there for stranded tenants. Alicia and David moved
temporarily into the dwelling, but they weren't very
happy. "There were roaches coming out of the plumb-
ing. It was disgusting. We had to stay there about
three weeks while renovations took place at the apartments." Their own apartment had been devastated.
Pervasive water damage had ruined it. Sand had
forced its way through the sliding doors and accumu-
lated from wall to wall, leaving a thick layer packed
underneath the carpets.

Moving back in left everyone disillusioned. The
beautiful beach had been completely eroded away,
leaving only a base of dark lava rock. Landscaping had
been destroyed and the pool was a muddy mess. Several tenants, including David and Alicia, began considering relocation.

A force of nature had struck the first blow in the
young couple's lives. The force of human nature would
be even more devastating.

14

Cuckold or Killer?

With the knowledge that "T. Legg" had booked a flight from Hawaii to Los Angeles on June 22, Detective Ron Jones made plans to be at LAX when the flight arrived. Maybe that passenger had some connection to the murders, thefts, and fraudulent use of Brian Legg's credit cards. Maybe not. Legg is a rather uncommon name, so a strong probability existed that this person could be the missing David Legg. Jones had no intention of skipping the opportunity to find out.

It puzzled Jones that the U.S. Army still had not pinpointed the location of either Specialist David Legg or Specialist Daren Maloy.

Jones next contacted the Bank of America and learned the check issued to Daren Maloy for the diamond ring had been cashed. A manager promised Jones he would look into the possibility of a security video camera having recorded the transaction.

In addition, the detective wanted to learn more about a payment made to the 48th Street apartment manager on June 10. Maloy had paid overdue rent with a cashier's check in the amount of $2,000, drawn on Bank of America. It had been issued after the $7,000 check for the ring was cashed. This added a link to the chain connecting Maloy to the crimes.

One more development interested Jones as well. At his request, another detective had visited the hotel where Maloy had charged a room on June 10, and collected the registration documents. Maloy had checked in after midnight and left early that same morning.

Credit cards belonging to the Leggs had been a provider of riches for both Maloy and the person using Brian Legg's name in Hawaii. They had racked up expenditures with no less than six cards: one from First USA Visa, one from Macy's, two from American Express, one from Sears, and a gasoline card from Unocal Oil Company.

Both victims' checking accounts also had been a fountain of cash for the travelers in Hawaii. Each balance looked like a drained reservoir, leaving only small puddles of mud at the bottom.

Jones and his team found that David Legg carried a checking account. They already knew, from a checkbook found in the 48th Street apartment, that Daren Maloy had one. But the balances for both men were small. Neither of them had financial reserves to cover charges on the cards for expensive electronics, luggage, airline tickets, rental cars, a hotel, or other travel-related expenses.

Unless a card user had won the lottery or inherited a large estate, it was not a good idea to run charges up

to astronomical heights far in excess of available assets. Yet, between the day Jeannie and Brian Legg died, and June 15, at least sixty-nine attempts had been made to charge purchases to their credit and debit cards. All but five of the transactions had been successful. Each of those five failures had been attempts to withdraw cash at ATM machines. Other ATMs had been more generous—not only draining all available funds, but also maxing out overdrawn limits.

One of the more extravagant credit card expenditures reflected the purchase of a laptop computer. It had been bought in a Honolulu store, Computer City, at the price of $3,161.

By Friday, June 21, Ron Jones hadn't yet firmed up a positive murder suspect. But the continued mysterious absence of David Legg provoked a great deal of thought. With each passing day, the need to find David and ask him some serious questions grew more intense. Jones said, "Starting at ground zero, we had no suspect information at all. Then, in a combination of three events, we started to feel suspicious about David Legg. That's different from naming an actual suspect in the murders."

Traditionally, the word "suspect" had been used for decades to describe someone who might possibly have committed the crime. Eventually law enforcement agencies would invent a new politically or legally correct term for someone under suspicion, calling the individual "a person of interest." In 1996, Jones still used the old-fashioned term in saying they didn't have a confirmed suspect yet. But they did want to learn more about David Legg. "We based this on the credit card use in Hawaii in the name of Brian Legg, on June tenth. That was the first information we had, followed

up with something we learned indicating that David Legg at one time had lived in Hawaii, while serving in the military. And third was his whereabouts at that moment from the army, because he was absent without leave. He was not where he was supposed to be. So those three actions led us to believe we should probably suspect him being involved."

The first really solid clue, Jones noted, came from follow-up information on the credit card used in Hawaii at the Dollar Rent A Car, located at the airport. The person had signed Brian Legg's name, used an American Express card issued to Brian Legg, but had presented a driver's license for David B. Legg as identification.

When Jones saw that airline tickets for two people had been bought with Brian's credit card, it looked even more to him that "the person improperly using this card is someone who is either involved in the murders, or has knowledge of that involvement."

This supposition grew even more likely when the purchaser changed names on the tickets of the female companion flier. Jones explained, "Based on the airline policy of requiring positive photo ID, this would indicate that the name of Kimberly Maloy was more correct than the previous name, Kimberly Miller."

Since Kimberly Maloy's name had shown up in the apartment on 48th Street, the connection in Hawaii made more sense. Jones explained, "Interviews with the family in regard to David's girlfriend, named Kimmie, was consistent with the flying companion's name, Kimberly. And in the apartment search, finding the name of Cecilia Kimberly Pierce-Taylor, and a signature of Cecilia Maloy on at least one piece of

paper, led us to believe that she was probably the one with David Legg in Hawaii."

Daren Maloy's involvement still remained unclear. Was he part of the murder scheme? Or was he a participant only in the financial fraud? Had he deserted from the army? Was he in Hawaii, or had his wife, Kimberly, gone over there with David? Was he a cuckold or a crook? Maybe the full trio had been a part of the murder plot, or perhaps they had acquired the credit cards and the diamond ring from yet another person, who had done the dirty work of killing Brian and Jeannie. These questions remained unanswered so far.

It helped considerably when Jones acquired security videotapes from the Phoenix Bank of America, where the $7,000 check for the ring had been cashed, and a $2,000 cashier's check purchased. The face of a young woman showed clearly. Jones had seen those features before.

Racing back to his office, Jones reexamined photos that had been borrowed from where they hung on a wall in the home of Brian and Jeannie Legg. He zeroed in on one that George Price, Jeannie's son, had identified as David and his girlfriend, Kimmie. Jones compared the young woman's face to that on the security tape. *Bingo!* Kimberly appeared to be part of the financial fraud. At last, investigators could use her real full name, Cecilia Kimberly Pierce-Taylor.

15

Why Is Your Husband
Taking My Wife?

Hurricane Iniki had ripped through the islands with devastating force, leaving a huge swath of destruction. It struck with breathtaking swiftness and then moved on with equal speed. In contrast, damage to Alicia and David's marriage began gradually, and took its toll over a period of thirty months.

Problems started soon after Alicia's arrival. She couldn't believe it when David began showing signs of disinterest in affection, intimacy, or sex. This man who would one day be diagnosed as "hypersexual" seemed to have lost all interest in lovemaking. "He was not interested in me at all that way. I would beg him, 'Can you please just touch me? A little bit? I mean, just a caress or something. Can you maybe just kiss my shoulder?'"

Three or four months would slip by without sex.

David seemed to be amorous only on nights preceding a field exercise that would keep him away for several days, sometimes a few weeks. "Suddenly," said Alicia, "making love was the most important thing in the world. It didn't matter what else was going on in our lives."

These field exercise absences also gave Alicia reason to wonder. "Sometimes they would last a month, like if he went to Korea or Japan. As far as I know, they were legitimate." The confused bride had no one to ask about the frequent trips. She and David had befriended only one couple, David's fellow soldier Larry Parsons and his wife, Angie. No one else was allowed into their narrow lives.

In a marriage, trust is even more important than sex. That, too, began to erode when Alicia discovered David's pattern of lying. "Once, he brought home an expensive stereo. To cover up buying it, he said he had installed an even better one in his buddy's car. As payment, the guy had given him this one. Later, I found out that he had forged my signature on credit applications to buy it. It was the beginning of a long series of elaborate lies he would tell. Pretty soon, I began to wonder if he was lying all the time, but there was never any way I could prove it. Every time I would try to call someone to check out his story, people either wouldn't talk to me or they would cover for him. 'Don't worry, Mrs. Legg, you are just overreacting.'"

It seemed to Alicia that David's superiors at Schofield Barracks would say anything to protect him. In her mind, they believed that wives served the single purpose of giving support to their husband-soldiers, but shouldn't meddle in anything or ask questions.

The object of David's affection, she thought, was no longer his wife, but his car. He bought a new red

Ford Mustang. "That car was David's true love," Alicia later lamented. "He called the Mustang his 'baby' and would not allow me to even have keys to it. I could drive the old pickup, but was prohibited from touching the Mustang when he was away. Sometimes he would park it at one of his buddy's houses to make certain I didn't try to drive it. He carried a rag around to buff away any spot of dust or dirt. He was loving and kind. To her!" Absolutely no food or drink was allowed inside. It didn't help that monthly payments of $650, plus $400 for insurance, consumed nearly all of the pay a private in the army earned.

At least, Alicia didn't have to remain isolated in their residence. Not long after joining David in Hawaii, she found a job, through a temp agency, working twelve-hour graveyard (midnight to noon) shifts doing data entry for the Federal Emergency Management Agency (FEMA) loans. This lasted a few weeks, after which she joined a mortgage company processing loan documents for a Honolulu broker. Nine months later, Alicia moved to another broker in downtown Honolulu, commuting two hours daily from Makaha. Eventually these long hours away from home grated on David's possessiveness, and he found a part-time opening for her with a credit union on the Schofield Barracks complex. This gave him more control of her time and activities.

Slipping gradually into depression, Alicia felt alone and helpless against David's increasing demands and control over every aspect of her life. "I wondered why we didn't have any friends, yet I would have been embarrassed to have people come over. I didn't want anybody to see that I had to vacuum with lines twelve inches equidistant from each other, along four-foot

tracks in the carpet, and that the car had to be washed every Saturday morning at eight. At meals, we had to have each course served in order, with every dish in place. No dust was allowed to accumulate anywhere in the house. Everything had to be exactly as specified. 'Don't wear your hair this way. Don't wear makeup.' I mean, he was in command of every single thing in our life. The only friends we had were Larry and Angie Parsons, and they were really his friends. I was never allowed to hang out with them myself."

At times, when things looked the darkest and most depressing, Alicia would find a tiny bit of relief by digging out her treasured Gemeinhardt flute and playing some solitary music. She couldn't believe it when David, running short of cash, hocked her flute for $30.

David did maintain his personal interest in music with high-quality stereos in his cars. In *From Here to Eternity,* Private Robert E. Lee Prewitt was an expert bugler, while David concentrated his talent on his drums. Prewitt had the honor of once playing "Taps" at Arlington National Cemetery. David's dream would be to perform one day with the heavy-metal band Metallica.

Alicia's hunger for emotional nourishment found some satisfaction with a Christmas visit from Brian and Jeannie Legg. Their presence gave her a fresh outlook and a sense of being loved again. David's behavior changed, too, back to the loving husband.

As if on a vacation, the four of them drove all around Oahu in a rented convertible, stopping at scenic spots, such as Hanauma Bay, the Halona Blow Hole, the Pali Cliffs Lookout, and Punchbowl National Cemetery, where more than thirty thousand American war veterans are interred.

On Christmas morning, everything seemed back to normal for Alicia as they gathered by a decorated tree to unwrap presents. Alicia's gift from David mystified her. He had bought a computer, far more expensive than they could afford. She wondered just how deeply in debt they were.

Since the apartment had only one bedroom, Brian and Jeannie stayed in a hotel. The next day, the foursome flew to Maui for two more days and nights of touring.

Any joy Alicia had felt vanished soon after the parents left, and David resumed his strict, domineering routine. She accepted her inferior role in an attempt to avoid conflict, but she resisted one demand. David told her he wanted a gun to keep in their residence for "self-protection." Firearms terrified Alicia. David's lifelong fascination with weapons and his expert marksmanship intensified her fears, and she protested. "I absolutely refused and told him I would get rid of it if he ever brought one home." As far as she knew, he yielded to her wishes on this issue.

Searching for something to appease her unpredictable husband, Alicia thought she found a perfect first-anniversary gift. She had once heard Jeannie speak of a friend who knew Kirk Hammett, lead guitarist for Metallica. Alicia knew that David loved the band's music, and she noticed how it had captivated him when Jeannie's friend snapped a photo of Hammett at a family barbecue and gave David a copy. Alicia contacted the woman and asked if she could use her influence to acquire backstage passes at a concert scheduled in Hawaii on March 13, 1993.

With the understanding that the passes could be picked up at "will call," Alicia and David attended the

concert. Remembering it, she said, "Of course, there weren't any passes waiting for us. We enjoyed the event, anyway, and decided to walk around and see if we could sneak a peek at the band in an open area behind the arena. We saw a big party going on, but couldn't get in without passes.

"After standing around about twenty minutes, we had an incredibly lucky break. Someone walked out of the party and slapped a pass on David's shirt. Well, he just walked in without me. I waited outside a long time, until he finally came out and told me how cool it was in there. Finally we started asking other people who left if we could buy one of their passes and got one for twenty dollars. We ended up meeting David's idol, drummer Lars Ulrich, and vocalist James Hetfield. It was so great to talk to Lars, and I have to admit that I was very smitten—even though I was surprised he wasn't a very big guy. My crush on him lasted a long time. For David, it was a dream come true. Of course, he never bothered to express any appreciation for the anniversary gift. Instead, he complained about not getting a top-of-the-line stereo component he wanted."

On nearly every decision affecting them, David ruled. He decided the beachfront apartment no longer suited their needs, rationalizing that he didn't want to risk the danger of another hurricane hitting the island. So they rented an apartment on the outskirts of Makaha at the top of a narrow, winding road on the slopes of Kamaileunu Ridge. The remote location made Alicia feel even more isolated and lonely. She found a little solace in adopting four stray cats. At least, they seemed to love her.

In late October, Alicia received a phone call from

her brother, Christopher, who had just turned sixteen. Sounding desperate, he told her that their mother had kicked him out after he got in trouble for being a graffiti artist, albeit a highly skilled one. He had been living on the streets in Berkeley, California. Could he possibly come and stay with her and David for a while? Alicia knew her husband would not welcome the boy, but after days of pleading, she finally gained his reluctant consent. She sent Christopher an airline ticket.

Predictably, the teenager's presence led to anger, fights, and more unhappiness. "It was a disaster from the beginning. From the moment Chris stepped off the plane, David started referring to him as 'a baggy-pants punk with an attitude.'"

The six months Christopher spent with Alicia and David turned into a classic study in human conflict between a control freak and a rebellious nonconformist.

Simmering anger between them almost turned physical when Christopher observed David's treatment of his sister's cats. Alicia described it. "I loved my cats, but if they did something wrong, David wanted to kill them. He would pick them up and twist their backs and bend the poor little things in horrible ways, and strangle them until they couldn't breathe, with their little tongues poking out of their mouths. One of the poor little kitties limped sideways for three weeks while healing from the injuries. It made me really scared. Really scared!" The mistreatment infuriated Chris, but he could do nothing except run out of the apartment and sleep on the beach for a few nights. He had entered high school, where he excelled in art, but he struggled with other courses.

Typical of the pattern often displayed by wife abusers,

David demonstrated starkly contrasting personalities. After a period of extreme cruelty, he would turn generous and loving. Once, he followed up several days of harsh dominance by taking Alicia on a driving trip, and even allowed Chris to tag along with a camera. They made a stop at the luxurious Turtle Bay Hilton resort, and Alicia posed for a photograph next to an interior fountain that featured a pair of turtles basking on rocks. It reminded her of her jade pendant and the hope it gave her for long life and stability. If she ever needed stability, it was at this point in her life.

It didn't come, though. Within a month, the most devastating event of her marriage occurred.

One afternoon, not long after David's promotion from private to specialist, he came home early with his close buddy, Larry Parsons. It surprised Alicia to see them wearing civilian clothing instead of uniforms.

David began packing a suitcase and announced that he was being deployed on a covert mission to another country, where the army didn't want an obvious military presence. "I believed him. Didn't have much choice. I was never supposed to ask any questions. Larry seemed kind of shy about it. They left in the Mustang so he could park it at Larry's place and deny me any access. I didn't care. Actually, I thanked God he would be away for a week. I wouldn't have to vacuum the carpet under his inspection at eight Saturday morning, and I could have some quality time with my brother, Chris."

Three days later, Alicia came into the house and found Christopher sitting on the floor, crying.

"He told me that a man had called and said some awful things, and would call again soon."

A few minutes later, the phone rang and Alicia

snatched it up. A man's voice asked, "Do you know where your husband is?"

"Of course, I do. Who is this?"

"This is [he gave a name] in Illinois. I don't think you do. Because he just came and picked up my wife and drove away in a Mustang. And your phone number has been on our bill for the past three months, and I'm wondering what the hell is going on. Why the hell has your husband taken my wife away?"

In shock, Alicia had no answer, and she could only listen as the man continued. "Do you know your husband has a child? He took the little boy, too, with my wife."

A tidal wave of confusion and anger rushed over Alicia. The man's voice sounded furious. "I have a shotgun. I'm going to sit here in the dark, and when they come back to get her stuff, I'm going to kill both of them. You can stay on the phone if you want and hear them die."

Speaking of it years later, Alicia still winced with anguish. "I tried to say the right things and talk him out of it. We talked for nearly an hour. He described David perfectly, and said that his wife, Dawn, and David had been carrying on for months with phone calls, letters, and even exchanging pictures. He gave me a telephone number, where he thought they might be staying. After I hung up, I called several times and left messages for David.

"He had told me long before about his high-school girlfriend getting pregnant, but adamantly claimed he was not the father. At that point, I realized my marriage meant nothing."

David finally called Alicia back and apologized, but he offered the rationale that Dawn's husband had been beating her and the child. So, said David, he had

flown to Illinois, rented a Mustang, and gone to rescue them. He stunned Alicia even more by proposing that he bring Dawn and the child to Hawaii, and they could all live together as a happy family. Alicia's response couldn't even have been aired on a Jerry Springer show. Absolutely no way in hell!

It amazed Alicia when David returned alone a week later. Dawn and the boy had stayed with relatives in Illinois. None of his baloney mattered to her anymore. She wanted nothing now but a divorce. David's expensive trip to Illinois had put them even more deeply in debt, and it would take some time for her to save money to return to the mainland.

"David came home, and all we did for weeks is fight. And my poor little brother was in the middle of it. David wouldn't even let him sleep in the house, and he spent quite a few nights in the pickup." A couple of months later, he returned to Hayward, California, to live with his mother again, in one of the city's roughest neighborhoods.

At times, during the ensuing months, Alicia sometimes wondered if she should actually sever the marriage. David's behavior changed, and he seemed more loving than ever. They moved to different apartments twice.

Coincidentally, at about the same time, David's parents also moved. Brian sold the Blackhawk home and, with another round of creative financing, purchased a new desert-style residence outside of Phoenix in a community called Ahwatukee. Jeannie continued her Physicians Placement Incorporated business from an upstairs bedroom converted to an office. And Brian found part-time employment in the family planning division at the Gila River Indian Community Health

Services department. He, too, conducted most of his duties from their new home.

David's army enlistment ended in November 1994, and he thought seriously about returning to civilian life. Struggling with the decision, he consulted his father. Brian did everything he could to persuade David that a military career would undoubtedly be the best possible future for him. At last, David agreed and reenlisted for another three-year hitch.

A crisis in the Caribbean brought matters to a head for David and Alicia in January 1995. Political and military unrest in the island nation of Haiti created the need for U.S. and allied forces to prevent outright war and uncontrolled violence. Beginning in late 1994, "Operation Uphold Democracy" sent army and marines into the country for a "peacekeeping mission." The 25th Infantry Division was deployed in January, and Specialist David Legg left Hawaii for a three-month tour of duty.

"I felt such a relief, such a weight lifted off of me. I found myself free to make friends and I began to understand how restrictive and obsessive David had been," Alicia said. "He wrote every single day, as he had during boot camp. In my unhappiness, I had gained over forty-five pounds, so I started working out, eating correctly, and seeing a psychologist on base for counseling. With my weight loss, a new confidence set in that I was doing the right thing in getting out of an abusive, terrifying relationship."

If any doubts existed, the final straw came when the army post office forwarded all of David's mail from his base quarters to their home. Alicia couldn't believe what it included. "There was a love letter from a seventeen-year-old girl in South Carolina, with photos

and all kinds of sexual references. He had never allowed me to see our phone bills, so I did some research and found hundreds of calls between them over a period of three months before David went to Haiti. I called, and let her know I was his wife. She started crying and informed me of all the lies he had told. She thought he was eighteen, and lived with three male roommates. They had met on the Internet. So I finally knew his very selfish reason for giving me that expensive computer."

The phone bills revealed something else. David had amassed a bill of $1,800 for calling sex-line numbers.

No doubt remained in Alicia's mind. She borrowed $500 from the aunt who had given her the turtle pendant and bought a plane ticket to Concord, California. Next she composed a letter to David informing him that she wanted to end the marriage. Instead of mailing it to him, she read it aloud by telephone.

An officer contacted Alicia a short time later to inform her that David had reacted strongly, and his weapon had been taken away from him so he wouldn't do anything irrational. During the following month, in more telephone conversations with David, she let him convince her to remain in Hawaii until he returned so they could at least say good-bye face-to-face. She reluctantly agreed, and booked her flight for March 20, 1995, a few days after his scheduled arrival back at Schofield.

"But, on the day of his return, I got so scared, I went to his commander and requested that he be required to stay on post. I was afraid he would kill me. In the past, he had threatened, 'If I can't have you, no one can.' It took me almost five hours of begging to

convince an officer to keep him on base that evening. I spent the night in a hotel, anyway."

The next morning, trembling in fear, Alicia confronted David. "He was rational and calm. He told me that he had booked a flight so he could accompany me back to California."

Stunned, Alicia thought fast and concluded that he couldn't hurt her on the plane. "I played along, and we sat silently for the complete five-hour flight. Some friends picked me up at the airport and drove me to my sister's house. They took David somewhere else. I don't know how long he was in California, or with whom he stayed, and I didn't care. I was free! I had played my cards right and survived."

David returned to Schofield and remained there a few more months. He wrote to Alicia, taunting her with descriptions of his new girlfriend, the Porsche he claimed to be driving, his wonderful days on Waikiki Beach, and the terrific life of being single. This continued until the army reassigned him to Fort Bliss, Texas.

Fort Bliss straddles the border between Texas and New Mexico near the Lone Star State's westernmost corner and city of El Paso. Just across the Rio Grande lies Mexico's Ciudad Juárez, a frequent destination for soldiers in search of excitement.

David's hunger for fun and female companionship began his descent into a volcano of trouble and strife.

16

The Search Narrows

On the morning of Saturday, June 22, Detective Ron Jones had no way of knowing that it would turn out to be an explosive day in his quest for a killer. Continuing the pursuit of clues related to financial fraud, Jones called a Sears store at the Fiesta Mall in Mesa, east of downtown Phoenix. He asked a security manager about the use of Brian Legg's Sears card on June 10. The cooperative employee confirmed what Jones already knew from a receipt Ken Hansen had found inside the Ford Escort. The card had been used at about two fifteen in the afternoon of that date to purchase top-of-the-line luggage.

Before lunch, Jones drove to the JCPenney store where he had previously picked up a security video that proved to be the wrong one. Apologetically, the manager gave the correct tape to the detective.

Back in his office, he popped the video into a

player and viewed a variety of shoppers strolling through the store on Sunday, June 9. Jones's heart skipped a beat when, during a half-hour segment, he spotted faces that looked familiar from photographs he had seen in the crime scene home. He recognized Brian, Jeannie, and David, but wasn't certain about the teenage girl at David's side. It could have been Kimberly. Jones stopped the video in a freeze-frame mode and noted the date and time registered on-screen: June 9. The crucial twenty-four minutes occurred from 3:33 through 3:57 P.M.

The video provided more proof that Brian and Jeannie had still been alive that Sunday afternoon. On their last day of life, they had been shopping with their son David and probably his young girlfriend. Jeannie's diamond ring had been sold the next day, June 10.

The victims' bodies had been decomposed, and the coroner had estimated time of death to be four or five days before discovery of the corpses. It looked fairly certain that the shooter had killed them on that same Sunday night after they had enjoyed a day of shopping with their son.

With a growing sense of satisfaction from this important development, Jones made a check of the office fax machine. It produced a photo sent from Hawaii. He examined the images closely and allowed himself a little triumphant smile. A clear picture showed Kimberly using one of Brian Legg's cards to obtain cash from an ATM.

At last, the detective now had enough evidence to support at least one of the goals he had been pursuing since first stepping into the home of Brian and Jeannie Legg a week ago. He contacted the county at-

torney's office and obtained warrants for the arrest of Kimberly Maloy, Daren Maloy, and David Legg. Not for suspicion of murder, but for fraudulent use of the victims' credit cards.

Now, at five o'clock on Friday afternoon, with developments breaking rapidly, Jones needed to know if the person who had bought a ticket from ATA Charter Airlines—from Hawaii to Los Angeles in the name of T. Legg—intended to use it. He called the carrier's 800 telephone number. An agent told him that a flight had just left a short time earlier. No one by the name of T. Legg was on the manifest list. But, he said, Cecilia and Daren Maloy were aboard!

If Jones's heart had skipped a beat when he spotted the victims' faces on a videotape, now it pounded like a trip-hammer. The ATA plane was scheduled to land at LAX, Los Angeles, in a little more than five hours, at approximately ten thirty that very night!

In his recollections of that pivotal Saturday, Ron Jones said, "When I made that call to ATA Charter Airlines at five o'clock in the afternoon, the person I spoke to said that a Cecilia and Daren Maloy were aboard the flight headed for Los Angeles. No one named Legg was on the plane. It was scheduled to land in just a few hours. I started to scurry, looking for a way to get there before they arrived."

Jones had hoped to hear from someone at the airline as soon as anyone named Maloy or Legg checked in at the Honolulu terminal so he could have a comfortable margin of time to reach LAX ahead of them. But the arrangement had somehow slipped through a crack, leaving Jones and Hansen in a desperate race against time. They launched a furious search for air

transportation that would beat the ATA wide-body jet to Southern California.

Miraculously, the detectives found seats on a carrier scheduled to leave at nine o'clock. It would be tight, but with any luck, they could be waiting in terminal number six at LAX when the Hawaii flight would pull into its assigned space. A hurried call to the Los Angeles Police Department (LAPD) set up arrangements for coordination of procedures to be followed upon arrival.

As usual, when travelers are in a big hurry, the plane is not. A couple of short delays put the race in jeopardy. Jones and Hansen fidgeted for the full one hour and twenty minutes in the air, and virtually leaped from their seats when the airline landed at ten thirty. Jones recalled, "Before our plane quit moving, we were requested to go to the front ahead of other passengers. And when the door opened, there was a uniformed L.A. airport police officer there asking for us. He shouted, 'Let's go.'"

In a full run, the two Phoenix cops followed their L.A. host through the Jetway, into the terminal, out a side door, and down a flight of steps. The officer told them the ATA plane had just landed, and at that very moment was taxiing toward its slot at terminal six. The trio leaped into a black-and-white cruiser. Jones remembered it vividly: "A wild ride across the tarmac at night is an adventure, believe me. We were really moving."

By the time they reached the terminal and rushed through the arrival Jetway, the ATA plane had docked and the passenger door had started to open. A pair of uniformed officers, one of them a sergeant, stood there on guard. Jones recalled, "The doors opened and I went inside. There's a good distance from one

side of the plane to the other, and I immediately walked across that space." A quick conference with the supervising flight attendant identified the seats in which Daren and Cecilia Maloy sat. Jones scanned the sea of approximately 220 passengers' faces and spotted the young couple about five rows from where he stood. "They were looking at us. In fact, everybody in there was looking forward. I'm sure the uniformed officers drew their undivided attention." Jones saw Maloy and Cecilia exchange glances with one another, but he could not hear anything they might have spoken.

While passengers remained seated as instructed over the intercom, Jones, Hansen, and two officers walked directly to the young couple. Maloy started to rise, but Jones ordered him to sit for a few moments; then allowed each of them to step into the aisle separately. Maloy muttered something that sounded like, "How did you find me?" With no response from any of the officers, he reached into the overhead bin and grabbed a piece of luggage, a black bag holding a laptop computer. Instantly Jones took it from his hands and handed it to one of the other men. The sergeant snapped handcuffs on both suspects, and Cecilia obeyed instructions to follow him off the plane. As she made her way toward the exit door, Jones spoke to Maloy. "I told him that he was under arrest, and to please follow another uniformed officer. We would explain everything in detail."

The local cops escorted both suspects and the visiting detectives through the exit door and into the Jetway. Instead of proceeding toward the terminal, they turned at an open utility door, just outside the aircraft, walked down the stairs to the floodlit pavement,

and over to three black-and-white patrol cars. Cecilia entered one with the LAPD sergeant, while Hansen climbed into a second vehicle. As Jones and Maloy stood outside the third one, the suspect asked, "Where's she going? Where is my wife going?" Without waiting for an answer, he inquired, "What's this all about?"

Jones replied, "These officers are with the Los Angeles Police Department. We are following their policies and procedures. They need to do certain things. When they have control of the situation, I will tell you in detail why you are under arrest and what I'm doing here. Let's let them do their job first and then we'll deal with that issue."

As they sat side by side in the backseat of the patrol car, the young man asked, "Can you tell me at least what the warrants are for?"

After thinking about if for a few seconds, Jones advised him, "We have a warrant for fraud schemes and suspicion of murder."

The reply came instantly. "I know what this is about. And I know that you are not going to believe me when I tell you." Their brief conversation ended when the vehicle halted outside an adjacent terminal. The occupants of all three cars stepped out and walked in single file through a passenger area to the LAPD airport substation.

In an incredible coincidence, Larry Parsons, the soldier who had been David Legg's best friend in Hawaii, happened to be in the terminal and saw the amazing procession. He recognized the handcuffed young man as his old buddy, but he didn't approach him or try in any way to interfere or question the obvious arrest.

The two suspects were placed in separate holding

rooms inside the substation. Officers retrieved their
checked bags, which would have to wait for issuance of
a search warrant before being opened. The computer
case, a wallet, and Kimberly's shoulder-strap leather
purse were examined to make certain they carried no
weapons. No knives or guns turned up, but other contents, piece by piece, began clearing up a lot of questions in the minds of Detectives Jones and Hansen.

The sleuths first found confirmation of their suspicions that this young man was not Daren Maloy. Instead, he was very obviously the missing soldier—the
murdered couple's absent son, David Brian Legg. The
young woman was not Cecilia Maloy. A certificate of
marriage in her purse identified her as David's wife.
The ceremony had taken place in El Paso County,
Texas, on January 24, 1996. Before that, she had been
Cecilia Kimberly Pierce-Taylor.

Ron Jones had been wondering for some time
about the Maloy-Legg connection; he breathed a sigh
of relief to have achieved some clarification finally.
The whereabouts of the real Daren Maloy and questions about his involvement in the crimes remained
a mystery, though—something that would require additional investigation when they returned to Phoenix.

An assortment of plastic and paper in the two suspects' possession added to the unfolding story. From
a side pocket of the black computer case, the officers
retrieved documents belonging to Brian Legg, David's
murdered father, along with a black cowhide wallet
containing the victim's Arizona driver's license and
his Social Security card. Among the twelve credit
cards in Kim's purse, they found one from Unocal,
which had been used to purchase gas on June 10, the
day after Brian was shot to death. The officers also

inventoried the victim's cards from Pentagon Federal Credit Union, Macy's, Sears, Hertz, Chevron, United Airlines, Bank of America, USA Visa, and American Express.

One other odd business-type card came from Kimberly's purse. It contained an imprint of 98KUPD.

The name "Daren Maloy" appeared on other cards in David's computer bag. These included one for cashing checks, one from Incredible Universe, and credit cards from Wells Fargo, Bank One, and a driver's license.

Some of the plastic belonged to David, including a Visa and one from General Electric Capital Insurance Services Group.

Among the numerous money-related documents, Jones found a peculiar exception. He bagged a business card from a veterinary hospital in Mesa, Arizona, a few miles from Phoenix.

Included in the telltale papers, documents related to the purchase of tickets for the ATA Charter Airlines flight showed up. They had been purchased from a travel agency in Honolulu, in the names of Daren and Cecilia Maloy, for $764 in cash.

David had been wearing a Gucci wristwatch and a braided gold chain necklace, both of which the officers bagged and tagged. Subsequently, with a search warrant examination of the checked baggage contents, a receipt for the watch would turn up. It had been purchased at a major department store in Honolulu and paid for with one of Brian's credit cards. Another receipt showed additional use of Brian's credit for the purchase of the laptop computer David had carried onto the plane. He had paid $3,161 for

it on June 13, at a Honolulu store, while the bodies of
Jeannie and Brian were yet undiscovered.

From Kim's small carry-on bag, seized by Detective
Hansen, another important paper was found: a copy
of the Dollar Rent A Car contract made in Hawaii.
When David had signed it, he had used his father's
name, but he had produced his own driver's license
as identification. Jones examined it and later commented, "The signed name is Brian, and the middle
initial looks like a backward *E*, with the last name of
Legg. The printed name underneath is Legg, David
Brian." In the upper portion of the document, the
customer's name and telephone number had been
entered. Both corresponded to the apartment on
48th Street that Hansen had searched, the one David
and Kim had rented as Daren and Cecilia Maloy.

Other receipts would substantiate a variety of expenditures: payment for a room on the night of June
10 at the Marriott Hotel in Phoenix (with a check-in
time of 3:46 A.M. and checkout just a few hours later),
purchase of expensive luggage at Sears in Phoenix,
dinner at the Red Lobster restaurant in Honolulu on
June 11, a stay at the Turtle Bay Hilton in Hawaii, and
the cash payment for an inter-island cruise aboard a
Hawaii-American ship.

Jones already knew that usage of the credit cards
had stopped on June 15. After that date, the expenditures had continued, but all in payments of cash.
Mentally tabulating the extravagant use of Brian and
Jeannie Legg's money, Jones shook his head in disgust. He recalled that "Maloy" had received a check
for $7,000 in return for the diamond taken from
Jeannie, and cashed it at a Bank of America. More
funds, approximately $2,300, had been drawn from

ATMs. So more than $9,000 had filled the pockets of
this couple, and they had brought back about $4,000
in cash. Another receipt indicated David had paid
up the overdue apartment rent shortly after cashing
the check for Jeannie's diamond. In addition, the violent death of David's parents had paid for a terrific,
fun-filled vacation. Had David or Kimberly actually
perpetrated the murders? Could any son of loving
parents carry out such cold-blooded executions for
nothing more than wanton greed? Jones found himself almost hoping that it had not happened that way.
Whoever had done it, Jones unequivocally wanted to
find the killer, or killers, and bring them to justice.

While Ron Jones oversaw collection of the checked
baggage and examination of the carry-on contents,
Ken Hansen interviewed Cecilia. He set up a recorder
to tape their conversation. When later transcribed, it
covered fifty-eight pages. In his easygoing manner,
Hansen began by putting the young suspect at ease,
asking if she needed anything to eat or drink, and
making certain she felt comfortable.

Cecilia told him that she was from Mexico, and that
people usually called her Kim or Kimmie. To Hansen,
she seemed to understand the English language quite
well, and she demonstrated an ability to express herself adequately. She tripped on a few words, and the
officer gently clarified definitions or pronunciation.
"I know that during the time I was advising her of her
rights, there were some words she had trouble with. I
read the Miranda advisory to her verbatim, and took
the time to explain any parts she didn't seem to com-
prehend." Just to be certain, he also handed Kim a

translation in Spanish and allowed her to read them for herself.

Experienced investigators develop finely honed techniques for conducting interviews, and Hansen's skills matched anyone's. He carefully worded each question to avoid giving her any clues regarding how much he already knew, all with one objective in mind. "It was a means of me trying to get information from her, her possible involvement in the events we were investigating, or her personal knowledge of it."

A few minutes into the session, he casually mentioned the shooting of David's parents just to gauge her reactions. Kim said she had no idea what he was talking about. To his inquiry regarding her whereabouts on Sunday, June 9, the last day Brian and Jeannie were known to be alive, Kim said she had been home all day and night.

Hansen asked, "Do you remember the day you left for Honolulu?"

"Oh yeah," Kim replied.

"Did you see David's parents on that day?"

"No."

"Did you see them the day before?"

"No."

"Did you see them at all on the day they died?"

"No."

"Are you telling me the truth?"

"Yes."

Kimberly's facial expression showed irritation and impatience as she told Hansen she had been home all day that Sunday, June 9, at the apartment she shared with David.

Hansen had seen the videotape showing Brian, Jeannie, David, and a young woman who appeared to

be Kimberly shopping together on that Sunday. If she had not been involved in the murder, Hansen wondered, why was she lying about seeing them?

With Kim's denial of knowing anything about homicide, Hansen made an easy transition to the next inquiry, asking if she had ever fired a gun. Kim said she had not.

"Did you ever see David fire a gun?" he asked.

"No."

"Have you ever seen a gun in the place where you lived with David?" Hansen referred to the apartment he had searched. Kim denied ever seeing any firearms in their residence or any bullets in their closet.

As the minutes ticked by, Kim seemed to grow agitated and finally asked, "What is going to happen to David?" Hansen assured her that he would not be mistreated. Still, Kim continued to express her concern for him. A short time later, she began to express anxiety about something else. "Are you going to tell him everything I say?"

Hansen explained that eventually she would probably be required to testify in court, which would allow David to hear her statements personally. The detective didn't mention an enormous issue that would soon loom like thunderclouds on the horizon. A marriage certificate had turned up in her purse. Longstanding legal precedent prevents forcing a wife to testify against her husband in criminal trials. If the case against David and Kim could ever be brought to court, a jury would probably never hear testimony from her. But, for now, Hansen focused his concern on obtaining as much information as possible.

A day planner belonging to Kim had been retrieved from inside her purse. When the detectives

opened it, they discovered several credit cards in Palma Legg's name, along with the victim's driver's license and nearly $2,000 in cash. Asked if she had ever used any of the cards, Kim stated she had not. Security video from at least one ATM in Hawaii had shown Hansen that Kim was lying.

He asked, "What if I tell you we have pictures of you taking money out of a machine?"

She twisted in her chair and grunted, "Uh-huh," and then haltingly added, "Maybe—maybe I took it. I didn't put the card in."

After nearly an hour of conversation, close to midnight, Hansen felt he had gained Kim's respect and trust. So he returned to the issue of guns. Still hedging, Kim admitted that maybe she had seen such a weapon in the apartment, perhaps a week before they flew to Hawaii. Her description indicated that it had been a semiautomatic handgun. But she claimed to have no idea of where it might be.

Turning to Kim's relationship with David, Hansen learned that after she and David had been married by a justice of the peace in El Paso, they planned on a subsequent formal wedding in Mexico. But it never took place, because his parents had shown up in Juárez and taken him away. It had hurt and angered her.

While Ken Hansen talked to Kimberly, Ron Jones sat down with David Legg in a separate room and began interviewing him shortly after midnight. The conversation didn't last very long. David grimaced, frowned, and admitted that he had stolen credit cards and had withdrawn cash that belonged to his parents. But he insisted they were dead when he arrived and

walked into the house. "I'm really scared right now," David moaned. "I know they are dead, but I swear to God I didn't do it." In a shaky voice, David said that he and Kimmie had gone over to visit, found the door unlocked, walked in, and "found them the way they were. They were dead, all covered up on the couch."

Without any questions from Jones, David continued to explain. "I was AWOL from the army, and didn't know what to do." He acknowledged being a fugitive and that he had been facing a court-martial for writing bad checks. So he couldn't call the police when he found his mother and father dead. Nothing horrified him more than the thought of going to jail—except perhaps losing his wife. Now, facing the gruesome scene of his parents sitting there on the couch, covered by a bloody blanket, he panicked. "I knew it would look like I did it."

David made eye contact with Jones, perhaps trying to measure the acceptance of his words, and then continued. "I calmed myself a little bit. Then I went into the bedroom and saw their wallet and purse, and took them. I did that, but my wife wasn't part of it. She had gone outside after I saw them on the couch. . . . And I couldn't stand to look at them anymore, so I went upstairs and I got another blanket from the guest bedroom and I put it over the top of them, because if I didn't . . ." His voice trailed off for a moment. "I don't know who did it. And I did not do that. I could not kill my mom and dad. My mom and dad!"

Tears welled up in David's eyes and spilled out. "They were like stiff and purple and gray and stunk so bad. I sat there a few minutes. Then I went upstairs for the other blanket, so I didn't have to see them anymore." He paused again, sniffling. "There was broken

glass everywhere. I picked it up off the floor, trying to make it neat. I really don't know why. . . . I was crying, and I didn't know what the hell was going on. It was just like everything happened so fast, it just seemed totally unreal to me that this could actually have happened to my mom and dad." Following another few moments of silence, David told Jones he had vomited in the guest bathroom, after which he had closed all the windows, shades, and shutters because he didn't want anyone to find his folks that way.

It surprised Jones when David admitted taking his mother's purse and rifling drawers to grab checkbooks. But the next statement sounded fishy. David claimed to have gone into the bathroom to throw up again, and then he spotted a pair of rubber gloves and his mother's diamond ring on the sink. He threw the gloves in a clothes hamper and pocketed the ring. After that, David said, he had tried to say good-bye to them, but couldn't manage it, so had turned off all the lights, walked outside, and locked the door behind him.

Detective Jones's delivery of the Miranda advisory was loud and clear. David decided that he didn't want to say any more, and announced he wanted a lawyer.

It had been a long Saturday, and the clock crept into the wee hours of Sunday morning. Both Hansen and Jones wound up their interviews, and Jones began preparations for transporting David Legg and his young wife, Kim, along with their baggage, back to Phoenix.

17

Disastrous Decisions

As soon as Jones and Hansen brought the arrested couple back to Phoenix, and placed them in custody, they began assembling a history of David Legg. The chronology of events traced a rapid downhill slide into inexplicable behavior after David and Alicia flew from Hawaii to California together and then separated.

The letters he wrote to Alicia, in which he bragged of driving a Porsche and enjoying a new girlfriend, turned out to be true. In correspondence with his father, David also boasted of owning a Porsche. He would one day explain that he wanted to make his dad proud of him for owning such a nice vehicle. David didn't mention that he had frittered away everything of any value he had possessed, including his beloved red Mustang, and he paid for the sports

car with a check for $8,000, which bounced. But by the time the fraud was discovered, he had left Hawaii.

Before departing the Islands, he asked the new girlfriend to marry him, and even made her the beneficiary of his military insurance policy, despite counseling from his commanding officer. She did not accept his proposal.

Perhaps for his own good, the army decided in late September 1995 to ship Legg back to the mainland. They assigned him to a unit in Fort Bliss, Texas, with the 6th Air Defense Artillery (ADA) Brigade, 56th Regiment, 1st Battalion. He arrived there with the rank of "specialist" (SPC), which is the same as a two-stripe corporal at pay grade E-4.

It didn't take David long to discover the excitement available across the border in Ciudad Juárez, Mexico. With no car, he had to depend on other soldiers, or on public transportation, for rides. In October, during one of his frequent forays in search of good times on the other side of the Rio Grande, he met a cute young girl and began a romance with her.

Kimberly Pierce-Taylor, Mexican born in November 1980, was only fourteen when they came together. Her parents, though, seemed to accept the liaison with the American soldier, despite his being ten years older than the childlike girl. Slim, with brown eyes, dark curly hair, and a broad smile revealing a tiny gap between her prominent front teeth, and standing five-four, Kim looked more like a high-school freshman than a prospective date for an army man in his twenties. Still, within a short time, the romance turned serious and intimate.

When David learned that Kim loved cats, he charmed

her by pretending to share her affection for felines.
(He didn't mention his harsh mistreatment of Alicia's
cats in Hawaii.) In November, close to Kim's fifteenth
birthday, David took her to Phoenix, where they spent
three days with his parents.

Back at Fort Bliss, he desperately needed transportation to Juárez for visits to his pubescent para-
mour. According to army documents, Legg's solution
to the problem was not a wise one. He openly admired a Cadillac belonging to Sergeant First Class
(SFC) James Hobson, and offered to buy it. After
some negotiation, Hobson agreed to sell the car for
$2,700. David wrote him a check, and drove the
Caddy to see his girlfriend.

The military crimes charge sheet stated:

> *SPECIFICATION 1: SPC David Legg, U.S. Army,
> did, at or near Ft. Bliss, Texas, on or about 29 Oc-
> tober 1995, steal a 1986 Cadillac Sedan DeVille,
> a motor vehicle of some value, the property of SFC
> James Hobson.*
>
> *SPC David Legg, U.S. Army, did, at or near
> Ft. Bliss, Texas, on or about 29 October 1995,
> with intent to defraud and for the procurement of
> a 1986 Cadillac Sedan DeVille, a thing of value,
> [did] wrongfully and unlawfully make and utter
> to SFC James Hobson, a certain check upon the
> Ft. Bliss Federal Credit Union in words and
> figures [for $2,700].*

Generously, David left the Cadillac with his girlfriend's family, and hitched a ride back to the base.
Three days later, he wanted to make another trip

across the border. Having been successful in finding transportation earlier, he resorted to the same tactics:

> *SPECIFICATION 2: SPC David Legg, U.S. Army, did at or near Ft. Bliss, Texas, on or about 1 November 1995, steal a 1985 Chevrolet Blazer, a motor vehicle of some value, the property of Staff Sergeant (Retired) Hector Gonzalez.*
>
> *SPC David Legg, U.S. Army, did, at or near Ft. Bliss, Texas, on or about 1 November 1995, with intent to defraud and for the procurement of a 1985 Chevrolet Blazer, a thing of value, [did] wrongfully and unlawfully make and utter to SSG (Retired) Hector Gonzalez, a certain check on the Ft. Bliss Federal Credit Union, in words and figures [for $3,500].*

Once more, in another burst of remarkable generosity, David left the Blazer with Kim's family and rode back to base with another soldier.

This pattern worked so well, Legg repeated it again, on November 15. This time, he targeted Sergeant Dirk Wessel, a member of the German Air Force on temporary assignment to Fort Bliss. David had always had a passion for Ford Mustangs, so he "bought" a 1989 model from Wessel.

Maybe realizing that three strikes would end the game, David decided against returning to his army post. Going AWOL, he stayed in Mexico, living with Kimberly's family. A sergeant in David's army unit knew about the romance and where Kim lived. He drove to Juárez, found David, and begged him to return before he could be charged with desertion. But David refused. A few days before Christmas, the army classified the missing SPC David Legg as a deserter.

Despite protests from Kimberly's father, and a worried look on her mother's face, David took Kim to El Paso on January 24, 1996, accompanied by her mom. He located a justice of the peace, and married his young love. Recognizing the risk of being caught, he, nevertheless, chose to have the marriage ceremony north of the border so Kim would become an American citizen. Never mind that he and Alicia had not divorced.

Remarkably, David kept in contact with his own parents through all of his misdeeds, and he told them of his "marriage." He even hoped they might be able to attend a church wedding ceremony he and Kim planned to have in Mexico. Extensive preparations had been made, including selection of a priest, a banquet, and invitations to about twenty people. Brian and Jeannie responded with enthusiasm, saying they would certainly be there for such an important occasion. They didn't reveal their true motive for making the trip.

On February 16, the parents arrived in Juárez for the reunion with their son. After chatting with Kim and meeting her family, Brian and Jeannie pulled David aside for a serious talk. Using logic, persuasion, and perhaps a few threats, they finally convinced him to face the music back at Fort Bliss.

Guests had arrived, the priest stood ready, and the banquet had been prepared. Just fifteen minutes before the vows were scheduled to start, Brian, Jeannie, and David drove away. They took him back to the army base and escorted him into the battalion headquarters. David telephoned Kim to apologize for leaving so abruptly.

Satisfied about having done the right thing, Brian

and Jeannie returned to Phoenix, optimistically hoping everything would turn out okay for their errant boy.

Pursuant to his return, army officials issued orders changing David's status. He had been classified as "dropped from the rolls." Now he was "returned to control," and assigned to a different battalion in the same regiment he had left. Five days later, on February 21, the judge advocate general (JAG) issued charges against SPC David Legg. He would face a general court-martial under the Uniform Code of Military Justice (UCMJ); article 121, larceny for the theft of three vehicles, and article 123(a), fraud for knowingly writing bad checks to obtain the three vehicles he was accused of stealing. His military attorney reportedly told him that he faced a possible sentence of seven or more years in prison.

During the period of time prior to commencement of the court-martial hearing, David's commander pondered the option to keep him behind bars or simply confine him to his quarters. The benevolent officer chose the latter and ordered SPC Legg to be assigned, under "house arrest," to a regular barracks in which soldiers were housed two men to a room.

David drew a room with SPC Daren Maloy.

The paired soldiers got along well, even though they shared little in common, other than being in the army. Maloy, a native Californian, almost four years younger than David, had been undergoing complex technical training as a tactical control assistant, in which he would man a computer van used to monitor and fire missiles. An intelligent, serious young man, he was held in high regard by officers, who could see a bright future for Maloy. Even though Legg and

Maloy shared living quarters, they did not socialize, since David's orders stated he could not leave the building or the post. Maloy didn't even know of the legal charges against David or of his restrictions.

In the first week of March, Maloy received orders for a transfer to Korea and left on a furlough to California, planning to visit his parents and celebrate his twenty-first birthday. He later spoke of his time with David Legg. "I had just gotten a room to myself and they brought Specialist Legg in. He and I became roommates for approximately five days or so. At first, we hit it off pretty good. We talked, and everything. When I received orders for a change in assignment, I went to my home in California for about five days to visit my family before leaving for Korea. During those five days, I was cleaning through my wallet and didn't find my California driver's license. At first, I assumed someone stole it from a box I had mailed to my father for safekeeping." Maloy also discovered that his Wells Fargo Bank debit card had vanished.

On March 6, Maloy's birthday, David Legg made another disastrous decision. Facing a probable prison sentence, he chose to walk out of the barracks and leave the U.S. Army forever. Later commenting on his actions, David said, "I freaked out. I called my dad and he said he would help." David hitched a ride into El Paso, and walked into a Ford sales agency. Strolling among the used cars as a prospective buyer, he spotted a dark green Ford Escort. Perhaps the Hawaii license plate caught his attention. The vehicle had probably been shipped from the Islands for a soldier transferred to Fort Bliss, and later sold to the dealer. When a sales representative approached, David expressed interest in buying the Ford. They agreed on a

price, and in the sales office, he produced a driver's license and bank card in the name of Daren Maloy. An hour later, David drove out of the lot toward Juárez and his young bride. Within a few days, the couple said good-bye to her parents, and headed to Phoenix. From that moment on, they became Daren and Cecilia Maloy. David even took her to the Arizona DOT to obtain an identification card in that name.

Years later, it amazed people who knew David's father when they learned that Brian Legg apparently had aided and abetted his son's desertion from the U.S. Army. According to David, his father guided him in forging documents to change his identity to Daren Maloy, and Brian pretended to be his uncle while vouching for him to obtain a credit card. The driver's license ruse succeeded in April. Brian had also coached him to claim falsely, on a Social Security card application, that he had lived with grandparents in the mountains. David and Kimberly moved in with his parents for several weeks. The whole scheme was reminiscent of the experiences Brian had described to David about meeting someone in a bar, stealing documents and identification cards, and then assuming that individual's identity.

Using the Maloy guise, David found a job with a telemarketing firm. It lasted all of twenty-four hours, after which he quit. On April 27, he and Kimberly rented the apartment under their assumed names, and they paid the deposit and rent with a check from an account he opened under the Maloy name. Of course, the check bounced as soon as the manager attempted to deposit it. David made up an excuse and promised to come up with the money soon. The impoverished couple depended on help from his parents

to furnish the apartment, including moving a small television set, a table with two chairs, dishes, and a bed from David's room in the Legg home.

Apparently dissatisfied with such sparse trappings, David and Kimberly soon plunged into debt by purchasing an entertainment center, a larger television, a desktop computer, assorted decorative items, and stuffed toys for her.

An aviation company took a chance on employing David on May 9. The job lasted three days before he deserted it. Terminix, the pest control firm, hired him near the end of May, but they had to send an employee to recover the abandoned company van within a week. With no regular income, David and Kimberly ate with his parents nearly every evening.

Even though he could not, or would not, keep a job, David talked frequently to Kim about taking her to Hawaii so they could finally have a real honeymoon. She would later deny these conversations. Perhaps he thought the fantasies offered a pleasant diversion from their growing tendency to quarrel. Just as he had with Alicia in Hawaii, David's controlling demands grew more stringent each week. He particularly hated for Kimberly to wear makeup, and she felt naked without it. He demanded that she wear her hair in a loose style, hanging down rather than tightly pulled back. Kimberly would later say, "He would always tell me what to do. He treated me as if he were my dad. He never treated me like I was his wife." To avoid conflict, she often found escape by chatting on the Internet, going outside to skate, or sitting by the complex's swimming pool.

Never having been away from her parents before, Kimberly missed her mother sorely. So she and David

drove the Ford Escort to Juárez and brought the
woman to Phoenix for a four-week visit. Her stay at
the apartment required the purchase of an additional
bed, on credit. In a show of generosity and affection
for his bride, and perhaps to impress the mother,
David scanned newspaper ads, found what he wanted,
and took Kim with him to buy her a pair of cats, one
brown and one black. It pleased the mother, and she
seemed happy when David and Kim transported her
back to her home in Juárez on the first day of June.
They arrived back in Phoenix on June 3.

By this time, financial problems for the irresponsible couple piled up like a mountain of sand in an Arizona windstorm. They needed money, and they
needed it soon.

18

Mickey Mouse
or Mexican Mafia?

In the opinions of Detectives Ron Jones and Ken Hansen, David and Kimberly had certainly found a solution to their need for money. And it obviously came from his dead parents. No question existed about their involvement in the perpetration of criminal fraud. The larger issue of murder, though, remained for investigators and the Maricopa County attorney to resolve.

With that in mind, they intensified the investigation. If the detectives had been forced to name a suspect at that point in time, they would have pointed to David Legg as the probable killer. But no forensic evidence had been found to support the theory. And nothing existed to tie Kimberly to the slayings.

Kimberly's age presented a problem. She had obviously participated in spending the ill-gotten money,

but was she just following David's bidding or could it
be shown that she deliberately committed crimes?
Should she be charged as a juvenile or an adult? Another complication muddied the waters. She had married David, and believed herself to be his wife. But a
check into California records revealed that he had
married Alicia in 1992, and they had never divorced.

The issue of legal marriage between David and
Kimberly loomed large.

In U.S. law, a tenet called the spousal testimonial
privilege, or the marital communication privilege,
prevents wives from being required to testify against
their husbands in criminal trials. It originated in English common law, and was integrated into federal
and state evidentiary rules in this country. The U.S.
Supreme Court ruled in 1934 that this matter was "regarded as so essential to the preservation of the marriage relationship as to outweigh the disadvantages to
the administration of justice." In other words, the
sanctity of personal communication between wedded
couples took precedence over identifying and convict-
ing a killer or any other criminal. Exceptions are extremely limited. Such testimony may be allowed in
divorce cases, for example.

If a wife chooses to testify, the defendant cannot
prevent her from taking the stand. But she cannot be
forced to do it. An important condition exists. The
privilege cannot be invoked *unless the marriage is recognized as legal.*

The Maricopa County Attorney's Office, in weighing possible prosecution of David Legg and Kimberly,
decided to deal with the testimonial privilege issue
right away. If the marriage to David could be declared
invalid, it would enable the state to subpoena Kim

and question her in court about David's financial fraud and perhaps even the homicides.

Kim had lied several times to Ken Hansen during the late-night interview at LAX, but she finally had acknowledged seeing a gun in the apartment before she and David departed on the Hawaii trip. None of the search warrants or other investigations had turned up a firearm related to the slayings, which made the challenge even greater for Jones and Hansen. The absence of a murder weapon left a huge gap in the investigation. Exploring possible methods to solve the problem, the detectives realized that indirect, divergent paths can sometimes lead to the same destination.

Jones began with telephone records of every call made from the "Maloy" apartment in the week prior to the night Brian and Jeannie Legg were shot to death.

The first call to catch Jones's attention went to a veterinary service on June 10, about twenty minutes after midnight. A follow-up visit to the vet revealed that David and Kim had dropped off their two cats to be boarded while they vacationed in Hawaii.

Two more dates virtually leaped from the pages of telephone records, due to the volume of usage on the afternoons and evenings of Thursday, June 6, and Friday, June 7, so Jones concentrated on those. He traced each of the numbers to identify names and addresses. At least five of the contacts had been made to travel agencies, but no pattern showed up for the remainder. On a hunch, Jones went to a Phoenix public library, and spent hours searching microfiche files of classified newspaper ads, published on the Wednesday and Thursday preceding the murders, listing guns for sale. He found that a staggering thirty-nine calls from the apartment had been directed to gun sellers. After

making photocopies of the classified ads, including one for a Ruger Mark II pistol, .22-caliber semiautomatic, the detective immersed himself in the process of sorting the ads for more analysis.

One of the telephone numbers popped up three times. The first of those calls took place on Thursday at 5:36 P.M., and two more occurred on Friday, June 7, at 3:09 and 5:46 P.M. Just two minutes prior to that final call on Friday, another one had been made at 5:44 P.M. to a pawnshop. Jones sent Detective McIndoo to visit the establishment. He learned that David, aka Daren Maloy, had hocked his desktop computer. It brought to mind the empty space Ken Hansen had noticed on a hutch in the apartment David had rented as Daren Maloy. When McIndoo asked to see the computer, the proprietor told him it had already been sold.

Obviously, David had needed some money at about the same time he telephoned a gun seller. It didn't take a math whiz to figure out why. Ron Jones keyed in the number David had reached three times and talked to a man named Ed Johnson. Johnson confirmed that he had, indeed, advertised several guns for sale, including a Ruger Mark II pistol, .22-caliber, long-rifle, semiautomatic pistol. According to Johnson, the handgun was brand-new, still in the box, and had never been used.

Through subsequent investigation of the sale, and some interviews, Jones reconstructed exactly what took place: David and Kim arrived at Johnson's home at seven o'clock on the evening of June 7. Inside, David spoke to Ed, an elderly, heavyset, full-faced man with a built-in scowl, thin white hair slicked straight back, amber-colored plastic-rimmed glasses, and a

whiskey voice. Ed's son, also named Edward, stayed in
the room but said little. They directed David to a display of several firearms laid out on a couch, on a
table, and a few mounted on the wall. David explained that he was interested in buying a pistol, but
he wasn't exactly sure what kind he wanted. Kim kept
silent. The seller's son would later say that both his
father and David were quite talkative, so the room
filled with their chatter. Part of it, the son thought, indicated that David wanted to buy a gun and give it to
Kim for her self-protection.

Examining various handguns, David first expressed
interest in an Austrian Steyr-Hahn nine millimeter,
which, Ed explained, was a collector's item from 1912.
Modern semiautomatics use ammunition loaded into
a removable magazine, but with this one, each round
had to be inserted through a slot into an internal clip.
Another pistol also caught David's attention: a Ruger
.22-caliber semiautomatic. The seller's son observed
David's focus on the second weapon, and later said,
"He handled the gun, checked out the weight and
heft, checked where the safety was, seemed to be interested in just how it felt, and looked down the barrel
to see if it was clean." The younger Ed thought David
seemed more experienced with weapons than most
customers he had seen. If so, the skills undoubtedly
came from his military training.

The conversation lasted about forty-five minutes,
and the son would recall that Kim also handled the
Ruger. Ed, the father, remained seated on a bar stool
most of the time, while Dave and Kim moved around,
looking at other firearms on display. Finally David
told the father that he would like to have the Steyr-

Hahn nine-millimeter pistol. The elderly man said, "Okay, it's yours for five hundred dollars."

The price seemed to jolt David. He said he couldn't afford to pay that much, and took another look at the Ruger, priced at $225. After a few more minutes of discussion, David agreed to buy it. He paid in cash, funded from selling his computer at a pawnshop. He and Kim left, with a specific plan in mind for the next day.

Having reconstructed David's acquisition of a gun, perhaps the murder weapon, Jones took it a step further. Since examination of telephone records provided a positive path, the detective continued in that direction. Scrutinizing the voluminous activity from the apartment phone, Jones found that one call had been made on Saturday, June 8, at 11:37 A.M., to a shooting range in Mesa. He contacted the company's owner, Ken Woodall, and arranged for an appointment. Jones stated, "I drove to his business, met with him in his office, and discussed this matter, face-to-face, with him." The outcome of this meeting showed that David and Kimberly had gone to the shooting range on Saturday at midday. He bought a box of .22-caliber ammunition and a pair of targets. Both of them practiced shooting the Ruger for a full hour, and then they paid for another hour to sharpen their skills even more.

Satisfied with the information about the gun purchase and the couple practicing their marksmanship with it, Jones turned to another matter. As soon as David and Kim had been brought back to Phoenix from Los Angeles, and processed into jail, both of them had been fingerprinted. The detective knew that print expert Joseph Silva had found latent

images on a Pepsi can taken from the murder scene, on a checkbook box, and on a page torn from a Yellow Pages directory advertising pawnshops. But the prints hadn't matched any exemplars on file. Silva had been asked to see if the new samples from David and Kim might be the missing pieces of the puzzle. Eager to hear the results, Jones paid a visit to the expert.

Silva wore a big smile on his face. He said, "That latent print on the torn Yellow Pages [page] identified to Mr. David Brian Legg." It had apparently been made by his left thumb. In addition, prints on the boxes of checks and the Pepsi can turned out to be from Kimberly.

Even though the circumstantial evidence of a handgun purchase by David, the proof that he and Kim had practiced using it at a shooting range only one day before the murders, and the fingerprint matches seemed to point the finger of guilt at the young couple, Jones knew he still needed to find considerably more hard evidence before a jury could ever hear a case against either of the suspects.

The torn-out page inspired another idea by Jones, and he wondered why he hadn't thought of it before. He drove to the Marriott Hotel where David and Kim had stayed a few hours before the flight to Hawaii. Escorted by a manager to the actual room the couple had used, Jones opened a drawer in a bedside stand and pulled out a Yellow Pages book. He flipped alphabetically through to the section listing pawnshops. *Bingo!* A page had been torn out. With the book in his possession, Jones raced back to headquarters, retrieved the page Silva had examined, now discolored by the Ninhydrin process, and held it against the spot

where someone had torn out the pawnshop listings. It fit perfectly!

The time had arrived, in Jones's opinion, to ask the county attorney to charge David Legg with murder.

Former football player Glenn McCormick, as the deputy county attorney assigned to prosecute the Legg case, had been keeping up with every step of the investigation. He had issued warrants for the arrest of David and Kimberly in Los Angeles. Now, while Kim resided in a juvenile facility, and David occupied a cell in the ten-story Madison Street jail, McCormick faced a key decision. Did enough evidence exist to charge either of them with murder?

Making decisions had never been a problem for McCormick. He had wrestled with many of them during his life. Born and raised in San Diego, California, and blessed with good looks to complement a powerful build, he had utilized his athletic skill for years, including his tenure at San Diego Mesa College for three semesters in 1978 through 1979. In the spring of 1980, McCormick transferred to the University of Arizona (U of A) on a football scholarship. Playing at the center position, he became a starter in his junior and senior years. (McCormick delights in reminding University of Southern California Trojans fans that his Arizona Wildcats defeated number one ranked USC in 1981.) His skills earned honorable mention in the Pac-10 Conference for 1982, and his selection to play in the annual Blue-Gray senior all-star game.

Reaching an important crossroad in his life after graduation, McCormick made a big decision. Rather than continuing his education, he chose to follow the

beckoning call of professional sports. The recently formed United States Football League (USFL) offered him a slot with the Arizona Wranglers. He played for them in the 1983 season, and then with the San Antonio Gunslingers in 1984, the year he married his wife, Alisa. The couple would eventually have two daughters and two sons.

The football career came to an end in 1985. McCormick had been invited to join the NFL Cleveland Browns. He recalled, "I was in training camp until being cut after the third preseason game. After breakfast, but before the first practice of that fateful day, I was asked to get my playbook and go see the general manager. He gave me the bad news, wished me well, and I hung up my cleats for good. Time to get a real job."

Back at the University of Arizona, McCormick completed his last semester of coursework and graduated with a B.S. in business administration, with a major in finance, in December 1985. With Alisa and their first baby, he moved to Northern Virginia, just outside of Washington, D.C., and took a job with a bank. But he felt a different calling, and pondered another decision. During his time at U of A, he had taken two business law courses, and recalled the law aspects being far more interesting than the business parts. So McCormick relocated again, this time to Portland, Oregon, and enrolled in the Northwestern School of Law, of Lewis & Clark College. He earned his Juris Doctor (J.D.) degree in May 1990 and joined Maricopa County Attorney's Office that same year. Immediately after passing the Arizona bar exam, he became a deputy county attorney.

Following tours in the Criminal Trial Division, then the Gangs and Repeat Offender Bureau, McCormick

moved to the Homicide Bureau in early 1996. In June, he inherited the Legg murder case.

Facing the decision of filing murder charges against David Legg or Kimberly, McCormick weighed several issues.

In the matter of Kimberly, he wondered if she would choose to cooperate with law enforcement. But if she did, it would be entirely up to her own conscience, because McCormick would not offer her any special treatment in exchange. Even though his case looked like it would be based on circumstantial evidence, McCormick stuck with his policy of rejecting deals with defendants. In regard to charging her with murder, the prosecutor didn't believe the evidence would support it. She had obviously participated in financial fraud, and McCormick readily agreed to charge her with those law violations.

Another challenge relating to Kimberly came from the "marriage" to David. Before any trial could take place, McCormick said, he wanted to prove "that David Legg was not legally married to Kimberly Taylor, due to his failure to legally divorce his first wife [Alicia], so that we could use Kimberly as a witness. She would have otherwise been precluded from much of her testimony due to spousal privilege."

Regarding David Legg, the prosecutor hoped some forensic evidence might still surface. An additional matter needed clearing up before taking David to court. David had illegally stolen the identity of fellow soldier Daren Maloy and used it so extensively that it could confuse a jury. McCormick needed strong proof, preferably from Maloy's own statement in the form of a deposition or direct testimony, that he had nothing to do with the crimes. Maloy, though, had

been transferred from Korca and deployed on a special mission. The U.S. Army didn't seem particularly eager to allow contact with him.

Most murder cases are cluttered with obstacles, but this one seemed to have more than its share. Glenn McCormick, weighing all available information, evidence, and logic about charging David Legg with murder, recognized the problems, but he knew what he had to do.

19

Tough Duty

Detectives in law enforcement agencies don't always have to work in the grimy, dangerous underworld, as might be perceived by the general public. Sometimes they are assigned duties that take them to glamorous sites or playgrounds for the wealthy, perhaps to Miami Beach, Beverly Hills, or even to Hawaii.

Because David and Kimberly had used credit cards illegally in Honolulu, Ron Jones realized that to satisfy rules of evidence in court, it would be necessary to interview vendors and personnel at businesses where the purchases had been made. Tough duty, but someone would have to do it! Jones needed to stay in Phoenix and continue to coordinate the ongoing legwork. Ken Hansen was in the middle of working long hours to complete a variety of details. Brian McIndoo had been working with the duo, and although he couldn't really be spared, he drew the duty

to visit the most popular tourist site of the entire Pacific region.

He would be accompanied by a representative from the Maricopa County Attorney's Office. Glenn McCormick couldn't get away, due to other pressing matters. Later speaking of it, he said, "I brought in one of the other DCAs from the group, Steve Lynch, as co-counsel. I assigned the fraud aspects of the case to him to prepare for and present at trial. Of course, that meant he got to take the trip to Hawaii to interview witnesses." With a chuckle, he added, "I guess I didn't think that through very well."

In mid July 1996, the detective and the prosecutor flew, coach class, from Phoenix to Honolulu. They made their initial stop at the Ala Moana Center. Located west of Waikiki, and across the boulevard from a park, both bearing the Ala Moana name, the huge mall was the most popular shopping venue in the state. Two levels of stores, separated by an outdoor promenade featuring lush foliage and koi ponds, offered almost any product tourists or local residents could possibly need.

Liberty House (which later became a Macy's in 2001) occupied the east end of the complex. McIndoo and Lynch entered the giant emporium and kept a previously made appointment with Matthew Souza, its security manager. Affable and cooperative, he told them a little bit about his employer. "We have been called the Nordstrom of Hawaii. Liberty House has been in business for over one hundred fifty years. It was here when Hawaii was its own independent kingdom, and survived since then. Now there are fifteen stores in this state." Souza said he had been with the company for two years.

The pair from Phoenix asked Souza if hard copies of transaction receipts were kept on file. Yes, said Souza. Not the originals, which went with the customers, but clear copies. He had already pulled receipts related to certain purchases, using an American Express card, on Thursday, June 13, and Saturday, June 15. Souza courteously agreed to make photocopies for them.

Information imprinted on each receipt could identify not only the date and time when it was sold, the price plus tax, but also the name of the salesperson, and even the register at which it was completed. Information about the credit card used included data to reveal whether the card had been swiped through a magnetic reader, plus an approval code. Souza explained, "In Hawaii, because we are a tourist destination, there is a high incidence of credit card fraud. People's hotel rooms get burglarized. That's not something I am proud to say, but it happens at most tourist destinations. So we have an arrangement with our bank called an approval service. As the card is swiped through, that information goes to a phone bank and those people are watching the card. So if someone's room had been burglarized and the card was stolen, and they notified the police right away, we would know. It would come up and the bank would know as well. That way, if it turns out the card was stolen, but we have been given an approval code by the issuing bank, we have the opportunity to say, 'Hey, you told us it was fine. Here's the number. You gave us an approval code. That means we are not out the money, you're going to be out the money.'"

McIndoo and Lynch enjoyed the folksy commentary and the pleasant manner of Souza.

The two receipts showed imprints of the name "B. E. Legg" from an American Express card, and corresponding signatures by the person who made the purchases. The one from June 15 had drawn the attention of Souza while the customer was still in the store. "I was on the main floor, which is the second floor of our building, and I got a signal from a salesperson that a card had not been approved. I happened to be the closest security person to that register, so I just casually walked over to see what's up. Frankly, it's rare for the individual to still be present, because they generally know something's up with the card and they leave. If they are still there, it's usually a customer who was way over their limit—easily solved.

"In this case," said Souza, "it was a code four, which means the problem was originated by the bank. See, the credit card belongs to the company that issued it, not to the customer. I mean, we go through this every day. They think they own the card, but they don't. For example, if the Bank of Hawaii has issued a Visa card, and they call and say, 'Hey, pick up this Visa,' our contractual obligation to the bank requires us to do that. As much as the customer might be upset that we're taking the card, it's actually the property of the bank. So we pick it up.

"So American Express had directed us to take this card. But it was after the sale had been completed. I went to our salesperson and she pointed toward a couple of people walking away, exiting the store."

"Were you able to make an identification of who they were, other than the name on the card and the signature?"

"No," said Souza. "In my business, we look at hundreds, maybe thousands of people a day, you know. I

wasn't actively looking for anybody, just responding to the cashier. I would have simply asked them for the card and taken it to the office for verification. They hadn't really done anything wrong."

"Do you have any security video cameras in the store?"

Souza said they did, and he had reviewed the tape. But the image was of the couple's backs as they walked out. "If we had gotten an image worth preserving, we would have made a print, a hard-copy photo, and saved it. But what we had was worthless, so we didn't keep the tape."

David and Kimberly had each brought a Gucci wristwatch back from Hawaii with them, and McIndoo knew the purchases had been made at the Liberty House. At his request, Souza took them to meet employee Diane Tagoshi in the fine-jewelry department who had served "B. E. Legg" and his companion on June 13.

The diminutive woman, no taller than four feet ten inches, greeted them with dignity, if a little nervously. She told them she had worked for Liberty for six years. Souza had followed company policy soon after being contacted by the Phoenix PD to have Tagoshi prepare a report of the sale to Legg. This helped her remember details to answer questions from McIndoo and Lynch.

She easily recalled that the customers had been a young man and woman. Asked to describe them, Tagoshi said, "The man was tall." McIndoo smiled as he noted her answer. David, at five-eight, would not have looked "tall" to most people, but this tiny lady would have had to look up at him.

Describing hair color, she said, "Blond." That didn't

quite fit, either, but the detective noted it, along with her observation that he had a "fair complexion" and was "slim." Tagoshi recalled that the female companion had "short brown hair. That's all I remember." After a few minutes, the salesclerk seemed to relax. She said, "He asked me to show him a watch for her." She had presented a ladies' Gucci wristwatch, with a champagne face and stainless-steel band.

"How did he behave? Was he courteous, happy, or sad?"

"He was nice." But the female, Tagoshi recalled, didn't say anything.

After looking at the watch for her, they had wanted to examine men's watches, too. The male also chose the Gucci brand and paid for both of them with an American Express card. The sale went through without a hitch, including approval from the bank. Tagoshi said she had compared his signature on the receipt with one on the card, and it matched. She couldn't recall asking him for identification.

McIndoo produced a sheet containing six black-and-white photos of male faces. He asked Tagoshi if any of them looked like the customer she had served. She immediately selected the picture of David Legg. The Phoenix men thanked her and said good-bye.

Souza next introduced the duo to another salesclerk, Soomie Choi. She, too, had made a written report for Matthew Souza after encountering Legg and the girl with him, on June 15 at 10:52 A.M.

McIndoo knew that David and Kimberly had boarded a ship that afternoon, at the nearby harbor terminal, for a seven-day inter-island cruise. So the morning visit to Liberty House fit the time line of events.

Choi answered McIndoo's questions in more detail

than her colleague had, albeit with some broken English syntax. Describing David, she said, "I thought he looked about twenty-seven years old. He may be five-seven, very well mannered. The lady [was] much younger than him, maybe twenty. Shoulder-length hair, with permanent, very shy."

"What kind of items were they looking for?"

"The gentleman was looking for a gold bracelet for the young lady."

"Did she participate in selecting it?"

"She actually did not communicate with me, but they were looking and they were deciding. She was part of making a decision at the end." Answering a question about the couple's demeanor, Choi said, "They appeared very much in love, generous to each other. . . . They were unselfish and very loving and gentle."

According to the salesclerk, the couple showed interest in a gold chain bracelet that was marked down from $500 to $250. "The gentleman offered more expensive, more better-looking, maybe wider."

To Choi, it seemed a little odd that the young woman would never address her directly, even when asking to look at another item from the display case. "She would tell him she wants to see the next one, instead of asking me to show her. That's why I had impression she very shy. She pay attention to what we talk about, but say nothing to me. I ask them, 'Are you newlywed?' She listen, but he answer yes. And they end up buying little tiny hug-and-kisses bracelet. Much less expensive than gentleman was offering."

"Did they buy anything for him?"

"He wanted gold rope chain for himself. It had diamond cut. That means it has little etches on the chain, makes it shine better." She said they had paid

for the bracelet and the chain with an American Express card. Pointing to the third line of data on the sales receipt, "D/C Rope," Choi explained, "That means diamond-cut rope."

Moments after the sale, a code 4 had requested the card to be picked up, but the customers had already headed for an exit door.

As he had with Diane Tagoshi, McIndoo brought out the two six-packs of photos, but Choi could not recognize any of them as the customers to whom she had sold the jewelry.

McIndoo and Lynch thanked Choi and Souza, inserted copies of the receipts into a briefcase, and left the Liberty House. They walked along the promenade, past only seven storefronts, before reaching a Guess store.

As a well-known purveyor of upscale clothing, Guess characterized its own brands as "adventurous, sexy and all-American with an international flair." Inside the store, McIndoo and Lynch met with a manager who, after a few minutes of conversation, introduced them to salesclerk Shaleen Mosher. She took them on a brief tour, pointing out that the lower level contained clothing and accessories for women. Near the entry, she explained, were their "young contemporary" fashions, including the basic Guess jeans. Shoppers going to the back section would find what Mosher called "the Collection—all of our suiting and sweater sets." The second floor displayed styles for men.

Not really expecting a "yes" answer, McIndoo asked Mosher if she could remember a young couple who made some purchases the previous month, on June 12. The attractive clerk surprised him with a strong

"yes." She recalled them quite well because they had distinguished themselves in two ways. First, their behavior had been somewhat peculiar, and second, they had bought quite a bit more than most Caucasian tourists do.

That comment caught both visitors off guard. Did Caucasians usually buy less? Mosher explained that her observation had nothing to do with racism, but simply a matter of economic reality. She said, "Okay, basically the Ala Moana Center is targeted to Japanese tourism. When Japanese people come into the store, they usually make purchases for their friends and families back in Japan. They'll walk through the store and they will purchase fifteen T-shirts from the men's section and fifteen from the women's department, and they will have big stacks of purchases, which is not unusual." Caucasians, tourists or locals, almost always buy only one or two items, Mosher said.

Considering her sharp recollection, McIndoo hoped Mosher would be able to describe David Legg and Kimberly. She didn't disappoint him. "The female was about five-three and she had short blond hair. They were both wearing shorts. He was about five-ten and, like, in his midtwenties. She looked quite a bit younger." McIndoo made notes of the portrayal, and entered a question mark about the female's "blond" hair. He wondered if Kimberly had worn a wig, or perhaps had bleached her dark brown hair. Diane Tagoshi in the Liberty House had described Kimberly's hair as brown.

"Did you help either one of them?" the detective inquired.

"Well, when they entered, he went upstairs and she didn't want any help. She was picking out merchandise,

and she didn't want to try anything on. She didn't seem to want anyone to bother her."

"Were you close by her?"

"Yes. She came into my area first." Mosher explained that the store is divided into zones and each one is covered separately by a salesperson who receives commissions for purchases made in that zone. "So we try to help the customer, get them into a dressing room with merchandise from your own zone in order to get the sale and the commission." The female, she said, was picking up a lot of merchandise and "just flopping it over her arm. Everybody was trying to help her and get that huge sale. It was very competitive." The customer, however, didn't want to try on anything. "She shopped for about twenty minutes. We ended up stacking a pile of her merchandise, almost a foot thick, on the back of a counter, and she waited for the male to come. When he did, he handed her a credit card. I ran upstairs to see if he had bought anything up there and found out there was a huge purchase on an American Express card. The substantial sale ended up being divided up between four of us." At checkout, the male signed the credit card slip.

Other than the odd rejection of any offered help, McIndoo asked if Mosher had observed anything else about the couple's behavior. She replied, "They were pretty quiet to each other. They weren't talking to us. They weren't obnoxious or anything, just quiet in their conversation with each other."

Once again, McIndoo produced the photographic lineup of faces. Shaleen Mosher had no difficulty in picking out the shots of David Legg and Kimberly. This time, the detective also showed her photos of several items of Guess clothing that had been found

in the couple's luggage. She recognized six of them, including blouses and shirts from the store. Receipts matched them to purchases made with the AmEx card.

Two more Guess employees spoke to the visiting investigators. Yung Ju Lim told them her recollections of the couple's visit. "I remember both of them coming into the store, and I did help the girl. She was wearing a cropped yellow top. I commented on it because it was from our Guess collection, and was really cute on her. I also helped her at the denim wall. She didn't want to try anything on. She just kept saying, 'Yes, this is my size. I want this.' I remember it was a huge sale. I think the man went upstairs."

Salesclerk Tri Ley corroborated the others' accounts of the young female customer's voracious shopping. "She kept grabbing a lot of clothes without looking at the prices and without trying anything on. Most people look at the price and then want to try the clothing on."

"Did she seem to have the freedom to do what she wanted, and to buy anything she chose?"

"Yes. She was going into the front of the store, junior clothes to women's classics. Usually people stay in one or the other sections. She seemed like she must have a lot of money."

"What was her demeanor when you tried to help her?"

"Well, I thought they were both kind of rude, actually. They were kind of hard acting, and she was kind of aloof. She wouldn't really let you help her with the dressing rooms, like she didn't need to try stuff on. Usually that's how we help. But she was just holding on to her items." Ley had tried to engage the girl in conversation, but felt rebuffed. "She was kind of bitchy."

Ley's selections from the photo lineups matched the others.

Before leaving the Ala Moana mall, the pair of investigators also paid a visit to the travel agency where Kathleen "Kit" Hansen worked. She told them the details of booking a cruise for Daren and Cecilia Maloy, and identified images of the couple from the six-pack photographic lineup.

Again expressing their appreciation for the help, McIndoo and Lynch left the shopping plaza. They headed west on Interstate H-1, drove past Honolulu International Airport and Pearl Harbor, before pulling off into another shopping mall, the Waikele Center. Only three years old, the complex stood on land that had been a sugarcane field for generations. Their first destination was another Guess store.

Assistant manager Melanie Silva greeted them and answered their questions. She said she recalled a young couple coming in on June 14, a little before their 7:00 P.M. closing time, and wanted to exchange four items of Guess clothing, bought for $104 at the Ala Moana store. Along with the exchange, they had also purchased two pairs of jeans, two shorts, and a denim vest. She personally observed the man fill out the exchange slip with his name, address, and phone number, then sign it as Brian Legg.

Describing him, Silva said, "He appeared to be in his midtwenties, had short brown hair, feathered in the back, and was about five-nine. He wasn't overweight or skinny, just a medium build." His demeanor in talking to her was "pleasant." The girl, said Silva, "was young, with shoulder-length, dirty blond, wavy hair, maybe with a permanent. She was quite a bit shorter than he, maybe about five-four, and slender."

"Do you remember how she was dressed?"

"Yes, very maturely and provocatively. She had a short miniskirt and a top that showed her stomach, kind of crisscrossed over her breasts. She looked pretty young, but by the way she was dressed, and her makeup, and by the way she was acting, it was hard for me to determine her age. She just looked young."

The detective wanted to know how they interacted with one another. Silva said, "They both seemed happy and upbeat, and they were hugging and kissing. So my first impression was that they must be on their honeymoon."

Silva seemed to remember the Legg name, and McIndoo asked how she had such detailed recall. The woman smiled and explained, "My fiancé at the time and I would go to this karaoke club, and it was called Peg Leg, so when I read the name the customer signed, I thought it was kind of amusing. I even talked to them about it and said they had an unusual last name."

Just as the other store personnel had, Silva picked out pictures of David Legg and Kimberly from McIndoo's photo lineup.

In the same shopping area, McIndoo and Lynch entered a Computer City store. General sales manager Allen Moore took them to salespeople Marloun Bayari and Fran Morrison. This stop buttoned down the use of an American Express card David used to purchase a computer, carrying case, and associated software at a cost of more than $3,000.

A few stops at smaller establishments garnered additional receipts and identifications.

The Phoenix team rounded out their Hawaiian journey with two more contacts. They visited the Dollar Rent A Car agency near the airport and spoke

with two employees, but this probe netted very little information.

Finally the duo drove to Oahu's north shore and found the Turtle Bay Hilton. There they spoke to the resort's head of security, Alan Nakamura, who provided them with copies of receipts for meals and the room occupied by David and Kimberly.

The trip to Hawaii had provided exactly what Detective McIndoo and DCA Lynch had hoped for.

20

Courtroom Capers

With outside July temperatures blazing in Phoenix, Glenn McCormick set the mechanics in motion for David Legg to face a jury on charges of murdering his parents. It would be a frustrating and long process. The Sixth Amendment to the U.S. Constitution provides certain guarantees to criminal defendants:

In all criminal prosecutions, the accused shall enjoy the right to a speedy and public trial, by an impartial jury of the State and district wherein the crime shall have been committed, which district shall have been previously ascertained by law, and to be informed of the nature and cause of the accusation; to be confronted with the witnesses against him; to have compulsory process for obtaining witnesses in his favor, and to have the assistance of counsel for his defense.

A speedy trial, to some, might mean within a few weeks, or no more than a few months. But people familiar with the American jurisprudence system understand

that the definition of "speedy" can be stretched to years. McCormick girded for the long haul.

At a mid-July arraignment, conducted by Maricopa County Superior Court judge Ronald Reinstein, David Legg pleaded not guilty to two counts of first-degree murder. He would be defended by a skillful Phoenix attorney specializing in criminal cases, Michael B. Bernays. Close to six feet tall, weighing about 175 pounds, with a thick mane of dark brown hair curling up over his collar, high cheekbones, masculine smooth-shaven face, and lightweight oval eyeglasses, Bernays created a powerful presence in the courtroom. And he knew his way around the law. McCormick would say about him, "Mike is a good guy, very thorough and effective at argument." At his side, acting as co-counsel, would be articulate, bright Tonya J. McMath. Her striking appearance, blue eyes, and blond shoulder-length hair, complementing an eye-catching figure, often seemed to distract their client David Legg.

The defenders also faced a long, harrowing period of preparation and independent investigation. If Las Vegas oddsmakers took bets on the possible outcome of David's pending trial, they would probably favor the defense team, since the prosecution's case would depend so heavily on circumstantial evidence.

At least, the long wait would give Detectives Ron Jones and Ken Hansen more time for additional investigation.

Meanwhile, Glenn McCormick tackled the issue of David's two marriages. He located Alicia LaFlesh in California and made a telephone call to her.

* * *

Alicia had left David on March 20, 1995, when they flew together from Hawaii to California. She walked away from him at the San Francisco airport and subsequently spoke to him only by telephone. Those calls were attempts to recover some of her personal property and to talk about the smothering debts he had incurred. Making a new life for herself, she had found a job with a finance company, lived for a while with her sister in Concord, and found peace.

Later talking about it, she said, "I didn't file for divorce right away because I still wanted some of my things that were still in his possession, and I knew I would never get them if I filed. He finally shipped a lot of boxes to me just before he was assigned to Fort Bliss in Texas. We talked for a few more months and I kept in contact with his parents the whole time, even after they moved to Arizona. They were understanding and nice to me. But for some reason, they didn't want me to know they were seeing David on a regular basis. I guess they wanted to keep the relationships separate. I felt like I was their daughter, but knew that it would be different since David and I had split up."

In November, David told Alicia about his new girlfriend from Mexico. In his version, she was almost eighteen. "I could sense that he was lying. After I received my household goods, I wanted to file for divorce. But he went AWOL, and I couldn't file legally because I didn't have a place to serve him the papers." Alicia knew of provisions to publish the filing in a newspaper, but she couldn't afford the prohibitive costs, so she had to wait.

Her wait came to an end when DCA Glenn McCormick reached Alicia by telephone. He gently informed her of the murders and said that David was the chief suspect.

Alicia's newly found serene existence exploded. She felt as if Hurricane Iniki had returned, and she was struck head-on with its full force. This just couldn't be. The beloved parents she had finally found, and revered, had been shot to death? By David? It was a nightmare too devastating to believe. Her tormented thoughts beckoned her back to Hawaii, when David besieged her with demands to own a handgun "for protection." Tears and unbearable pain nearly drowned her. Alicia had withstood a long series of difficult times in her life, but this hit her the hardest. She couldn't shake the feeling that if she hadn't married David, maybe this would never have happened.

Fifteen years later, tears would still well up in her eyes when she spoke of the horrible events.

Alicia agreed to help McCormick in any way she could. The next day, she filed for divorce. A short time later, she traveled to Phoenix and served papers to David at the Madison Street jail. It really didn't surprise her much when David avoided any mention of his parents' death. Nor did he make any effort to resist the divorce. Instead, he spent most of the time complaining to Alicia about the filthy lockup conditions.

To her dismay, Alicia also learned that David had incurred more than $50,000 of debts, for which she held joint legal responsibility. This forced her into another civil action; Alicia had to file for bankruptcy.

With confirmation that David's marriage to Alicia had legally existed when he took Kim for his bride, and committed bigamy, the county attorney's office concentrated on issues related to Kim. First they prepared legal motions to have the El Paso marriage declared in-

valid. Next DCA Tom Glow addressed superior court judge Maurice Portley requesting a change in Kim's status as a juvenile so she could be prosecuted in an adult court. Portley held a hearing at which Detective Ken Hansen testified of Kimberly's presence during the sale of Jeannie Legg's diamond to a dealer. Both she and David carried out the transaction under false names, which is a crime: trafficking in stolen property.

Kimberly's mother spoke from the witness stand telling the judge that her daughter had performed extremely well in a Juárez school. She had been a happy girl, but all of that had changed when David Legg came into her life. The weeping mother said David had dominated and controlled Kimberly's every move. Asked if she had approved the marriage, the woman acknowledged allowing it, but only because David seemed to protect Kim like a daughter rather than a prospective wife.

Tom Glow argued that Kimberly had behaved with adult motives of greed and duplicity. She had full knowledge of the murder but chose to cover it up. She also willingly participated in profiting from the slaying.

Kimberly's defense attorney, Marcus Westervelt, protested that she had feared the possibility of David harming her if she reported the crimes, and that she followed his demands in using credit cards and cash stolen from his parents.

Neither the testimony nor the oral argument convinced Judge Portley of Kimberly's maturity. He ruled in her favor, reaffirming that she would be treated as a juvenile. Still, he refused permission for her to return to Juárez with her mother. Instead, she had to

remain in a juvenile facility pending her trial, set for late August.

The trial would never take place. On August 16, Kimberly returned to Judge Portley's courtroom to offer a plea of guilty in charges of felony theft. The judge promptly ruled that she could go home to Juárez with her parents on one condition: she must return to Phoenix on September 16 for sentencing.

DCA Tom Glow asked the judge to hold her locally for three days so she could give a deposition, and he was granted the temporary hold. But it turned out to be useless because a clerical problem delayed completion of necessary police reports. So the deposition had to be postponed. Kimberly left on the following Monday morning. Prosecutors and detectives expressed deep concern about ever seeing her again.

During her four weeks of absence, another court hearing took place about Kimberly.

True to her word, Alicia LaFlesh showed up in Phoenix on Friday, September 6, to testify in superior court judge Louis Araneta's court that she and David Legg were married in California on February 22, 1992, and that union remained intact when David illegally married Kimberly Pierce-Taylor. Supporting documents presented by DCA Glenn McCormick corroborated Alicia's words. The judge ruled David and Kimberly's wedding invalid.

This finding would prevent Kimberly or her attorney from invoking the spousal privilege. It cleared the way for Kimberly not only to give a complete deposition upon her return from Juárez, but also to testify regarding anything she knew about the murders of

Brian and Jeannie Legg. But McCormick couldn't allow himself to be very optimistic about what Kimberly might say. Her attorney, Marcus Westervelt, announced that his client would rely on the Constitutional Fifth Amendment and refuse to answer any interview questions.

If authorities were concerned about Kimberly's return for the sentencing and subsequent deposition, they breathed a sigh of relief in September. She came back to Phoenix from Juárez as promised.

On Monday, September 16, Kimberly stood once again before Judge Portley, the same magistrate who had accepted her guilty plea to felony theft. Apparently taking into consideration her status as a juvenile, he delivered what some regarded as a slap on the wrist. Kimberly would be required to perform 150 hours of community service and to pay $7,810 in restitution. She would also be on probation for two years. Finally, through powers of subpoena, Judge Portley ordered her to return once again to the United States when David Legg's trial commenced, and to testify.

Four days after the sentencing, September 20, Kimberly showed up for the deposition, and she swore to tell the truth. At her attorney's request, the judge issued an order granting her immunity against future prosecution for anything she might say in the deposition. Facing a battery of questions, she repeatedly denied ever firing a gun, and claimed never to have seen a gun fired. Asked if she had ever seen David Legg handle a firearm, she said no. And she adamantly denied going to a firing range with him.

More to the point, she responded to inquiries

about the night of the murders. Kimberly testified
that she had been in the Leggs' house with David on
the evening of Sunday, June 9, visiting his parents.
Later that night, she stated, she had left them all in
the family room and walked outside to the car to retrieve a sanitary napkin from her purse. There, she
turned on the radio, according to her customary
practice. She could specifically remember a song she
heard, "Don't Cry," by Guns N' Roses. It was one of
her favorite pieces of music. While listening to it, she
asserted, she heard four loud noises, "like gunshots."

Although she could no longer recall which radio
station she had listened to, Kimberly thought it was
one for which she carried a business card in her wallet
at the time. The DCA questioning Kimberly knew that
a card had been discovered in her purse during the
search at LAX upon the couple's return from Hawaii.
It was imprinted with 98KUPD.

Asked why she never notified the police about
hearing gunshots on that night, Kimberly testified
that she was afraid to tell law enforcement because
David might hurt her.

While Glenn McCormick and Steve Lynch took
some comfort in Kimberly's keeping her promise to
return from Juárez, it disappointed them that she had
been untruthful. On several points, her tale had included outright lies. Kimberly's version of events
didn't appear to be of much value for the impending
murder trial of David Legg. At least, she hadn't refused to testify as her lawyer had predicted. Her excuse
for not contacting the police—fear of David—seemed
duplicitous. From what DCA Lynch had seen and
heard in Hawaii, and from viewing the video David
had taken during the honeymoon cruise, she had

Jeannie and Brian Legg sitting in a loveseat, similar to how their killer confronted them. *(Courtesy Alicia LaFlesh)*

David Legg spent thousands of dollars calling sex-line telephone numbers. *(Courtesy Alicia LaFlesh)*

Alicia LaFlesh thought she had found paradise when she met and married David Legg. *(Courtesy Chris LaFlesh)*

Brian Legg and David after David's completion of U.S. Army boot camp at Fort Benning, Georgia. *(Courtesy Alicia LaFlesh)*

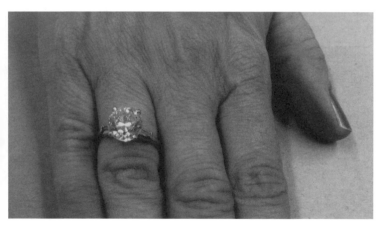

The 3.3 carat diamond ring Brian gave Jeannie on their twenty-fifth wedding anniversary was pulled from her finger by their killer. Here, the ring is modeled by an employee of Maricopa County Superior Court. *(Author photo)*

David Legg and his parents, Brian and Jeannie, prior to his departure for Schofield Barracks, Hawaii. *(Courtesy Alicia LaFlesh)*

Jeannie holds a needlepoint message from her daughter-in-law Alicia on Mother's Day. *(Courtesy Alicia LaFlesh)*

Brian Legg with a Christmas present from Alicia. *(Courtesy Alicia LaFlesh)*

David in front of the Hawaii apartment where he and Alicia first lived. Hurricane Iniki inundated the building and stripped all the sand from the beach. *(Courtesy Alicia LaFlesh)*

Alicia, Brian, and Jeannie during a visit in Hawaii. *(Courtesy Chris LaFlesh)*

Angie and Larry Parsons with Alicia in Hawaii. Alicia was not allowed to socialize with anyone else. *(Courtesy Chris LaFlesh)*

In Hawaii, David grew cold toward his wife and exercised extreme control. *(Courtesy Alicia LaFlesh)*

Alicia collected turtle symbols for good luck and enjoyed a visit to the famous Hilton Resort. *(Courtesy Chris LaFlesh)*

David with his Ford Mustang. Alicia believed he loved the car more than his wife. *(Courtesy Alicia LaFlesh)*

While David and Alicia were still in Hawaii, Brian and Jeannie moved to this upscale home in the suburbs of Phoenix, Arizona. They were later murdered inside it. *(Author photo)*

Back yard of the Legg home in Phoenix. When Jeannie's son and his wife couldn't contact them, they peered through a back window and saw blankets on a loveseat. *(Maricopa County Superior Court Records)*

The distraught relatives called police. Detectives entered and found the blankets covering the murdered bodies of Brian and Jeannie.
(Maricopa County Superior Court Records)

The killer had peeled twine from this roll to bind blankets on the bodies. *(Maricopa County Superior Court Records)*

The murder weapon was never found, but detectives learned the type of pistol by ballistic tests and from a catalogue in the possession of a gun seller. *(Maricopa County Superior Court Records)*

Clues led to a suspect calling himself Daren Maloy. Detectives found this driver's license for Maloy in the possession of David Legg, with David's photo on it. *(Maricopa County Superior Court Records)*

Merchants in Hawaii identified David from this six-pack as the person using Brian Legg's credit cards. *(Maricopa County Superior Court Records)*

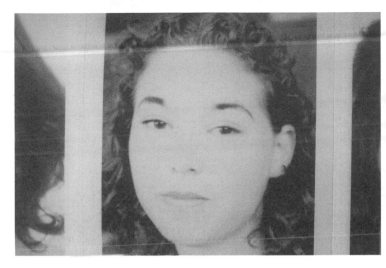

A young woman with David was identified from this six-pack photo. Kimberly was David's 15-year-old wife by an illegal marriage. *(Maricopa County Superior Court Records)*

David and Kim had pawned the diamond ring for $7000 and were recorded in a bank kissing while they cashed the check. *(Maricopa County Superior Court Records)*

Reporter Doug Murphy followed the case and wrote numerous articles about the murder and the ensuing trial. *(Author photo)*

David Legg faced a murder trial by Judge Michael Wilkinson in this Phoenix courthouse. *(Author photo)*

The killer had left this Ford Escort in a parking building at Sky Harbor Airport in Phoenix. *(Maricopa County Superior Court Records)*

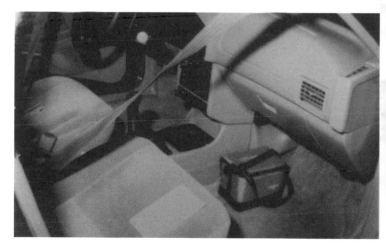

With a warrant, detectives towed the Ford to an impound lot and searched the interior. A key clue on the passenger side floor had contained music CDs. *(Maricopa County Superior Court Records)*

A security camera had recorded Brian Legg, along with his wife, David, and Kim shopping on the last day of Brian's and Jeannie's life. *(Maricopa County Superior Court Records)*

David and his young "wife" returned from a trip to Hawaii and were arrested for credit card fraud. She pleaded guilty to lesser charges and received a light sentence. *(Maricopa County Superior Court Records)*

When David and Kimberly were arrested, they carried Brian's credit cards and thousands in cash withdrawn from ATMs. *(Maricopa County Superior Court Records)*

Alicia, after divorcing David, made new friends, including Playboy Playmate Keri Furman and her boyfriend, Taylor Helzer, who was later convicted of multiple murders. *(Courtesy Alicia LaFlesh)*

ample opportunities to make a report with a telephone call, and certainly did not appear to be frightened.

After the deposition, Detective Ron Jones telephoned radio station KUPD and talked to its nighttime disc jockey, Larry Mack. Jones reported, "I was given Mr. Mack's name as the disc jockey at KUPD, the most probable radio station playing hard-rock music at the midnight hour. In speaking with Mr. Mack, I asked if he recalled playing a song titled 'Don't Cry' on or about the night of June 9, 1996. He first looked through the records for that date, and then advised that he was sure he wouldn't have played a song like that at that time frame. The shows during the late hour are much more hard rock than a song like 'Don't Cry.'"

After the deposition, authorities again allowed Kim to go home to Juárez and wait for David Legg's trial to begin. Press releases by the county attorney's office stated it would commence in October 1996. Their optimism would soon give way to frustration at one delay after another.

21

Another Case of Parenticide?

Michael Bernays and Tonya McMath needed time to review the evidence against David by examining every aspect of the murder investigation. She also made a trans-Pacific trip to personally interview witnesses in Hawaii who had spoken to Brian McIndoo and Steve Lynch.

The October schedule for David's murder trial evaporated. At a December hearing before Judge Araneta, Bernays claimed that DCA Glenn McCormick hadn't handed over documents regarding the prosecution's investigation, as required by disclosure rules. The judge ordered both sides to prepare a joint memorandum detailing exactly what discovery material had been exchanged. To allow enough time for this to be completed, Araneta set a new trial date of January 21, 1997. That, too, would be postponed.

It soon became evident to McCormick what strategy

Bernays planned to employ. Using what is known as a "third-party defense," attorneys for the defendant often attempt to convince a jury that someone other than their client had committed the murder. Bernays and McMath apparently would insist not only that David was innocent of shooting his parents, but that Kimberly might very well have been the killer.

Like a powerful football player might do, McCormick rushed forward to block the kick. In a motion presented to the court, he stated his objections: *Although the state has not been provided with notice of a third party defense, [we are] moving* in limine *to prevent the defense from introducing evidence that suggests Kimberly Pierce-Taylor or others murdered the defendant's parents.*

"In limine" is a Latin term often used in legal documents meaning "at the threshold," or before the trial begins.

The prosecutor realized that David must have told his lawyers that Kimberly pulled the trigger that awful night. Continuing his protest, McCormick wrote: *It is undisputed that Kimberly was at the victims' home when the murders were committed. However . . . Kimberly had no motive to kill the defendant's parents. She was only fifteen years old when she married Mr. Legg. The marriage was actually null and void because he had never divorced his first wife. Kimberly had no legal rights to his parents' inheritance. Her only access to them was through the defendant. There was no sign of forced entry at the crime scene. It was also the defendant who was in complete control during the purchase of a weapon and the pawning of his mother's jewelry after the murders. It was the defendant who repeatedly used his parents' credit cards. It was the defendant who was trained in the military.*

Kimberly testified at a deposition that she had nothing

to do with the murders and that only she, the defendant, and the victims were at the residence at the time of the murders. Therefore, the only witness who could testify that Kimberly, or some other person(s), committed the murders is the defendant.

Citing legal precedents, McCormick explained that before evidence may be introduced indicating someone else possibly committed the crime, *the defendant must show that the evidence has an inherent tendency to connect such other person with the actual commission of the crime. Vague grounds of suspicion are not sufficient.*

Countless defense attempts to point the finger of guilt elsewhere have been derailed by that crucial point: the insufficiency of vague grounds of suspicion. McCormick presented examples of other cases in which judges have issued orders precluding the "third party" defense.

But in the David Legg trial, Michael Bernays and Tonya McMath intended to do everything in their power to persuade jurors that the entire package of evidence collected by investigators against David could apply equally to Kimberly.

The news media, enraptured by a good-looking young man being accused of murdering his parents and using their money to take his young "wife" to Hawaii, covered every step of the investigation and court proceedings. Some of the reporters drew a parallel to a highly publicized crime that took place in Beverly Hills, California, seven years earlier.

On Sunday evening, August 20, 1989, entertainment executive Jose Menendez and his wife, Kitty, lounged on a plush couch in the family room of their

multimillion-dollar Beverly Hills mansion, watching a James Bond movie on television. They both dozed off before the clocks chimed the hour of ten.

Newspaper readers could see the eerie resemblance to the circumstances of Brian and Jeannie's murder.

In the Menendez home, two young men carrying shotguns quietly eased into the front entrance and tiptoed through a lavish hallway. They heard the television blaring and moved toward the sound. One of the gunmen raised his weapon, aimed it at Jose's head, and pulled the trigger. A thunderous blast echoed through the home, waking both sleepers. The shooter had barely winged Jose, who yelled in alarm. A second shot destroyed the back of his head.

Kitty Menendez, horrified at the sight of her husband's exploding flesh, bone, and brain tissue, sprang upright. The lethal weapons barked again, sending pellets into her legs and arm. Collapsing on the floor, she crawled and then made it to her feet again. Two more shots toppled her to the floor, but miraculously she still had enough strength and will to live. As she struggled, the inept gunmen sprinted to a car parked outside, reloaded, and raced back to the severely wounded woman. With the barrel tip touching Kitty's face, one of the killers delivered a shot that ended her life.

Over an hour later, the murdered couple's two sons returned to their home. The elder boy, Lyle, age twenty-one, usually recognized as more handsome than his sibling, entered with the taller, somewhat awkward, eighteen-year-old brother, Erik. They would later describe their reaction to the scene of violent carnage. Lyle said he overcame the emotional jolt long enough to call the police. Erik reported a feeling of almost paralytic

shock and the need to look more closely at the bodies of his parents.

On the 911 call, Lyle sobbed into the phone, "We're the sons . . ." before his throat constricted. The dispatcher asked what the problem was. In a quavering falsetto voice, Lyle yelled, "They shot and killed my parents." While the dispatcher tried to calm him, Lyle shouted garbled commands to his brother. Finally he began to answer questions falteringly.

When the news broke the next morning, overwhelming sympathy for the two orphaned boys spread across the nation. Although they didn't seem as heartbroken as some might expect, they did appear to be grieving.

Lyle and Erik Menendez had grown up in a luxurious, though highly controlled, environment. Their father strongly expressed his expectations for his sons' success. He also made it clear that he would be in complete charge of the planning and implementation of their goals. A few insiders thought the two boys were never allowed to be normal children. Education at the right schools was a must, so Lyle attended Princeton University, but he struggled and was suspended a year for cheating. Erik settled for the University of California at Los Angeles, UCLA.

In the relationship between the brothers, Lyle had shown considerable dominance, while Erik seemed less aggressive, perhaps more sensitive. But they appeared to have a tight bond despite the difference in self-confidence. Lyle exhibited an almost arrogant ability to control events and people, while Erik was sometimes judged as insecure. Both boys were competitive in sports. Lyle won a regional tennis championship in his age class, and Erik responded with a similar win for younger players. It angered their father

when Lyle mentioned he would like to quit school to become a tennis professional.

Prior to the killings, in the summer of 1989, people close to the Menendez family whispered suspicions about the existence of dark problems. Lyle's reckless behavior had upset his father repeatedly. Erik seemed to be brooding. Their mother appeared to sense something was wrong.

A massive investigation of the murders dealt with rumors of a drug hit, jealous business dealings, and other wild speculations. Some observers expressed quiet concern about the boys going on extravagant spending sprees—buying an expensive new sports car, making impulsive investments, and traveling world-wide. The sons had made a remarkably speedy recovery from the grieving process, and this puzzled many acquaintances.

Homicide investigators had been wondering about the same things and became increasingly suspicious that Lyle and Erik were the mysterious killers of their own parents. The theory grew when a screenplay turned up, cowritten by Erik Menendez and one of his close friends. It told the story of a wealthy family in which the egotistical eighteen-year-old son kills his parents, inherits a vast fortune, and later dies with a complacent smile on his face.

But the sleuths needed more than a fictitious script. In March 1990, a female friend of a psychologist whose clients included the Menendez brothers contacted investigators with a stunning development. She said she had overheard the boys, in a private session with her friend, yelling about killing someone. Erik, she revealed, had sobbed, "I can't kill anymore."

According to the informant, her psychologist pal had taped the session.

On March 8, a swarm of detectives arrested Lyle Menendez at the mansion. Erik, playing tennis in Israel, flew home to surrender voluntarily. The defense wanted separate trials for each of the brothers, but the judge compromised by conducting one trial with two juries.

Prosecutors presented the theory that the greedy, spoiled brothers committed murder to inherit the family fortune, valued at $14 million. In the highly publicized proceedings, the brothers admitted shooting their parents, but they tearfully claimed they did it out of fear that Jose Menendez was going to kill them to prevent the boys from revealing that he had sexually molested them for years.

The district attorney countered by suggesting the boys, eighteen and twenty-one at the time of the murders, were certainly capable of getting away from any parental abuse. After weeks of emotional testimony, one jury and then the other failed to reach a verdict. A second trial, jointly prosecuting both defendants with one jury, became necessary in 1996. As in the earlier trials, the controversial confession taped by a psychologist played a pivotal role. The prosecution pointed out that not once in the revealing tape could anything be heard about sexual abuse being inflicted on either of the brothers.

Ruling on the hotly disputed issue of self-defense, the judge stated that evidence did not show the boys to be in imminent danger on the night of the shootings. Lawyers for Lyle and Erik, he said, might assert that Jose Menendez had been killed in the heat of

passion, but no evidence existed regarding any threat
of death from Kitty Menendez.

In the summation, the prosecutor argued that the
brothers clearly premeditated the murder as shown by
their carrying loaded shotguns into the house that
night, then stepping outside to reload. "How could
they shoot their mother like this?" he asked.

Their defense acknowledged that the boys fired the
lethal shots, but they asked the jury to find them
guilty of manslaughter instead of murder.

On March 20, the jurors returned with verdicts that
both brothers had committed first-degree murder
with special circumstances. In April, the judge sentenced Lyle and Erik Menendez to spend the rest of
their lives in prison without the possibility of parole.

The horrific case of parenticide came to a close in
April 1996, just two months before Brian and Jeannie
Legg faced a similar fate in the family room of their
home. News watchers and readers couldn't help but
wonder: Had David Legg killed them? If so, had he been
inspired by extensive coverage of the Menendez murders? Did he believe that he could learn from mistakes
made by Lyle and Erik, and commit a perfect crime?

Everyone waited eagerly for the trial to begin, and
for answers to these questions.

22

Secret Mission

A serious and complex matter that could confuse a jury needed to be resolved before the trial. Glenn McCormick understood the need for perfect clarity of evidence presented to jurors, and realized that David's extensive use of Daren Maloy's name might complicate matters. To prevent this, he needed to provide crystal-clear assurance that the real Daren Maloy was absolutely innocent of any complicity in the murders.

The best way to deal with it, McCormick knew, would be to summon Maloy and put him on the witness stand. But this turned out to be impossible. The U.S. Army would not allow it.

Explaining the problem to the court, McCormick noted that Maloy's testimony would be material to the state's case. He explained that David had shared living quarters with Maloy at Fort Bliss for a very short time while under house arrest in February 1996. Later, Maloy

had noticed the absence of his personal identification documents.

Attempts to contact the soldier had met with failure because Maloy had been transferred to Korea, then to Germany, and was currently deployed to Saudi Arabia on a special mission. In legal motions, McCormick wrote, *The State has made every effort to obtain SPC Maloy's presence. However, because of his unique occupation and expertise in the military, the United States Government has refused to honor the State's request.*

Specialist Maloy's occupation, wrote McCormick, required him to work a tightly constructed schedule of duty. Even during the off-duty periods, the army expected him to participate in training activities: *His superior officer, Commander Brian Gibson, has informed this prosecutor that it is absolutely imperative that Specialist Maloy remain in Saudi Arabia for national security reasons. . . . He cannot be returned to the United States to testify at trial.*

As an alternative, the U.S. Army would allow Maloy's presence for a teleconference deposition, which they offered to videotape. The conference would be transmitted via relay.

For this deposition to be presented to the jury, the judge would have to make an official finding that Maloy was unavailable, and that the recorded testimony would "bear adequate indicia of reliability."

Despite objections by the defense, the judge handed down the necessary ruling. McCormick coordinated the intricate arrangements, and assembled the participants in a Phoenix office. They included Detective Ron Jones, defense attorney Michael Bernays, David Legg, defense investigator Thomas Breen, a legal assistant, and a legal secretary.

At the other end of the satellite hookup, a pair of officers sat with SPC Daren Maloy; these were the command judge advocate Major Joe Fetterman and Captain Brian Gibson, Maloy's unit commander. SPC Bobby Pierre, a legal specialist, joined them to do the videotaping.

The conversation began with mutual greetings and introductions on speakerphones at both ends. With that accomplished, Maloy was asked to stand, raise his right hand, and be sworn in.

McCormick explained to everyone that Michael Bernays would kick off the session with a short interview of Maloy before the actual deposition started. Bernays asked Maloy to state his name and date of birth, and describe his assignment. Maloy complied with the basic information, and said, "I am currently a fourteen echo, which is a TCA operator in the Patriot field."

No one in Phoenix had any idea what that meant, so Maloy explained, "TCA means tactical control assistant. I assist an officer in doing Patriot missile acquisitions."

His commander spoke. "Sir, this is Captain Gibson. I can probably give you a little bit more concise job description, if that's all right." Bernays welcomed the help and Gibson continued. "Sir, he is one of three soldiers with the unique job description inside my unit. He is the actual soldier who mans the computer van that monitors the radar, fires the missiles, and he's one of the three-man crew who mans the system on a twenty-four-hour basis every third day and continues that during the length of the deployment." At

Bernays's inquiry, Gibson added, "I have three crews, each consisting of three individuals. Each person has unique job titles, descriptions, and responsibilities that are not interchangeable. . . . It is a Patriot Missile Battery assigned to defense over here."

He made the army's refusal to release Maloy for attendance at trial crystal clear. Bernays asked, "How many such batteries are there?"

Gibson replied, "Sir, for classification purposes, I don't think I can discuss that on an open line."

Bernays shot right back, "Are you telling me that there are no backup personnel there for cases of injury or death in combat?"

"There is not in this situation. If there is a death during combat, I would go on worst case. I would have to go twenty-four hour on, twenty-four off, but obviously I could not sustain that for an indefinite amount of time."

Still pushing, Bernays wanted to know the current status of hostilities in the region. Another voice replaced Gibson's and sounded a little impatient. "Sir, this is Major Fetterman again. That is classified and we don't want to discuss that over an open line. We can just tell you that we're at threat condition Charlie. There are four levels of threat conditions; *A*-Alpha, *B*-Bravo, *C*-Charlie, and *D*-Delta. Delta would mean we are being attacked. Charlie means attack is imminent. But any specifics, sir, are not available for public dissemination for obvious reasons."

What about emergency leave in case of a death in the family? Bernays inquired.

Fetterman said that emergency leave would depend on the unit commander's analysis. He commented that four previous subpoenas for trials had also been

rejected because the soldiers were considered "mission essential." Maloy's presence was particularly important, said the major, because only three men in the entire unit were qualified to do his job.

After a few more minutes of exchanges on the subject, Bernays spoke directly to Maloy. "Do you mind if I call you Daren?" Maloy said that would be fine. "All right, Daren, tell me a little bit about your contact with David Legg?"

Again Maloy, by force of habit, spoke in abstruce military slang. "I was PCS from Fort Bliss after my eight-month AIT—"

"Wait! I've never been in the military," Bernays said. "You're going to have to translate some of those initials for me."

"I'm sorry. AIT is advance individual training. It's our job training. Like I said, I was getting ready to PCS from there to the Republic of Korea—"

"What's PCS ?"

"That is where you, kind of, a change of station. You move from one base to another." He didn't say what military jargon aficionados know: the initials mean permanent change of station. Maloy told of being quartered with Legg for about five days, leaving for California, and then discovering that his driver's license was missing. "There's not really much else I could say—I mean, other than I didn't, at first, trust Specialist Legg as a friend. And that's it." He couldn't recall the exact dates, only that it had been in March 1996.

"Did you ever meet any family of Mr. Legg's?"
"No. I did not."
"Did you ever meet any of his friends from Mexico?"
"No. I did not."

"Did you ever go out of the barracks with him?"

"No. I did not."

"Was he on some sort of barracks restriction at the time you met him, to your knowledge?"

"To my knowledge, no," said Maloy. "I didn't really get into his personal life as far as barracks restriction goes. It was just day-to-day army bs talk, if you want to put it like that."

Bernays said he had no more questions and turned it over to McCormick.

The prosecutor's first question was "Did you ever purchase a Ford Escort from [an agency] in El Paso, Texas?"

"No. I did not."

"Do you recall if you ever took out any loan papers or ever signed any documents relating to the purchase of a Ford Escort in El Paso?"

"No. I did not."

Referring to copies of documents that had been faxed in advance to Maloy's headquarters, McCormick asked him to look at the image of a California driver's license that contained Daren's name. Maloy said that the address, the height, the weight, and the signature were all his. But he couldn't recognize the photo. McCormick next asked him to examine the image of a Wells Fargo card. Maloy recognized it as one he had possessed while stationed at Fort Bliss. Another image showed a Bank One ATM card in his name, but Maloy said he had never owned it or anything from Bank One. Nor did he recognize a Social Security card or Arizona driver's license in his name.

"Do you know anyone by the name of Cecilia Maloy?"

"No."

The rental agreement for the apartment on 48th Street came next. Maloy said the writing on it was not his, nor was the signature. But the Social Security number in the upper right corner was his. This document and several others contained the name "Daren David Maloy."

"And your middle name is what?"

"Russell." He spelled it out.

"And it's not David. Is that right?"

"That is correct."

The same questions and answers applied to several more documents in question. McCormick directed him to look at a birth certificate for Daren David Maloy and asked, "Where were you born?"

"Mountain Valley, California."

"So there wouldn't be, or shouldn't be, in your understanding, a certificate of live birth for you in the state of Nebraska?"

"No." If David had forged the certificate, he had found it necessary to take a wild guess about the state in which Maloy had been born. The names of Maloy's parents were also completely wrong.

A check from an account at Norwest Bank came under scrutiny, and Maloy said, "I did have an account there while at Fort Bliss, but do not recognize that particular check."

"Daren, did you ever pawn anything at a shop in Phoenix, Arizona?"

"No."

"Where were you on June 7, 1996?"

"I was in the Republic of Korea."

Shown the photo lineup of females Detective McIndoo had used in Hawaii, Maloy said he had never seen any of the women. But he did recognize David Legg in the six-pack of male photos.

McCormick took Maloy once again back to his time with David at Fort Bliss. "Did you have many talks with him?"

"Not anything specific. There were a couple of times he mentioned he had a wife in Mexico. That I do recall. But other than that, it was just school or on-the-job training or just day-to-day chitchat. Nothing really important."

"Did he ever talk about his parents?"

"Not that I recall."

Glenn McCormick had no more questions and turned Maloy back over to Michael Bernays for a short cross-examination.

The defense attorney dealt with a few issues about handwriting, and then asked, "You never heard David Legg talk about wanting to see his parents dead, did you?"

"No."

"And you never heard him discuss any plans or ideas for killing his parents, did you?"

"No."

After disposing of a few logistical matters, and expressions of gratitude, the conference came to a close.

Daren Maloy's stolen identity might have misled investigators for a very brief time, but now his name was once again restored to pristine innocence in any matters relating to the murders of Brian and Jeannie Legg. He had absolutely no connection to the homicides or to any other crimes committed by David Legg.

23

Impossible Odds

After Alicia filed for a divorce and testified in the hearing at which a judge declared David's marriage to Kimberly invalid, she returned to Concord, California. Using her maiden name, LaFlesh, she began trying once again to reassemble her broken life.

Even though Alicia tried to erase bewildering visions of murder from her mind, she couldn't stop replaying events of the past. Like the old tale of a drowning person's history flashing before the eyes, Alicia's thoughts uncontrollably looked backward. She had been so deeply in love with the person she thought David was, but she realized he had lied not only in words, but in his actions as well. His entire persona was a lie. It turned her stomach to realize she had been blinded by his adoring behavior at the beginning of their relationship. When they exchanged marriage vows, she thought it opened a whole new

chapter of happiness, family, perhaps children, and companionship throughout a bright future. Alicia had basked in the warm love from her parental in-laws, whom she called "Mom" and "Dad," and returned the sincere affection unconditionally.

Now, with the dreams turned to nightmares, she blamed herself for failing to see the warning signs: David's mendacity with his parents about working a second job, his dishonesty about money, and his tendency to avoid discussing anything of importance with her. Alicia wondered if he truly possessed the capacity for loving anyone but himself.

A new strength had gradually established itself within her after she left Hawaii. Alicia had worked steadily, reaffirmed relationships with her siblings, and found a reasonable level of serenity. But the murder of Brian and Jeannie had jolted her world and shattered the self-confidence she had developed. Her childhood had been a disaster, and her marriage had turned out no better. Once more, she would have to start rebuilding from ground zero.

While David waited interminably for the trial to begin in Phoenix, Alicia gritted her teeth, gathered the remaining shards of strength, and accepted the risk of opening herself to new friendships. A gruesome, incredible murder had marred her existence. Surely, knowing an accused killer could happen to a person only once in a lifetime, and the odds of it occurring again would be just impossible.

If Alicia had owned a reliable crystal ball, and been able to look into the future, she probably wouldn't have believed what lay in store.

It started with a camping trip. Alicia and a few friends set up tents in a state park not far from San Francisco Bay and she took a walk to explore the scenery. People who enjoy nature are often friendly in a communal sort of way. A few campsites away, a tall man greeted her and they began chatting. His good looks, charm, courtesy, and relaxed demeanor set her at ease, and his infectious laughter was just what she needed. They found an instant camaraderie, not flirtatious or sexually oriented, just amiable conversation.

The stranger introduced himself as Taylor, and he said his girlfriend, Keri, would be there soon. With a nice smile, he told Alicia of his Mormon faith and his belief in joy, peace, and love. A couple of hours flew by before Keri Furman arrived and joined in the new friendship. Alicia thought they made an attractive couple.

Keri spoke of ambitions to model or find a place in the entertainment industry. An adventurous soul, she also said she wanted to try skydiving and bungee jumping. Alicia thought that Keri just might have a chance in the modeling world, in view of her glowing smile, great figure, five-eight height, and curvaceous 115 pounds.

Because Taylor and Keri so willingly shared information about their lives and preferences, and seemed interested in her, Alicia felt comfortable telling them all about David and the murder of his parents. The friendship grew, and they agreed to meet again soon. Alicia looked forward to it, and followed up by joining the couple for a picnic and visiting them at their home.

Taylor, whose full name was Glenn Taylor Helzer, talked about his younger brother, Justin, and their high-school days in Martinez, near Concord, where Alicia lived. In fulfillment of his Mormon mission, he

had traveled to Brazil. With ambitions to succeed in the field of high finance, he worked as a stockbroker. While Alicia listened, she snapped a photo of Keri holding a young boy. Keri wore a cleavage-revealing halter top and black scarf over her hips to cover a minuscule bikini bottom. Taylor knelt next to her, shirtless, grinning, his eyes hidden by sunglasses, and sporting the makings of a beard.

True to her ambitions, Keri eventually succeeded as a model. Using the name "Kerissa Fare," she posed nude for *Playboy* magazine and was chosen as "Miss September 2000."

Taylor's future pursuits took a far different path after he and Keri broke up. Perhaps as an offshoot from his experiences as a Mormon, and being excommunicated from the faith, he chose to build a business offering spiritual guidance to lost souls. God, said Taylor, spoke directly to him and he had no compunction about using his power as a chosen prophet. His views of religious morality, though, took a warped twist. With brother Justin and a restless woman ironically named Dawn Godman as partners, the trio decided that acquisition of funding for their enterprise should not be constrained by any ethical limitations. If lives had to be taken in pursuit of this goal, so be it.

One more person was drawn into the circle of evil greed. Taylor lured and romanced Selina Bishop, age twenty-two, in order to use her name for laundering money he planned to steal. She loved music, partly because blues guitarist Elvin Bishop was a close relative. Selina's mother, Jennifer Villarin, thought Taylor seemed nice. She dropped by his residence one day just to check him out. She had no idea it would end up costing her her life.

As a stockbroker, Taylor Helzer had acquired numerous clients, some with large fortunes. An elderly couple, Ivan and Annette Stineman, had not only trusted him with investments, but they had befriended him as well. In the final week of July 2000, brothers Taylor and Justin paid a visit to the Stinemans at their Walnut Creek home, just a few miles north of Danville, where Brian and Jeannie Legg had lived. Instead of financial documents in their briefcases, the Helzers brought handcuffs. After shackling the frightened couple, they forced Annette to telephone the manager of their brokerage house and tell him she wanted to liquidate their stocks. Next they demanded two checks be written for a total of $100,000 to Selina Bishop. Using the so-called date rape drug, Rohypnol, Taylor force-fed the victims what he assumed would be a lethal dose. It didn't kill them, so the brothers transported their captives to an apartment. Inside, Justin slashed Annette's throat, and Taylor beat Ivan to death. Using a power saw, they dismembered the bodies and stuffed the remains into duffel bags.

The checks to Selina Bishop were soon deposited to her bank account, which had been set up exclusively for that purpose so it could easily be converted to cash. With the scheme's finances now set, Selina's usefulness had ended. On the pretense of taking her camping in Yosemite Valley, Taylor drove her instead to the charnel apartment, where he and Justin fractured her skull with a hammer before using a razor-sharp hunting knife on her throat.

Concerned that Selina's mother, Jennifer, might know too much about him, Taylor decided she should also die. Late one August night, he crept into her

apartment, found her in bed with a man, James Campbell, and shot them both to death.

Taylor and Helzer had stuffed the chopped-up bodies of the Stinemans and Selina Bishop into three duffel bags, deliberately mixing the gory remains in a misguided effort to prevent future identification. They drove to a river and dumped them all into the murky water. The current carried them downstream, where all three bags were finally found in separate locations.

Too many people had seen the killers with their victims and reported their suspicions to investigators. Taylor, Justin, and Godman were rounded up and charged with multiple murders. Godman worked out a plea deal in which she agreed to testify against the brothers, and received a sentence of thirty-eight years in prison.

Among a gaggle of witnesses at the trial, *Playboy* model Keri Furman told of riding to Tijuana with Taylor, where he planned to buy Rohypnol. She also recalled Taylor talking about a wild scheme in which he might lure a woman by pretending to love her. Selina Bishop had filled that role.

Taylor Helzer surprised authorities by pleading guilty to five murders. Justin Helzer stood trial and heard a jury convict him on five counts of first-degree murder. Both men are on death row in San Quentin State Prison.

Alicia LaFlesh watched the television news in stunned shock. What kind of a curse had been inflicted on her? Would people think she was a magnet for murderers? Somehow, she managed to draw upon the resiliency she had earned the hard way, and moved forward again. Certainly, she had been a victim, but at least she had survived.

24

Lethal Love Letters

Sitting in jail while waiting for his trial to begin, David Legg hadn't given up on romance. He had professed to Alicia that she was the love of his life. Later, he had committed to Kimberly that she was the love of his life. While sitting in jail, he wrote nearly sixty letters to Kimberly between August 1996 and May 1997.

That all changed in August 1998 when he entered into a correspondence with a girl named Lynette, who happened to be in Texas prison. From his cell on Madison Street, David wrote passionate letters to this new love of his life.

One September evening, soon after she had been paroled and paid a visit to David, he wrote a fifteen-page letter addressed to "Lynette, My Life." In neat, small script on lined paper, he began by calling her "Princess."

In the first sentence, David made a declaration of

being scared to death—not afraid of the forthcoming murder trial, but frightened of losing her. Expressing regret for not having told her anything about events leading to his incarceration, David claimed he had wanted to confide in Lynette, but couldn't find adequate words. Stating his love again, he told of praying to "Father in Heaven" that Lynette would understand his reluctance to explain it all. To drive home his anguish, he revealed his inability to stop crying, shaking, and dying inside.

With references to the times she had visited him in jail, David rationalized his failure to share details of his plight by blaming his oversight on the brevity of their time together. He hadn't wanted to waste those precious minutes with mundane matters. Apparently realizing how flimsy this excuse sounded, he assured Lynette that his deep love for her would never allow him to lie.

Several other women in David's life had heard those same promises.

Telling Lynette of his confidence in their future together, David committed to fighting for it with everything in his being.

At the top of page two, he wrote: *I am going to tell you everything that everybody (my lawyers and investigators) have told me not to discuss because you never know who reads our letters.* Disdainful of the advice, he stated he didn't care, because Lynette was the woman he truly loved, and he wished to hide nothing from her.

In the next long, convoluted paragraph, he thanked her for a beautiful card, and referred to a detective who had probably given her a lot of information. Perhaps, David speculated, he should just wait to explain the charges against him until he won in the

trial, because "the case against me is practically non-existent." Still, he said, because he wanted to marry her, he needed to find a way to divulge all. Just in case the detective had told her too much, David made a plea to Lynette to believe him and not desert him.

Getting to the heart of the matter, David swore, *I did not, could not, would not, or in any way kill anyone or plan to kill anyone or have any knowledge of it happening until after the fact.* Evidently confident that he would be found not guilty, even if he did not testify, David told Lynette that he must do the right thing because the real killer needed to be behind bars: *I will get on that stand and testify to everything I know, darling. I promise you on my life that I can put enough solid evidence down to convict the person and totally prove myself innocent.*

David's next blunt statement pointed an accusing finger: *Lynette, the person who did this was my ex-girlfriend from Juarez. . . .* Without using Kimberly's name, and avoiding any references to having illegally married her, David shifted all the blame. He described her as a ruthless person and cryptically characterized her friends as "very dangerous."

Next, David moved on to tarnish his dead parents. Referring to himself as a very sexual person, he attributed it to carnal abuse by his parents he suffered as a child, and continued until he turned twelve. But, he said, he never understood it was bad, just part of life. Also, he claimed his family had brought drugs into the home: *They were really sexually messed up and I guess you could call them "swingers."*

At fifteen, David recalled, he had a girlfriend. One night he came home late from playing sports, and found her having sex with his parents! Distressed, he ran away and didn't return for a week. The incident

with his girlfriend never came up for discussion, and
he never saw her again. Pleading with Lynette again
to understand and accept his love, David told her he
joined the army to get away from everything so he
could try to have a normal life. Omitting any mention
of marriage to Alicia, he told of his parents moving to
Phoenix, where they began to deal "drugs on the
side." Benevolently, he said, he wanted to establish a
relationship with them during his stay in Hawaii because part of him still cared.

Finally acknowledging a misdeed of his own after
being transferred to El Paso, he admitted getting into
a habit of writing bad checks and "all that crap."
Bringing Cecilia into the picture, he described ventur-
ing down to Juárez, meeting her, and alluded to finding stuff available that would make his parents
overjoyed "at what I could get my hands on." With Cecilia tagging along, he often traveled to Phoenix, he
wrote, *to make them happy and at the same time destroying
my military career.*

With the army behind him, David told Lynette, he
and Cecilia moved to Phoenix, where he started a new
life and a new job. But he still had the "bad check
habit." Coming back to the present, David wrote, *I am
absolutely happy in life now because of you and the Lord.*

In Phoenix, said David, he worried about a problem facing him back in El Paso. To avoid getting
caught, he and Cecilia found an apartment where
people she knew dropped in now and then. After a
long talk with her, he decided to face the music back
in Texas on a Monday. But on the preceding Sunday
night, a couple of people came to the apartment, he
wrote, as *kind of a going to jail party for me.*

In David's account, he took one of the men home

at about nine o'clock. When he returned, a "friend" of Cecilia's was there, but she wasn't. The guy told him he should go over to his parents' house right away.

Taking a break in his story, David commented: *Lynette, my lawyers would freak out if they knew I was telling you all about this but I don't care because I want and need you to know the whole truth. Nothing on earth is more important to me than you. Understand and believe that. I love you.*

Returning to his narrative, David said that he arrived at his parents' home and knew something wasn't right. A car belonging to their Juarez "friends" was in the driveway. He entered the house and found Cecilia inside. The "little bitch" stood there with her gun in her hand. *She freaking pointed it at me,* he wrote.

At that point, penned David, *I saw what she did and it was bad. Lynette, I fell to the floor and I thought I died.* Describing how difficult he found it to tell all this, David stated that he still couldn't deal with it even after so many months. Despite all the hell he had gone through with his parents, he still loved them. Cecilia and her "friend" had taken them away from him forever.

Decrying his own stupidity for not telling police, David bemoaned the turn of events that landed him in jail charged with the murders. As soon as the trial started, he promised, he would give them everything they wanted to convict that girl and her friend who helped her. He had been a fool, David admitted, and had made a terrible mistake by helping the guy get away, and for fleeing from Arizona with Cecilia. He made the excuse that he was afraid for his own life, and for the lives of other people.

Dragging his correspondence back to the crime scene, David stated that by the time he figured out

what had happened, the killers had already grabbed everything of value. That included drugs, money, jewelry, and credit cards. Somehow, for reasons he couldn't understand, the other "friend" who had been at the apartment informed the police, which resulted in David and Cecilia being arrested by police in Los Angeles.

Cecilia's friends, said David, found a way for her to avoid charges, and they took her to Mexico.

Explaining again his confidence of being acquitted of murder, David admitted he might be convicted of fraud, but was certain the sentence would be no more than the time he has already served, especially if he provided evidence needed to bring the killers to justice: *I can give them the weapon with her prints and shell casings with her prints.* He could also identify the person from whom she bought the gun and even provide the motive. And the buddy he took home that night would provide him with a foolproof alibi. The timing, David asserted, was "indisputable."

Weaving even more detail into his account, David stated that a neighbor had heard the gunshots and noted the time. The woman had thought the noise came from firecrackers and had complained at a community meeting about someone making so much of a disturbance on a Sunday night.

In the next few paragraphs, David repeated his love for Lynette and apologized again for not confiding in her earlier. If he had, he claimed, she might have been subpoenaed to testify at the upcoming trial, and he didn't want to put her through "bs" like that. Instead, he wanted her standing by his side at the trial, as his wife.

Bringing up something he had previously told

Lynette, David begged her not to think he had lied
about inviting his parents to their wedding. He explained that he meant the parents of a dear friend
who had always treated him like a son. He had even
called them "Mom" and "Dad."

He filled another page with apologies and suppli-
cations before commenting that he couldn't wait to
see the prosecutor's face when David's attorney presented all of these exculpatory facts to the jury.

For some reason, David's account reverted to the
fraud charges, and he informed Lynette of what he
had already endured in the case against him. Furthermore, he asserted, one of the murder charges was
"scratched" at the hearing, and had he been found
not guilty, the other one would have been dropped.
But a "hung jury" wrecked the whole deal, and he still
had to face a murder trial.

Multiple paragraphs in his letter were devoted to
complicated legal proceedings. In David's stated opinion, these tangled matters could still cause the whole
case to be dropped. After still more vows of love and
pleas for Lynette's understanding, he turned his
wrath again to Cecilia: *No matter what that so-called
"family" of mine put me through, I honestly still loved them,
Honey. They did not deserve what she did to them.* He en-
gaged in a few passages of self-reproach for failing to
see in advance what might happen. If called upon to
testify against Cecilia, he would happily do it, and
would gladly see her put away forever.

Rhapsodizing again, he told his love that life would
be perfect for them, and he called her "Lynette Legg."
His love for her, David said, would last for eternity.
He concluded by begging his princess for forgive-

ness, understanding, and undying love. Under his signature of "David," he printed, *Your Husband*.

By all appearances, David had serious intentions for his future with Lynette after she earned parole, and he would be found not guilty. To Lynette's consternation, David telephoned her parents, who didn't seem to care much for his attention to their daughter. The father contacted authorities in the Madison Street jail, where David resided, and demanded they prevent him from making any more calls to them in the future. Lynette, too, objected. She wrote to David and instructed him to leave her parents out of it.

Perhaps to prove his good intentions, David even telephoned a travel agent and began making arrangements to take Lynette on a cruise.

Not long after David penned the lengthy letter to Lynette, he wrote one to superior court judge Michael O. Wilkinson, who would preside over his trial.

Hello Sir! My name is David B. Legg, he began. *I pray that you are well and that I spelled your name correctly.* After mentioning that he had been in custody for twenty-six months, Legg explained his purpose in bringing a matter to the judge's attention. He said that he and his fiancée, Lynette, were very much in love and desired to be united in marriage. A key policy, he said, demanded approval of the judge. As persuasion to obtain Wilkinson's permission, David pointed out that he had caused no problems, nor had he been in any trouble during his incarceration. Repeating his statement of love for Lynette, David urged the judge to grant his approval. Thanking him, David ended his request: *Take care and God bless always!*

Judge Wilkinson ruled that defendant David Legg could postpone any future plans until after completion of the trial.

David's impassioned words to Lynette might have touched her temporarily, but soon after the trial began, her presence in his life faded away.

25

Eagle Scout Hall of Shame

As an Eagle Scout, David Legg had reached the heights, joining some great luminaries of American history. Now, charged with killing his parents, he faced a trial that could drop him into the depths, along with ten other Eagle Scouts who committed or attempted murder. According to several websites, the trail of shame had started thirty years earlier:

1966: *Former Eagle Scout and U.S. Marine Charles Whitman, at age twenty-five, stabbed and shot his mother to death. Later that July 31 night, he killed his wife by stabbing her repeatedly with a bayonet. The next morning at the University of Texas campus in Austin, carrying a footlocker full of food, handguns, rifles, and ammunition, Whitman rode an elevator and then ascended several flights of stairs to the clock tower's top floor. On the way up, he split the skull of a female*

employee with his shotgun stock and used the weapon to shoot and kill a teenage boy and his aunt, plus wound other members of the family. From the observation deck, he took aim through a powerful rifle scope and shot thirteen pedestrians to death, while wounding thirty-one more. The slaughter ended when a pair of police officers cornered the killer and emptied a shotgun into his head and chest. Whitman became one of the most notorious mass murderers in U.S. history.

1970: *Former Eagle Scout Karl Armstrong parked a bomb-loaded car on campus at the University of Wisconsin, Madison. The explosion badly damaged a building but caused no deaths. Convicted in court, he was sentenced to serve twenty-three years in prison.*

1975: *Former Eagle Scout Daniel Alstadt, at age eighteen, had been a straight-A student in a San Diego, California, high school. No one could ever explain why he came home after midnight and attacked his family. Using an ax, he murdered his father, mother, and sister, and then inflicted grievous injuries to his brother, leaving him paralyzed. A jury found him not guilty by reason of insanity in the deaths of his mother and siblings, but convicted him of first-degree murder for slaying his father. Serving a life sentence, he used a shoelace to hang himself in prison in 2000.*

1975: *Former Eagle Scout Richard Holtje evaded capture for twenty-seven years. But Texas Cold Case Squad detectives caught up with him in a drugstore parking lot in 2002. Ironically, he was on his way to serve jury duty. In the mid-1970s, he had been living with his girlfriend and her sixteen-month-old boy. While*

she attended night classes at the University of Houston, Holtje babysat with the toddler. One hour after she had left one evening, Holtje drove the child to a hospital, but too late. His little body showed signs of abuse over several months. Death came from being scalded in boiling water and drowning. Arrested at age sixty-one, Holtje faced a judge and perhaps the rest of his life in prison.

1983: *Former Eagle Scout and honor student Arthur Gary Bishop, age thirty-two, was captured after a four-year crime spree of sexually torturing and murdering at least five young boys in Utah. The victims ranged from ages four to thirteen. Bishop had been excommunicated from the Mormon Church in 1978. Ten years later, he was executed by lethal injection.*

1985: *Former Eagle Scout Lesley Gosch, age thirty, attempted to extort money from a bank president in San Antonio, Texas. Holding the victim's wife as a hostage, Gosch grew impatient and fired six shots from a handgun into her head. Convicted of first-degree murder, he was executed at Huntsville Prison in 1998, just five months before the start of David Legg's trial.*

1994: *Former Eagle Scout Ronald Shamburger, a fifth-year senior at Texas A&M University, who claimed to be a devout Christian, was born on November 11, 1971, just one day before the birth of David Legg. At the end of September 1994, he broke into the home of a coed he had dated a few years earlier. When Shamburger heard her housemate in an adjacent room, he shot the victim to death. Trying to cover the crime, he set the house ablaze. Convicted of first-degree murder, he was executed at Huntsville in 2002.*

1995: *Former Eagle Scout Wendell Williamson, a law student at the University of North Carolina, carried a handgun as he walked the streets of downtown Chapel Hill on a chilly January day in 1995. Diagnosed as a paranoid schizophrenic, he had been undergoing psychiatric treatment. At random, he began pulling the trigger. The wild shooting killed two young men and wounded a police officer. In November, a jury found him not guilty by reason of insanity. Three years later, he sued his former psychiatrist and the jury awarded Williamson $500,000.*

1995: *Former Eagle Scout Larry Puckett, at age eighteen, broke into a mobile home in Petal, Mississippi. Finding a woman inside all alone, Puckett raped and killed her. A jury convicted him of first-degree murder and the judge sentenced him to death in August 1996. He is on death row at Mississippi State Prison, where he solicits pen pals online. One of his interests, he says, is the military. He tells of enlisting in the U.S. Navy and looking forward to basic training. However, his arrest, in Great Lakes, Illinois, came one month before his training was scheduled to begin.*

During the next decade after David faced trial, five more former Eagle Scouts would become murderers. Three of them killed one or both of their parents, and one murdered the parents of his best friend.

Would David Legg be counted among the shamed killers? A jury would soon weigh the evidence and make a profound decision.

26

Girding for Battle

On the possibility that it might become necessary to show that David's childhood may have negatively affected his adult behavior, the defense team wanted a comprehensive look at him by experts. Michael Bernays employed a "mitigation specialist," but the project didn't go very well.

The expert ran into obstacles early when she attempted to interview members of David's extended family. For some reason, they appeared to be torn between two desires. On one hand, they apparently wanted to cooperate in order to help David. On the other, they worried about violating loyalty to his dead parents. According to a written statement by the defense attorney regarding the expert's efforts, David's paternal grandmother *may have volumes to say about family dynamics which led to this crime. However, she has refused to talk to [our representative],* the report stated.

David's two half sisters agreed to be interviewed by the specialist, but they turned reticent during the conversations. One of the women did reveal some aspects of dysfunction in the nuclear family, and said she would be willing to testify on David's behalf, but she could not afford the costs of travel to Arizona. The other sister was "not as forthcoming about details" that concerned the family.

A maternal aunt in Boston spoke several times by telephone to the interviewer, but *was not available for consultation when the specialist made a trip east to talk to people,* the report noted. Attempts to contact other relatives produced similar results and limited background information.

Considerably more information came from probes conducted by a New York psychiatrist associated with a well-known university. She questioned David at the Maricopa County Jail on two different occasions. His enthusiastic cooperation inspired her to characterize him as "affable and loquacious." In her view, his mood of excitement, which included giggling and unexpected laughter while talking about depressing subjects, appeared "grossly inappropriate to his circumstances."

Investigators working with the doctor spoke briefly to one of David's sisters, interviewed his former wife, Alicia LaFlesh, and talked to the high-school girlfriend who had given birth to David's son. They also obtained information from two of his aunts, another ex-girlfriend, and one of his male friends. To complement these oral histories, the doctor reviewed records of police interviews with David and Kimberly, plus the videotape they made in Hawaii.

As a supplement for these sources, she reviewed David's school records, military documents, financial reports, and results of his hospitalization as a teenager in Illinois. Digging even deeper, she tried to explore a history of David's father through his military records, but she ran into the same problem thousands of individuals and investigators have encountered. A disastrous 1973 fire in St. Louis, Missouri, destroyed huge volumes of documents stored by the armed services.

Upon completion of her research, the doctor prepared a comprehensive report. In it, she concluded that it would be impossible to understand David's behavior on June 9, 1996, without an appreciation of *the erratic, punitive, and frankly bizarre household in which he was raised, and an appreciation of his father's severe psychopathology,* she wrote. Her commentary summarized Brian Legg's air force experience and his subsequent sharing with David facts about war, weapon usage, and covert efforts in gathering "intelligence," including identity theft.

These lessons, the psychiatrist noted, were "interesting" in view of David's subsequent "wild, illegal behaviors" in stealing another person's identity.

Sexual lessons from his father and mother had also impacted David, according to the doctor. From her interviews with him, she concluded that his parents "enjoyed sex" and had a collection of pornographic tapes to which David had access.

She also raised the possibility that when David wanted to enter the air force, Brian had *reportedly found a way to have David's earlier arrest records for writing bad checks sealed by the court.*

These remarkable assertions do not appear to have

any basis in fact and may have been formed largely from David's statements. A couple of David's siblings allegedly spoke to a defense team investigator. But in her report, the doctor admits they wouldn't talk to her. Readers of these conclusions wondered if her observations about Brian Legg's alleged misconduct came entirely from David. If so, the next part of the report seemed strange: *David was reluctant to speak ill of his father.* She acknowledged that records from Riveredge Hospital, where David had been treated in 1990, described his father, Brian, as angry, explosive, demanding, and domineering, as well as derogatory and critical of David. Once, according to David, Brian had lost his temper and kicked the boy's dog across a room, injuring it. An evaluation made at the hospital said that Brian had treated David in a "cold, intrusive, rejecting" manner. Those characteristics seemed contradictory to "explosive and angry."

Referring to beatings with a belt Brian supposedly inflicted on David, the mental-health expert wrote of scars on his back and buttocks for which he could not account. Years later, an author asked Alicia LaFlesh if she had ever noticed any scars on David's back. She said his skin was completely unblemished. Perhaps the alleged scars had healed over and vanished.

More commentary about Brian reportedly came from his stepdaughters, who, according to the doctor's investigator, called Brian "manic-depressive." David complained to the mental-health professional of his dad's impulsive decisions to move his family from place to place, tearing them away from schools and friends. The son also charged Brian with reckless spending habits in which he had felt it necessary to

possess the best of everything. The report observed: *David came by his own psychiatric disorders not only genetically but also by virtue of the examples set by his father.*

Expounding on her patient's earlier years, the psychiatrist lamented that David's medical and educational records were not available, and that family members refused to be interviewed. But she had somehow learned that he began suffering wide mood fluctuations while in junior high school, resulting in withdrawal and lethargy during depressive periods. He even considered suicide. At the other end of the behavioral spectrum, during manic periods, his mind raced "a million miles a minute" (presumably his words). The doctor wrote that David *became hypersexual and was involved in numerous simultaneous sexual relationships.* She cited his prolific telephone calls to sex lines by mentioning a time when David, at age thirteen, ran up a bill of about $2,000. For some reason, the report didn't mention similar conduct in his adult years.

The doctor reported that David's odd activities, which included stealing his parents' credit cards and using them to buy an expensive set of drums, plus writing bad checks to pay for a car, had led to psychiatric evaluation. The diagnosis characterized David as impulse-ridden, self-destructive, and noted that he showed signs of sadness and depression. These symptoms suggested the possibility that he suffered from bipolar mood disorder or perhaps even a brain tumor. More testing followed at Riveredge Hospital. During his seventeen days there, David exhibited "mood swings and instability," plus symptoms of obsessive-compulsive disorder. Medication appeared to stabilize him. After his discharge, he continued to

take lithium and Prozac for approximately nine months, until his parents made a decision to discontinue it.

The psychiatrist's report made brief references to David's army service, noting that his father had convinced him to reenlist for a second hitch, despite David's reluctance. She observed that he became increasingly manic and *found himself involved with several women simultaneously.* By 1995, David became "floridly manic" and started writing bad checks again to buy cars. In her interviews of him, he boasted of telling Brian Legg about purchasing a Porsche. She saw this as one example of how he often tried to make his father proud of him, *but never quite succeeded,* she wrote.

David's misadventures at Fort Bliss, El Paso, and Juárez showed up in the doctor's documentation, culminating in his "marriage" to Kimberly Pierce-Taylor and his desertion from the army. According to the writer, David's father had helped his son forge documents to create a new identity: *Brian Legg showed David how to make photocopies of his birth certificate, insert a different name, then create a raised seal on the paper by dampening it and rubbing it over one of David's mother's brooches.* David had told the doctor that his father ordered a rubber stamp to imprint "Health Department of Nebraska," but when it failed to arrive promptly, they had used the brooch method. She noted that both of his parents had participated in this "intelligence operation."

More allegations in the extensive report accused Brian Legg of giving David phony references, attesting to an inflated salary so he could get a well-paying job, and by pretending to be David's uncle, vouched for him so he could obtain a credit card and a driver's

license. *He counseled David to apply for a social security card by saying he was raised in the hills of Nebraska by grandparents who did not believe in "government." But David had abandoned the scheme at the Social Security Office "because the line was too long,"* the report asserted.

The doctor stated that those few weeks preceding the death of Brian and Jeannie Legg were the first time in David's life that he felt accepted by his parents. She noted, *David, his fifteen-year-old bride, and his parents spent almost every evening soaking in the Leggs" Jacuzzi, dining, and watching television.* In the first week of June, Brian *was sending David to hardware stores to buy tools for remodeling the patio, giving him a credit card and permitting him to forge Brian Legg's name.* The doctor commented that since David was hardly a good risk, it showed questionable judgment by the father.

Unfortunately, the doctor concluded in her report, David *fell behind in his rent and the cycle of bad checks resumed. It was in this bizarre context that the shooting of David's parents occurred.*

While Michael Bernays and Tonya McMath worked for long months assembling information to defend David, DCA Glenn McCormick invested equal labor preparing evidence to prosecute the accused defendant. His intense efforts sometimes precluded stopping for meals, and his Superman physique, which had been 275 pounds during the football years, gradually slimmed down to 240.

McCormick's friends and associates may have noticed a Clark Kent resemblance in physical terms, but they saw in his character something of far greater

importance. They described him as genuine, friendly, easygoing, and having a terrific sense of humor. He could get along with anyone, including cantankerous defense attorneys and overbearing judges. If asked to explain how he had developed these skills, McCormick attributed them to his years on the gridiron. In the camaraderie of athletes, he had developed a thick skin from growing up around trash talk in locker rooms and coping with screaming coaches. Those tribulations gave McCormick knowledge of how to separate the hyperbole of his adversaries in the courtroom, and in heated negotiations, from social exchanges in nonconfrontational settings.

Once asked in an e-mail about his cordial abilities with competitors, McCormick replied, **It's kind of like the post game handshakes with your opponents after having tried to kick the $#@% out of each other for the past sixty minutes.**

More than a few defense attorneys have told McCormick that although they professionally enjoy going to trial against him, they did not relish seeing how well he presented his case to a jury. He put them in mind of someone a Hollywood central casting agency would offer as the ideal prosecutor.

Before dealing with the David Legg case, McCormick had prosecuted nine cases of murder, mostly as the supervisor of the Gangs Unit. The issues involved with Legg presented sharply different obstacles.

At the top of McCormick's list of challenges stood the enigmatic figure of Kimberly. He had already disposed of a key matter by asking the court to declare her marriage to David invalid. This would free her to testify against him if she chose to. McCormick decided

not to depend on her. Later speaking of it, he said, "Because Kimberly Taylor would not, or could not, say in so many words that David Legg shot and killed his parents, we knew we would have to rely heavily on circumstantial evidence. Although circumstantial evidence is often very strong, juries sometimes have difficulty relying on it to convict."

Another aspect of Kimberly's interests had been part of McCormick's preparation. His own experience in the Gangs Unit made him cognizant of a tangential point. He anticipated the defense might try to claim that her collection of Mickey Mouse memorabilia had a special meaning. "It appeared they would somehow implicate her as part of the Mexican Mafia because of the M.M. initials. I was very familiar with the Mexican Mafia. And, fortunately, Detective Ken Hansen had investigated some Mexican Mafia homicides and knew enough about them to answer my questions. We were prepared to dispel any myth in that regard [that] the defense might attempt to have the jury believe."

An extremely thorny potential problem had been David's use of Daren Maloy's name. It disappointed McCormick that he would not be able to put the real Maloy on the witness stand to give the jury unequivocal proof that this upstanding soldier had absolutely nothing to do with the murders or circumstance surrounding them. Before obtaining Maloy's deposition via satellite connections, McCormick had worked on arranging a different alternative to having him appear at the trial. "We worked out an elaborate uplink through the air force and the army to have him testify by phone." But some technical malfunction prevented it.

As sometimes happens when trials are delayed for many months or even years, witnesses might die.

Edward Johnson, the man who sold David the Ruger pistol, which McCormick believed to be the murder weapon, passed away. Fortunately, though, Johnson's son, also named Edward, had witnessed the sale and would be available to testify.

These problems, among a hundredfold more, had consumed McCormick's time and energy for two years while David Legg sat in jail and his defense team worked on strategies for convincing a jury to find him not guilty.

The trial would be presided over by superior court judge Michael O. Wilkinson. A solidly built man, with a full, youthful face and dark hair looping down over his forehead, Wilkinson commanded respect among his peers and the attorneys who worked in his courtroom. He had served two years as a prosecutor with the city of Phoenix and then eleven years with the Maricopa County Attorney's Office, after which he went into private practice. Arizona governor Evan Mecham appointed Wilkinson to the bench in 1987. On the day he reported to the new job, the presiding judge assigned him to a triple homicide! Wilkinson subsequently handled at least fifty murder cases. Glenn McCormick said about him, "Judge Wilkinson is serious and maintains excellent control over proceedings. Prosecutors appreciate a judge with commanding presence, and one who plays by the rules." Wilkinson fit that picture perfectly.

A grand jury had indicted David Legg, and their charges would be read to the jury on opening day:

Count 1: David Brian Legg, on or about the 9th day of June, 1996, intending or knowing that his conduct

would cause death, with premeditation, caused the death of Brian Legg, in violations of applicable Arizona Laws. The State further alleges that the offense charged in this count is a dangerous offense because [it] involved the discharge, use, or a threatening exhibition of a gun, a deadly weapon or a dangerous instrument, and/or the intentional or knowing infliction of serious physical injury upon Brian Legg, in violation of Arizona Revised statute 13-604 (P).

Count 2: David Brian Legg, on or about the 9th day of June, 1996, intending or knowing that his conduct would cause death, with premeditation, caused the death of Palma Jean Legg, in violation of applicable Arizona laws.

Count 3: David Brian Legg, on or about the 10th day of June, 1996, without lawful authority, knowingly controlled Palma Jean Legg's diamond ring of a value of $3000 or more but less than $25000, with the intent to deprive Palma Jean Legg of such property, in violation of applicable Arizona laws.

Count 4 charged David with illegally selling the diamond ring.

Counts 5, 6, 7, 8, and 9 charged him with stealing and illegally using numerous credit cards.

After twenty-seven months of delays, legal arguments, and additional investigation, a date finally emerged for the trial to start: September 1998.

Newspaper reporter Doug Murphy had been following the case for the *Ahwatukee Foothills News*. In his role as staff writer and editorial page editor, he took a deep interest in the upcoming trial. Well qualified to dig out details of a compelling story, he had been a first-place

winner for general reporting from the Arizona Press
Club and the Arizona Newspaper Association.

With his reputation for fair and accurate coverage
of events in the Phoenix region, Murphy had established strong rapport with investigative agencies.
Police reports found their way to Murphy's hands in
record time.

Murphy reported in late September that the long
postponed trial appeared to be finally imminent.
Summarizing what David had told investigators,
Murphy mentioned that David had consistently
denied murdering his parents, claiming they were already dead when he and his "wife" arrived at the
house. In order to save anyone else the trauma of
seeing the dead bodies, he had closed all the drapes
and window blinds. As he moved through the house,
he had collected his mother's purse and taken checkbooks out of drawers and a file cabinet. Discovering
the mother's diamond ring on a bathroom counter,
he had slipped it into his pocket. In a police interview,
David had admitted pawning the diamond the following day and taking Kimberly to Hawaii. He had rationalized it as the only place he could think of to just get
away from everything.

The arduous jury selection process, which took several days, had been closely observed by Murphy. It
had resulted in seating a retired attorney, a mathemat-
ics teacher, an employee of United Parcel Service, a
flight attendant, an electrical engineer, a computer
programmer, a Motorola employee, a couple of re-
tirees, and three others with no specified occupation.
Some of the questioning from the prosecutor and the

defense attorneys had been puzzling, such as which sports teams the prospective jurors supported. None had admitted liking the Arizona Cardinals NFL team. The final picks appeared to satisfy both sides. Now the trial could finally get started.

27

He Cold-Bloodedly
Killed Them

Judge Michael O. Wilkinson's fourth-floor court-room filled quickly on Wednesday morning, September 23, 1998. Spectators and reporters, including Doug Murphy from the *Ahwatukee Foothills News,* eagerly awaited opening statements by the prosecution and the defense.

This introduction to the facts of the case, which lawyers expect the evidence to show, provides a sketch of the unfolding story. The judge had advised jurors in advance that attorneys' statements are not to be regarded as evidence. Anything they might say is nothing more than a road map of where the trial is headed.

As soon as his clerk completed reading aloud grand jury charges against defendant David Legg, Judge Wilkinson said, "Thank you, Judy. Mr. McCormick, your opening statement."

* * *

The tall attorney rose from his chair at the prosecutor's table and strode with an athlete's grace to a lectern facing the jury box. Wearing a dark gray suit, white shirt, and conservative red tie, he stood silent for a few moments and made eye contact with twelve freshly coiffed jurors. Faces of five women and seven men, plus two alternates, one of each gender, looked bright, alert, and ready to absorb every word. Glenn McCormick spoke in a deep, pleasantly resonant voice easily heard by court officers and spectators in the gallery, and he began with a deliberately blunt dictum.

"May it please the court, counsel, ladies and gentlemen of the jury. What the evidence in this case should show is that David Brian Legg took a twenty-two-caliber Ruger pistol from near to contact, shot his mother in the head three times from close range and his father in the head two times from close range, up close and personal!

"Now, from there, a ring with a diamond in it, that is three-point-three carats in weight, was taken. The evidence should show that Palma Jean Legg never took that off, and that ring was taken from her lifeless finger." It would also be made clear to the jury, said McCormick, that Brian Legg's pockets were turned inside out and his wallet containing credit cards had been stolen. Other credit cards, along with checkbooks, were also taken on that tragic June night.

McCormick's speaking style—getting right to the point and avoiding unnecessary rhetoric—appeared to keep jurors riveted. He said he planned to explain the evidence against David Legg in three story lines.

The first phase would be the family members who

had the misfortune to discover the bodies. Second would be the police investigation. The third phase would be "from another person who was present at the residence when this happened. That's the story line coming from Cecilia Kimberly Pierce-Taylor."

Without a pause, McCormick launched into the traumatic experience of Jeannie's son by a former marriage. He told of the horrific experience in which George Price, along with his wife and his cousin, had found the decaying dead bodies. Through Mc-Cormick's narration, jurors heard of Price's attempts to reach his mother and stepfather by phone, his trip to Ahwatukee, and finally the shock of finding them on a love seat, dead.

Scanning his audience's expressions and body language while he spoke, McCormick satisfied himself that he had each juror's full attention. He moved on to the investigation. "They processed the crime scene as they do, taking care with each step of the way. Initially there really wasn't much to go on as to who the suspect might be. But soon they found that credit cards were being used . . . at Sky Harbor Airport to purchase airline tickets round-trip to Hawaii for two people." Those tickets, he said, had been issued for Brian Legg and Kimberly Miller. Further investigation found that in Los Angeles, the female's name had been changed to Maloy.

Another use of the card popped up in Hawaii, said McCormick, for the rental of a vehicle at Dollar Rent A Car. David Legg had presented his driver's license with an address on 48th Street. McCormick couldn't hide the admiration he had for Detectives Ron Jones and Ken Hansen as he described the apartment

search, which turned up checkbooks belonging to the victims, along with other evidence.

About $2,300 had been withdrawn from ATMs, the prosecutor said, and hits kept coming on credit card usage, until June 15 when they suddenly ceased.

Eventually detectives at the last minute "found a couple by the name of Daren and Kimberly Maloy coming back on an ATA Charter Airlines flight on the twenty-second of June. Jones and Maloy jumped on a plane. They flew over to Los Angeles International Airport. They arranged with the L.A. police and security to have the plane detained when it landed. No passengers were allowed off. They entered the plane and made arrests of David Legg and Cecilia Kimberly Pierce-Taylor."

A major piece of evidence in McCormick's arsenal was Jeannie Legg's diamond ring. He explained in detail how David, posing as Daren Maloy, along with Kimberly, had pawned it for $7,000. If jurors felt disgust or loathing at the idea of a man killing his mother and selling her diamond ring the next day, their facial expressions didn't reflect it. They remained true to form, adhering to the universal code that people serving jury duty must maintain poker faces.

McCormick took the avid listeners through Detective Jones's systematic tracing of phone calls made from the apartment. "And what do you think they found from the sixth and seventh of June, two days before the homicide? They found several calls to people who had guns for sale, advertised in newspapers. They came upon one Ed Johnson, who, in fact, had sold a Ruger twenty-two to a young couple who had come to his house. Mr. Johnson, the man who actually sold the gun, has passed away since this happened, but his son, whose name is

also Ed Johnson, was present. And he can talk to you about the transaction, and the fact that both the male and the female handled the weapons for sale." The evidence would also show that "on the eighth of June, the couple went to an indoor shooting range, rented a lane, and fired a weapon."

Keeping a perfect pace, not confusingly fast or tediously slow, McCormick knew the prosecutor's maxim. Experience told them never to waste the moment early in a trial for grabbing the jurors' interest. That window of opportunity was fleeting, and must be utilized for full effect.

Retracing the victims' last day of life, McCormick said, "On the ninth of June, in the late afternoon, around four o'clock or so, Mr. and Mrs. Legg were at JCPenney's. And with them were a young couple, David Legg and Cecilia Kimberly Pierce-Taylor." A few soft murmurs could be heard in the gallery, expressions of astonishment that the young man accused of killing his parents had gone shopping with them in those final hours. Could he really have been so cold-blooded? Were investigators absolutely certain they had that timing correct?

As if anticipating that question, McCormick stated, "They are on videotape taken by a surveillance camera, so you can see the time and date they were there. The family . . ." He paused momentarily and then said, "I won't go there for right now. These are some of the activities that lead to the charges we are now talking about."

During the months leading up to the trial, the defense's primary strategy became obvious to McCormick: They planned to convince jurors that Kimberly could have been the killer. If Michael Bernays

and Tonya McMath could persuade just one person among the twelve to believe their theory, it could result in a mistrial. And if they could tilt more jurors in that direction, it could result in a verdict of not guilty. Some observers, considering the paucity of forensic evidence and the prosecution's need to rely completely on circumstantial evidence, expressed confidence in David Legg being exonerated.

Kimberly came up next in Glenn McCormick's reconstruction of a murder case. "Now, let me talk about Kimberly Pierce-Taylor. She is a citizen of Mexico. She has an Anglo name, but she was born in Mexico, and Spanish is her primary language. She also speaks English. As a young girl, she met David Legg in October of 1995 and began a relationship with him, which resulted in a marriage ceremony in El Paso, Texas. Not a church, just a justice of the peace–type setting.

"The evidence will show that the reason David Legg was in the El Paso area is because he was in the army, stationed at Fort Bliss. And, as is common for a lot of servicemen, they will go across the border into Juárez—the city right across the Rio Grande—and I guess spend some time over there. That's where he met Ms. Taylor."

Soon afterward, said McCormick, David went AWOL and planned a church marriage ceremony with the teenager. But David returned to the army base, instead. "He was, at that point, placed in a barracks with another man, by the name of Daren Maloy."

If McCormick's presentation sought to clarify Kimberly's role, it also needed to assure that jurors

understood the role Daren Maloy *did not* play. David
and Kimberly's illegal use of the Maloy name had
seemed to implicate him during the initial week of
investigation, but detectives soon established Daren
Maloy's complete innocence. McCormick wanted
the jury to understand that in advance. He needed
to scrub from the jurors' brains any hint of complicity by Maloy, and make them realize that he had
been victimized in a clear case of identity theft.

With that goal in mind, McCormick explained that
David had gone AWOL again in March, and at the
same time, Maloy had been shipped to Korea. Soon afterward, Maloy had realized his driver's license and
ATM card were missing. "The evidence will show that
David Legg took those things and assumed Mr. Maloy's
identity," so he could successfully evade arrest by the
army. When he took Kimberly to Phoenix, she entered
into the fraud by also assuming the Maloy name.

In Phoenix, said McCormick, the couple moved
into an apartment and began a spending spree they
could not afford, since neither of them earned any
noticeable income. David worked briefly at a few jobs,
but abandoned them. "Then, on the ninth of June, as
was typical for Kimberly and David, they would go
over to his parents' house and have dinner and spend
some time with them."

McCormick had made no bargain with Kimberly
for her testimony. She had been subpoenaed to
appear, and the prosecutor knew she had made the
trip from Juárez. But he couldn't be certain what she
might say, so he had to tread carefully in these opening statements. He told the jury, "Kimberly should tell
you that they were in the Leggs' house watching television. She had fallen asleep on another couch—not

the one on which the victims were found—and at some point, she woke up. She was in her menstrual cycle and needed to go out to the car to get something in her purse. She went out there where the car was parked in the driveway, and while she was in the car, she either listened to the radio, or a CD, to one of her favorite songs. And while she was out there, she heard some noises. When she came back into the house, she walked into the entryway."

Describing the interior layout, McCormick painted a mental picture of Kimberly being able to see down the hallway where a mirror reflected the sight of two bloody bodies sitting on a love seat. "She was scared. She started crying and sat down on the stairway. She saw David coming down the hall with an intense look on his face. At some point, she saw a gun sitting on a table that's right by the stairway. She doesn't know what was happening. She will tell you that she was crying and didn't do anything until David said, 'Let's go.'"

No sound other than McCormick's voice could be heard in the courtroom. Jurors appeared engrossed in every word from the prosecutor's mouth, and spectators found themselves leaning forward, trying not to miss a single detail. "They got in the car and drove to their apartment, where David rushed around getting things together for them to go. He made a flurry of phone calls. Now, the telephone records show that calls were made to a veterinary clinic. They had two cats, which they needed to drop off before the trip. Two calls were made to airlines. Then they left. It appears they went to the veterinary clinic, dropped off the cats, then back to the apartment."

The timing of telephone calls had allowed investigators to construct a time line of events. McCormick's

narrative took the couple to the Marriott Hotel, not far from the airport, where they checked in, sometime after three. About six hours later, calls were made from the hotel room to the jewelry store where David sold his mother's diamond. "And the Yellow Pages book later recovered from that room was found to be missing a page. And that page contained the telephone number of the jewelry store."

Some observers might have pictured Kimberly as a timid companion under David's absolute control. But McCormick's description of her in the jewelry store perhaps altered that view. "During the transaction, David turns to the young girl and says, 'The offer is seven thousand dollars. Should I take it?' And she's like, 'Yeah.'"

Part of the money gained from selling the diamond, said McCormick, was used to pay the apartment manager $2,000 in back rent.

If jurors and spectators wondered why Kimberly was not on trial also, McCormick explained, "The evidence will show that Kimberly Pierce-Taylor was a juvenile, she was fifteen, and that she was prosecuted for theft and fraud-related offenses as a juvenile and is currently on probation."

People familiar with the case knew that David and Kimberly had taken a "honeymoon" trip to Hawaii after the death of his parents. This apparently heartless act had not endeared the couple to anyone, and news that they had used money stolen from the victims to fund the vacation made them even less sympathetic. McCormick spoke of the trip, outlining buying sprees at clothing stores and the purchase of expensive watches and jewelry. "The evidence will show the total run-up on an American Express card was twelve

thousand dollars. The Bank of America card was used for cash withdrawals totaling twenty-three hundred. A First USA card was used for a hotel room.

"Ladies and gentlemen, what this all shows is that the evidence the state expects is going to show you that Mr. Legg cold-bloodedly killed his parents, cold-bloodedly killed them so he could have money, so he could have a trip to Hawaii, so that he could have cash, so that he could go off and live a life of leisure without having to work for money, so that he could avoid the responsibilities that he had in life, responsibilities to the military. And the evidence will show that this was a devastating event in the life of Kimberly Pierce-Taylor, a young person who now must live with what she did after this incident.

"During the trip to Hawaii, they took a seven-day cruise. They paid cash for it. She went along. Fancy gifts were purchased. She, in fact, used the mother's debit card a couple of times at the bank. The greatest devastation has occurred to the family members who have lost their parents.

"Ladies and gentlemen, after his case is through, the state is going to ask you to return guilty verdicts on all counts. Thank you very much."

28

Kimberly Is the One

After Glenn McCormick's unusually brief statement outlining what he expected the evidence to show, Judge Michael O. Wilkinson turned to the defense table. He had been advised in advance that Michael Bernays would defer to his co-counsel for introduction of their case to jurors. He said, "Ms. McMath, your opening statement."

Tonya McMath, dressed in a gray pants suit with blue pinstripes, walked to the lectern, placed some papers on the slanted top, scanned jurors' faces, and began. "Ladies and gentlemen, the state's prosecution of David Legg on murder charges is about *assumptions*." She spoke the last word as if it left a bad taste in her mouth.

"Those *assumptions* began as early as June 15, 1996, when the bodies of Brian and Palma Jean Legg were discovered in their home. At that stage, the Phoenix

Police Department was forced to work off of *assumptions* because despite their best efforts, they had not uncovered any eyewitnesses with concrete information about what had happened."

Prosecutor McCormick listened carefully and took a few notes, but nothing McMath said surprised him. It had been obvious to him for months the defense team would shine a powerful spotlight on the total absence of forensic evidence, and try to convince jurors that circumstantial evidence was not enough to convict their client. McCormick also anticipated hard work by Bernays and McMath to suggest Kimberly Taylor's culpability, with strong hints that she might have been the shooter.

In crisp tones, McMath continued. Effective speakers know how to use repetition of a word or phrase to drive home a point, and McMath hammered hard with "assumed." She said, "So, by the time of David Legg's arrest at LAX, he had come to be a suspect in the deaths of his parents based on a number of circumstances. He was *assumed* to have been involved in his parents' death for one reason—because there was no sign of forced entry. There was no ransacking of Mr. and Mrs. Legg's home that would be indicative of a burglary by a stranger. It was *assumed* at the time of his arrest that he was involved in his parents' murders because of credit card usage." McMath cited several incidents of charges to the cards.

"It was *assumed* that David Legg was involved because he was traveling under a false name. By the time of his arrest, it was *assumed* that David Legg was involved in his parents' murders because by then, search warrants had been executed on the apartment on Forty-eighth Street." Listing items seized by

investigators, McMath included financial documents
and a pair of bloody shorts. "That was another circumstance on which it was *assumed* that David Legg was involved in his parents' murders. Finally, by the time of
David Legg's arrest, it had been discovered that Mrs.
Legg's engagement ring had been pawned at this jewelry store. That was another circumstance upon
which it was *assumed* that David Legg was involved
in his parents' murders."

Insiders recognized McMath's error in calling Jeannie's diamond an "engagement ring." It had been a
twenty-fifth-anniversary present from Brian. The
minor misstatement, though, had no relevance to the
case, and jurors understood the judge's admonition:
these introductory statements were not evidence and
must not be given any weight during deliberations.

Recapitulating the arrest in Los Angeles with
charges of theft and fraud, McMath sounded incredulous in stating that David was the only one eventually
charged with murder. Just as McCormick had anticipated, the defender made clear their key strategy: "All
of the circumstances known by the Phoenix Police Department upon which they might *assume* David Legg's
involvement in his parents' murders pointed just as
easily to Kimberly Pierce-Taylor as the guilty party."

With the foundational theme revealed, McMath
proceeded to build on it. "We can just as easily
assume . . . that Kimberly Pierce-Taylor was the guilty
party, based on the lack of forced entry into the home
and the lack of any ransacking. She was Mr. and Mrs.
Legg's ostensible daughter-in-law. She was welcome in
their home. She had free access to their home."

Prefacing more statements with "We can just as
easily *assume* that Kimberly Pierce-Taylor was the

guilty party, based on . . . ," McMath spoke of the airline tickets, the use of an alias, pawning the ring, and the Hawaiian shopping spree. She also pointed out that Kimberly's fingerprint had turned up on a box containing checks belonging to the Leggs.

The state's burden, said McMath, is to provide proof beyond a reasonable doubt, not *assumptions*. As an example, she referred to bloody shorts that the investigators had found in the apartment. Even though detectives had rightfully suspected they might be evidence, serological tests proved the bloodstains did not come from either Brian or Jeannie Legg. The word "assumption" factored heavily in her opening statement. "That was an *assumption* the Phoenix Police Department relied on to obtain warrants, and while that working hypothesis was reasonable, it came to nothing. Proof beyond a reasonable doubt requires more than *assumptions* or mere probabilities."

Reiterating the possibility that all of the evidence pointed to Kimberly as much as it pointed to David, McMath said, "These circumstances establish a real probability that Kimberly is the perpetrator of these homicides. And in so doing, they create a reasonable doubt as to David's guilt."

A long-used maxim in murder investigations, and trials, is called the MOM theory. It simply refers to the probability that a suspect had the *m*eans, the *o*pportunity, and the *m*otive to carry out the killing.

Certainly, McMath asserted, Kimberly had the opportunity to kill Brian and Jeannie Legg. By her own admission, she was present at the crime scene.

The prosecution's stated motive, said McMath, was greed. David wanted the use of their credit cards, wanted a Hawaii trip, and wanted to possibly inherit

his parents' worldly belongings. But, she said, "those motives apply just as easily to Kimberly. She went to Hawaii. She partook in the proceeds of the credit cards. She had every reason to believe, having married David, that she would receive any inheritance from the death of his parents."

Turning to a series of telephone calls made from the apartment, which she expected to be presented as evidence against her client, McMath said Kimberly could easily have been the caller. The phone contacts for the purpose of obtaining a gun, she suggested, were made while David was at work.

The purchase of that gun, McMath said, further supported the culpability of Kimberly. This would be shown through the testimony of the deceased seller's son. "Mr. Johnson will tell you that both Kimberly and David were involved in the transaction. Both of them held the gun, and it was his impression the gun was for Kimberly, based on conversation he overheard between David and Kimberly." In addition, they had looked at a larger nine-millimeter weapon and rejected it as being too bulky for this young woman.

If the Ruger .22 had been for Kimberly, it would have provided the third part of the MOM theory, by giving her the means to kill.

More evidence of Kimberly's motivation, McMath told jurors, could be seen in the extravagant shopping expeditions in Hawaii. "She herself used the ATM cards. When she was arrested, in her luggage and personal belongings were a number of Mr. and Mrs. Legg's credit cards. She was present at every transaction in which they were used. At least half of the purchases were for her. She got a Gucci watch at Liberty House and did a bunch of shopping at Guess."

Kimberly's behavior at the Guess store fueled the defense's theories. "Some witnesses will tell you that Kimberly was at the Guess shop at the Ala Moana mall, that she was effusive and jubilant about her shopping. She went from rack to rack, taking things and not even trying them on, just buying everything she could." The store employees would testify that Kim showed no nervousness, confusion, or discomfort during the shopping spree.

"While we're on the subject of these credit cards, let me pause here for a moment. After the discovery of his parents' bodies, David Legg did some very stupid, disgraceful things, not the least of which was using his parents' credit cards. David Legg does not dispute that, nor does he dispute the stupidity and disgracefulness of it. . . . The state would like you to believe that because David Legg used his parents' credit cards, ipso facto, he committed the homicides." McMath reasserted that the circumstances point just as readily to Kimberly as they do to David.

Escalating her allegation another level, McMath said, "But there's additional evidence that points only to Kimberly, starting with motives." The defender explained that Kim might have wished to get Brian and Jeannie Legg out of her life. One reason for this, McMath offered, related to the failed church wedding Kim and her family had planned in Juárez. "They had invited a number of people. To be married in a church was a very important thing to Kimberly, because she was a young woman, and at the time she met David, [she] was a virgin. When the day came for the church wedding, David Legg was nowhere to be found. Kimberly later came to believe, came to learn, that the reason David didn't show . . . was because his

parents, Mr. and Mrs. Legg, had come and spirited him off, had kidnapped him from marrying her. This made her very sad, very disappointed, at the actions of David's parents."

Building on that theme, McMath said, "When Kimberly and David moved to Ahwatukee, they lived at first with Mr. and Mrs. Legg, and then subsequently in the apartment nearby. They spent a great deal of time, virtually every day, at the Leggs' home. Kimberly will tell you that became a source of resentment for her, that she was jealous of the time David insisted they spend with his parents because she was a newlywed. She wanted to spend more quality time at home alone with David. In fact, the frequency of those visits to the Legg home became a source of contention between the couple."

At this point, McMath thought it important to tell jurors that Kimberly would be testifying under a grant of immunity, with a judicial order preventing any of her words from being used against her in subsequent prosecution other than for perjury. "You will also hear that in the absence of that immunity grant, you wouldn't have been hearing from Kimberly Pierce-Taylor because she would have exercised her Fifth Amendment privilege against self-incrimination." The immunity, said McMath, had been requested by the state.

"Speaking of Kimberly Pierce-Taylor's testimony, an additional, very important piece of the evidence you are going to hear that points directly to her is her previous false sworn testimony. She has already lied under oath about this case. When she gave her videotaped deposition three months after the homicides, she took an oath, a solemn oath, to tell the truth. Now, at that time, she had no way of knowing what

other information was going to come to light during the investigation——that investigators would learn she was present during the purchase of a handgun, that she held a handgun. She didn't know any of that. She very calmly, politely, and, without hesitation, lied."

Referring to a folder of transcripts, McMath read aloud from them. Kimberly's false testimony read:

Question: Okay, now, as we just discussed moments ago, you are not familiar with guns, right?

Answer: Yes.

Question: Had you ever seen David with a gun?

Answer: No.

Question: Have you ever seen David purchase a gun?

Answer: No.

Question: Have you ever purchased a gun?

Answer: No.

McMath paused, studied the jurors' faces, and let the falsehoods sink in. "And again, you will hear from Ed Johnson Jr. about the veracity of that sworn testimony of Kimberly Pierce-Taylor. As Mr. McCormick indicated to you, you'll probably hear some testimony about Kimberly and David going to a firing range and practicing with a handgun." Kimberly had deliberately broken her oath and lied, said McMath. "In many ways, Kimberly Pierce-Taylor is the state's case against David Legg. Kimberly is the one who's going to make David out as a murderer. Kimberly is the one who's going to claim that David confessed these murders to her. Kimberly is the only one who's getting a judicial grant of immunity so that she can testify before you. Her credibility is crucial in this case . . . to sustain the

state's burden of proof against David Legg. Because of this, you can expect that we, as Mr. Legg's lawyers, are going to come down on Kimberly in this trial and come down on her fairly hard."

Speaking more rapidly, and passionately, McMath said that Michael Bernays would cross-examine Kimberly and would not wear kid gloves. "And while that may initially cause you some discomfort, please don't hold that against David Legg because the state is relying on this young woman to convict him of two counts of first-degree murder. It's our job as his lawyers to cross-examine, to probe at the truth—or lack thereof—of Kimberly Pierce-Taylor's testimony.

"At the end of these opening statements, you still haven't heard any evidence. David Legg sits before you as presumptively innocent. It is the state that must prove these charges against him beyond a reasonable doubt. And I submit to you, at the close of this case, when we stand before you again during closing arguments, that Mr. Bernays will suggest to you that the evidence the state had been able to produce does not meet the burden of proof beyond a reasonable doubt and will ask you to return a finding of not guilty as to both counts of murder.

"Thank you for your attention."

As Tonya McMath strode back to her chair with her chin held high in a confident posture, the clock had reached high noon.

Reporter Doug Murphy scribbled in his notebook that the trial had all the makings of a made-for-television show.

29

I Was Afraid David
Would Do Something to Me

After the lunch break that Glenn McCormick requested, and was granted, the opportunity to discuss an issue out of the jury's presence arose. Kimberly Pierce-Taylor, the only person in the world who could say she had been with David at the crime scene when his parents were murdered, could possibly make or break the entire case. McCormick planned to call her to the stand as his first witness, but her attorney, Marcus Westervelt, had advised Kim to invoke Fifth Amendment privileges and refuse to answer any questions. The prosecutor referred to the deposition Kimberly had given two years earlier with a grant of immunity. "There's nothing in it," said McCormick, "that inculpates her as to the homicides. She [pleaded] in juvenile court as to the fraud and theft counts,

and therefore, the Fifth Amendment privilege would not apply."

Westervelt protested. "Judge, I disagree. My client was given immunity for a deposition. . . . There's nothing that would prevent her from being prosecuted for anything she says here today." He explained that her potential answers to questions about seeing or handling a firearm allegedly used in the murder might somehow link her to the crime. "For that reason, I'm continuing, on her behalf, to assert the Fifth Amendment. I don't think the state can compel her to testify."

Judge Michael Wilkinson reviewed the original immunity grant document, and surprised several people, including McCormick, by ruling that it extended to her testimony in this trial. She could not be prosecuted for anything she might say on the stand. The county attorney could, of course, make a decision to prosecute her if he chose to, but none of her testimony in this trial could be heard in future proceedings. Wilkinson's decision neutralized the argument about invoking Fifth Amendment privileges.

With that matter settled, the judge turned again to McCormick and said, "The record will show the presence of all members of the jury. You may call your first witness."

Murder trials sometimes call in excess of a hundred witnesses. This one would hear only twelve women and eighteen men telling jurors what evidence the state of Arizona had compiled in order to charge David Legg with killing his parents.

Kimberly Pierce-Taylor walked through the swinging gate separating spectators from court officers.

Now seventeen, she looked older. Her conservative apparel included a dark skirt and white knit short-sleeved blouse covered with a black vest, accessorized by gold earrings and a delicate chain looped around her slim neck. A recent permanent had curled her shoulder-length chocolate brown hair. During her time with David, he had allegedly prevented her from using makeup. Now her eyebrows and lips openly disavowed his preferences. Oval-shaped glasses covered her moist brown eyes.

Being so young, Kimberly had probably never heard of sixteenth-century French essayist Michel de Montaigne, who wrote: *He who has not a good memory should never take upon him the trade of lying.* She certainly could have used the advice.

As Kimberly swore once again to tell the whole truth, and nothing but the truth, her trembling voice betrayed her outward appearance of calm confidence. Even though she spoke English, Spanish-language interpreter Jennifer Fernandez stood close by and translated questions for the witness, as well as a few answers she gave in her native tongue.

A huge question hovered like a cloud in the courtroom. Despite taking an oath to tell the truth at her deposition and previous interviews, she had blatantly lied. Would she tell the truth now in open court?

Responding to the initial sequence of inquiries by Glenn McCormick, Kimberly said she knew David Legg and had met him through a friend in October 1995 in Ciudad Juárez, where she lived. They soon became "very close" and "physical." If jurors were taken aback by a girl of fourteen dating and having sex with a soldier who turned twenty-four in the first month of their relationship, they didn't let it show.

Most of Kimberly's answers to the prosecutor came in very few syllables, with an occasional sentence of a half-dozen words. She acknowledged the civil marriage in El Paso on January 24, 1996. They had lived with her parents, brothers, and sisters in Juárez periodically.

Showing the witness a notebook featuring Mickey Mouse on the cover, DCA McCormick asked if she recognized it. Yes, said Kimberly, it was her personal diary. She had started making entries in June, five months after the marriage.

Kimberly spoke almost robotically in her replies, but she appeared unsettled when McCormick asked about her plans for a church wedding. Arrangements had been made, invitations sent, a priest selected, a house prepared, food cooked, and a car rented. But it had never taken place because of David.

"What did he do?"

"He lied."

"Did he show up?"

"No."

"How long before the wedding was to take place did you find out he wasn't going to show up?"

"Approximately five or ten minutes."

Increasing the length of her responses, Kimberly said she remembered a phone call from David explaining his absence. "He told me he was calling from the army, that his parents had gone to pick him up to take him back to the army." She added that she had been "mad" at herself for believing him. But she had felt no anger toward Mr. or Mrs. Legg. David had returned soon after and they continued living with her parents until March, when they moved to Phoenix.

The trip was made in his Ford Escort. There, they had lived with David's parents "two or three months."

Through Kimberly's answers, McCormick informed jurors that David Legg had worked sporadically, with little income. She said she watched television a lot, played Nintendo, and got along well with Brian and Jeannie. When she and David moved to an apartment, they had borrowed a few items of furniture from the Leggs, but they also began buying some. McCormick lingered on that point for some time, establishing the acquisition of a television set, an entertainment center, and a stereo—despite having no source of income.

Nearly every day, Kimberly said, they had visited David's parents. Did she like going over there all the time? "Not always, because of the fact that I wanted to spend some time alone with David."

"How were you and David getting along during that time when you had the apartment?"

"Not very well. . . . We used to fight, because I wanted to use makeup and he didn't want me to, and because he didn't want me to pull my hair back. He always wanted me to have it down."

Alicia LaFlesh did not attend the trial, but when she later learned of David's controlling behavior over Kim—especially about the hair—it took her back to the misery she suffered with him in Hawaii.

"When David wasn't in the apartment and you were alone, what would you do?"

"I would sit at the computer, talking on the Internet. I would skate and go to the swimming pool." But she had no friends or relatives in Phoenix, and had contact with her mother mostly by telephone, with

the exception of a visit during which the woman stayed a few weeks in May.

Use of the telephone came up next in McCormick's questions. After they returned from taking Kimberly's mother home to Juárez, had she seen David use the phone to buy something advertised in a newspaper? Yes, she had. She couldn't recall the exact date, but it was before the trip to Hawaii. Nor could she remember exactly what he wanted to buy.

McCormick zeroed in on the matter. "Well, at some point, did you go with David to buy something at someone's house?"

"Yes. It was in June, but I don't remember what day."

"What did you go to purchase with David?"

Time seemed to stand still in the courtroom. Here was the first crucial question about which Kimberly had previously lied. Would she finally stick to the facts?

Her answer relieved the tension. "A gun."

"Why were you going to buy a gun?"

"According to him, for protection of the house and to protect me."

"Was the gun for you?"

"No."

With that important point made for the jurors, McCormick shifted gears. "Did you ever go to any pawnshops with David?"

"Yes, a lot."

"On the day the gun was purchased, did you go with him to a pawnshop?" Kimberly didn't hesitate. She told of pawning a computer, but she couldn't recall how much money it had brought. She did know that it had been used to pay for the gun. At the seller's home, she recalled, "maybe I could have held one

[gun], but not to see if it fit my hand, but just to look at it."

Anticipating that the defense would certainly portray Kimberly as a liar, McCormick opened the issue first. Referring her to the deposition she gave in September 1996, he asked, "Did you say you had never purchased a gun?"

She admitted saying it.

"Did you say you had never seen David handle a gun?"

She verified it.

"At the time, you knew that you had been to this gentleman's house for that purpose?"

Yes, she agreed.

"Why didn't you tell us about it back then?"

Kimberly frowned and said, "I was afraid."

"What were you afraid of?"

"I don't know. I was just afraid."

McCormick tackled another lie she had told during the deposition. "Did you ever shoot the gun?"

"Yes, two or three times, I think. It was at one of those places that you go for a hobby for shooting." Kimberly described it as an indoor range, said she went there with David, and admitted they both practiced using the weapon. David had shot many more rounds than she had.

With the gun practice locked in, McCormick jumped elsewhere. He wanted to know if she and David had planned a trip to Hawaii together or visited any travel agencies. Kimberly didn't think so, but she acknowledged that David always talked about Hawaii, and he often told her she would love it.

"Was that someplace you wanted to go?"

"Not exactly," she said, and volunteered that she

would have preferred Alaska, but had never mentioned it to David.

Kimberly Pierce-Taylor seemed fairly comfortable by this time, and her answers genuine. Glenn McCormick decided to take her to the crime scene. "Do you recall being with David, and with Brian and with Jeannie, on Sunday, the ninth of June?"

"Yes." But she could not recall exactly what time she and David had first arrived at the Legg home, and she guessed that it was before noon. Not long afterward, all four of them went to a store, she said. "I think it was a JCPenney's."

"Did you have dinner at David's parents' house that day?"

Kimberly thought so, but she couldn't say what time they had eaten.

"After dinner, what did you do?"

"We watched a movie." All four of them had sat around the television set, with David and Kim on a couch, and his parents, side by side, on a love seat. Again, Kimberly couldn't put the event in a time frame, but she did recall that it was dark outside. The movie's title also escaped Kimberly. She could only say it was old, and that she didn't see all of it because she dozed off on the couch. When she woke up, the movie was still playing. While David and his parents still watched the film, she went outside to the car.

"Why did you go out to the car?"

"I was on my period, and I went out for a sanitary napkin. My purse was out there, and I always left them inside it." Asked the reason she had left her purse in the car, Kim said, "Because of David, the way he was.

He would always tell me what to do. He treated me as if he were my dad. He never treated me like I was his wife. And he told me to leave my purse in the car."

"Well, when you went out to the car, did you get what you needed and come right back in the house?"

"No, not right away."

"Why not?"

"I stayed, listening to a song." Kimberly said she could not remember the song's title.

McCormick posed a series of questions reminding her of statements she had made in interviews and in the deposition. With those memory joggers, Kimberly thought she might have been listening to "Don't Cry" by Guns N' Roses. But she still couldn't be sure whether she had heard it on the radio or on a compact disc.

"Did anyone come and talk to you while you were in the car?"

"Oh yes, David did. I think he said something like, 'My dad's asking why you are taking so long.'" She had replied that she would go back in when the song finished. David left her in the car and reentered the house. "Don't Cry" by Guns N' Roses lasts a full five minutes and fifteen seconds.

"Did anything happen prior to you going back in after the song was over, something that drew your attention to the house?"

"Yes, I heard some gunshots." She added, "At that time, I didn't know if they were gunshots or firecrackers."

"How many did you hear?"

"Four." McCormick knew from the investigators and the autopsy reports that six shots had been fired, two of which struck Brian and three that killed Jeannie. One

had glanced off a magazine, pierced a wall, and wound up in an adjacent room. But perhaps Kimberly had actually heard only four. He asked her what she did when she heard the gunshots. Kimberly replied, "First I got scared, and I looked around me, thinking maybe something was happening outside." Seeing nothing, she got out of the car and entered the house, and stopped at the staircase near the entry.

"Why did you stop there?"

"Because David was coming, walking toward me. He didn't say anything, but looked scared, in shock."

"Did you go any farther into the house?"

"No. I got scared. David had blood on his shirt." She stated that she could see into the family room, where a mirror above the fireplace reflected something awful. "I saw blood where Brian and Jeannie were sitting." Kimberly insisted that she could not actually see either of them, even though she entered the family room and spotted a gun on a glass-topped end table.

"Can you describe the shirt David wore?

"Yes, it was a sleeveless shirt."

Rapidly scribbling notes for the article he would file that evening, Doug Murphy entered the quote from Kimberly that she had seen blood on David Legg's shirt. He noticed that almost every eye in the courtroom focused on the petite girl during her emotional testimony. The exception, Murphy observed, was *her former husband, who sat casually at the defense table flipping through transcripts and other documents even as his two attorneys listened attentively.*

McCormick utilized a large-screen television showing photos of the crime scene, and asked the witness to indicate exactly where David stood. She pointed to a spot only a few feet from the glass table, which placed

him close to her own location. In her recollection, he did not speak to her.

"What did you do?"

"I sat down on the stairs and I was crying."

McCormick wanted clarification about her being able to see blood but not the victims. "Could you see any parts of their bodies?"

"Yes, I think I could see their legs. I'm not sure." To observers, her answer left the issue vague. Where was the blood Kimberly had seen? To McCormick, little would have been gained by badgering her to be more precise. Instead, he established that Kimberly had not gone again into the family room, or anywhere else in the house. He also asked if anyone else had been present during the whole episode; to which, Kimberly said no.

The murder weapon had never been found. Kimberly testified that she had seen it on the table, but she had not touched it, moved it, or taken it with her. Oddly, she said that the gun was no longer on the table when they left. McCormick asked, "How is it that you could be right there and not see the gun removed from the tabletop?"

Tears ran down Kimberly's cheek as she replied, "Everything has erased. I was very scared. I don't remember a lot of things."

"Did David carry anything out of the house?"

"Yes, I think it was a black garbage bag. It seemed to have things in it."

Investigators had found a pair of kitchen gloves in a clothes hamper, but Kimberly could not recall ever seeing them, or knowing whether Jeannie Legg used gloves while working in the kitchen.

Kimberly did remember Jeannie's diamond ring.

She described it as very large, and said David's mother "always wore it." Trying to think of any time that Jeannie removed it from her finger, Kimberly said it might have happened once while the parents worked in their backyard building a barbecue. McCormick wanted jurors to know that Jeannie had not absent-mindedly left her ring lying around, perhaps near a bathroom washbasin, as he expected David to claim.

Capping Kimberly's recollection of events in the Leggs' home, McCormick asked, "What did David do when it was time for you to leave the house?"

Still dabbing a tissue at her eyes, Kimberly replied, "He grabbed my arm and we left. He said, 'Let's go now.'" They drove away, in silence, and went to their apartment. When they arrived, David carried the black bag in and then told her to get the cats ready to leave.

"Leave?" McCormick asked. "Where were you going?"

"He didn't tell me. The only thing he said was that we were not going to stay at our place that night."

"Did any of the things in the bag get taken out inside the apartment?"

"Yes. He dumped everything out on the living-room carpet." Kimberly could not remember seeing a gun, but she did recall noticing several credit cards, and maybe some checkbooks.

"Did those items just stay there in the middle of the floor, or did they get put somewhere?"

"I think they were put into a suitcase. I'm really not sure." Kimberly said she did not pack anything or help David do it. "He just threw some things into the suitcase."

When they left, Kimberly told the jury, she thought they delivered the cats at "a place where you leave animals," but she had no recollection of where it was.

After that, they went to a hotel, the name of which she could not remember, but thought it might be somewhere near the airport.

According to Kimberly's answers, she could not recall having any conversation with David that night or the next day about what had happened to his parents. Spectators in the gallery wondered if her memory had turned selective. Even though she spoke of being "scared," it seemed odd that no mention of the searing events took place between them.

Her memory sharpened somewhat about the next morning in the hotel. She told of David looking at a Yellow Pages book and calling a jewelry store. And just before they checked out, she had a vague picture in her mind of David taking with him "a paper from the directory."

"Where did you go from there?"

"To the jewelry store. David sold his mother's ring, pawned it." Kimberly denied talking to the buyer, but she said she did have a brief conversation with a female in the store. "I wanted to see if I could tell her what happened, but I didn't do it because I got scared."

"Why did you want to tell her what happened?"

"I was afraid that David would do something to me."

McCormick seized on that comment and asked if she had made similar attempts to tell anyone else what happened, at the hotel or elsewhere. Had she tried to make any phone calls? Kimberly shook her head and said she had not.

Another witness the prosecutor planned on summoning to the stand, Warren Williams, the jewelry store proprietor, would probably testify that David had asked Kim if he should accept the $7,000 offered for the diamond; to which, she allegedly said, "Yeah."

Now he wanted to hear her version. "In the store, did David at some point turn to you and ask a question about whether or not he should take a certain amount of money for the ring?"

"Yes. I think he asked me if he should accept a certain amount. I think it was seven thousand." Shrugging her shoulders, Kimberly said, "I went like that, but I don't remember if I said 'Okay,' or something." To observers, this brief incident may not have meant much, but to McCormick, it could go a long way in convincing jurors that Kimberly had testified honestly.

She told of leaving the store, arriving at a bank to cash the check, and going inside with David. Why had she accompanied him rather than waiting in the vehicle? Kimberly explained, "He wasn't going to leave me alone in the car." Her answer seemed to imply fear of David.

Anticipating an attack on her credibility by the defense, McCormick asked if she had been affectionate with David, either in the jewelry store or in the bank. She acknowledged that she had. Why? "I wanted him to think that nothing was going on, that I wasn't upset or something. I was afraid he would do something to me." Why? She didn't hesitate in saying, "Because he is not a good person."

That last comment drew a sharp objection from defense attorney Michael Bernays.

Judge Michael Wilkinson sustained it and advised jurors they must not consider it. Still, it opened the door for McCormick.

"Were you afraid that David might harm you?"

"Yes. He had already done it before."

A murmured gasp rippled through the gallery, and both attorneys huddled next to Judge Wilkinson's desk for a sidebar conference. Bernays complained

that he had not been forewarned of abuse by David Legg coming into play. McCormick countered that the defense had interviewed Kimberly for days, providing them with ample opportunity to learn of any physical abuse by David. "They are trying to say that she did [the killing], so the state should be allowed to meet that by showing she was afraid of David, and why." The judge ruled that her comment about "doing it before" could stand, but no details of the abuse would be allowed, since such information might be prejudicial against the defendant.

Resuming his questioning of the witness, McCormick asked, "Is there anything about what happened the previous day that caused you to fear David?"

"Yes, the fact that he had killed his parents."

Now the jury had heard it stated clearly. The only witness who had been at the crime scene had just said—in no uncertain terms—that David Legg killed his parents. But how much weight would it carry in deliberations? Kimberly had already admitted numerous previous lies. Was she now telling the truth, or just covering her own culpability? The defense team would certainly exploit that possibility.

For the remaining half hour of the day, McCormick elicited from Kimberly her recollections of events on the morning of June 10 before departing on a plane for the Hawaii trip. She said they returned to the apartment building office, where David paid $2,000 in overdue rent, using a cashier's check he had bought after cashing the check for his mother's diamond. She couldn't remember stopping for gas, as a credit card receipt had recorded, or at any stores.

After they parked his Ford Escort in a multistory airport building, they had walked to a counter and bought tickets to Hawaii, using the names Brian Legg and Kimberly Miller. She said she didn't know the name of the airline.

Several times, McCormick asked if any opportunities had come up in the airport for her to escape from David, but she replied that her "fear was too big." When they boarded the Delta flight, they couldn't sit together at first, but David had convinced a passenger to swap seats with him so he could join Kimberly.

At one point in the testimony, Kimberly said she had agreed to a Hawaii trip on one condition: that they could go to Juárez when they came back. Why? "Because I didn't want to be with him. In Juárez, I could tell a relative of mine to call the police to come and get him. I was going to have us go to my city, and there I was going to pretend that everything was okay, and then I would tell my grandfather to call the police in Phoenix and they could come find us in El Paso."

McCormick knew the jury would eventually see, many times, a videotape made by David during the inter-island cruise, in which Kimberly appeared anything but frightened. On the contrary, she acted flirtatious and excited, smiling and teasing him. Would this undermine her story of being in fear of David, afraid that he might harm her?

The Delta flight had landed in Los Angeles, and David had taken her to a counter, where they changed her name from Kimberly Miller to Kimberly Maloy. McCormick asked, "Why did you go by the name of Maloy?"

"Because David changed his name when he left the military."

From Los Angeles, they flew to Hawaii, sitting side by side.

Glenn McCormick glanced up at a large wall clock and suggested to Judge Wilkinson that it might be a good time for the evening recess. Jurors and spectators filed out into the hallway, heading toward the elevators, eager to hear more from this key witness the next day.

30

They Were Already Dead

Seats in the gallery filled up quickly again, on Thursday morning, September 24. Doug Murphy occupied the same spot he had taken on Wednesday, ready to take copious notes. He wondered if he would hear Kimberly's explanation of why she had helped charge thousands of dollars' worth of purchases in Hawaii.

As expected, Glenn McCormick resumed his direct examination of Kimberly Pierce-Taylor.

He began by showing her a box of bullets found in the apartment by Detective Ken Hansen. Kimberly admitted having seen them in her closet the day before the murders, along with the semiautomatic pistol David had purchased. Investigators had been unable to find the murder weapon, so McCormick showed Kimberly a brochure picturing a Ruger .22 semiautomatic pistol. She couldn't say it was identical to the gun she and David had fired at a shooting range.

The next exhibit brought out by the prosecutor made an immediate connection in Kim's memory. A blue flexible plastic case with black carrying straps, resembling an insulated cooler, had been kept in David's Ford Escort for storing music CDs, and she stated it was in there on the night of June 9. When detectives had searched the car, and taken the plastic case as evidence, it had contained a CD of the Guns N' Roses song "Don't Cry." Kimberly told McCormick that David always demanded that CDs be removed from the player and stored in the blue pack before they exited the Ford.

In Wednesday's testimony, Kimberly had said she and David did not talk about the murders of his parents on June 9 or the next day. Now McCormick asked if they talked about it in Hawaii. She said they did, briefly. "He comments to me, he said something like, 'I couldn't believe how much a person . . . how much blood a person can have inside their body.'"

With that small wedge offering an opening into Kimberly's previous reticence about the murders, McCormick sought more. "Were you having a conversation about what happened when he said that?"

"I don't know, but I was always asking him what had happened."

"What did he tell you?"

"He told me how it was possible he had done something like that."

"Was he upset about what he had done?"

Michael Bernays instantly lodged an objection. "Assumes facts not in evidence." Judge Wilkinson sustained it, and Glenn McCormick asked for a sidebar conference.

In a heated but whispered exchange next to the

judge's desk, McCormick said, "I'd like to know what facts this assumes so I can certainly do what I can to get them in."

Wilkinson, imperturbable as always, calmly replied, "That he killed both of them."

"She just said that."

"I didn't hear her say it."

"She said it yesterday. She said the reason why she was afraid of him was because he killed his parents. She said it again just now, quoting David telling her that he couldn't believe what he did."

Judge Wilkinson wasn't convinced. "I'm not sure she has. You can ask the question again. 'Did he tell you he killed his parents?'"

Bernays, unwilling to concede, interjected: "Judge, I am sorry, I would object to that on foundation. What is the basis for her saying—"

"It's overruled," Wilkinson snapped.

Still persisting, Bernays appealed, "Your Honor, if I may, it's the same as just bringing up a string of witnesses—'Do you believe he killed his parents?' 'Yeah, I do believe.' It's all opinion."

Unruffled, Wilkinson replied, "I don't believe it is. Next question."

Still challenging the issue, Bernays said, "My objection to it is, it's something I am incapable of cross-examining on. Allowing her to express beliefs violates the rules of evidence."

Judge Wilkinson still didn't agree. "Not to oversimplify for the court of appeals or supreme court here, but there were no other individuals [present]. She testified that no other individuals were there. She can

form a belief without seeing the actual act done. That's the basis of the ruling. Let's go."

Bernays returned to his chair, careful not to let the jury see any signs of frustration. McCormick approached Kimberly once more and jolted everyone in the room by asking, "Miss Pierce, did you kill David's parents?"

Obviously startled, Kimberly faltered. "I am sorry, the—"

"Miss Pierce, did you kill David's parents?"

"No."

"Did David kill his parents?"

Bernays couldn't resist. "Objection—foundation and relevance, Your Honor."

"Overruled. You may answer."

Kimberly didn't hesitate. "Yes."

"You previously said that David had stated something to the nature of not believing he could do that. Do you remember his words any better than that?"

"Yes. He said that he couldn't believe that he had killed his parents." She thought he made the statement while they were on the cruise ship. David seemed angry while discussing it, and at other times during their time in Hawaii, said Kimberly. They often argued.

"Did you ever say to him that he was going to get caught?"

Another objection came from Michael Bernays on the grounds of relevance, and the judge sustained it.

This time, McCormick asked for a sidebar. He explained what he regarded as the relevance. "It's my understanding that the witness will say David told her he wouldn't get caught because 'they don't know my real name.'"

Judge Wilkinson repeated, "Objection sustained."

Just as Bernays had been persistent at the previous sidebar debate, McCormick held his ground. "Your Honor, this goes directly to the heart of the reason why he felt like he could use the credit cards, et cetera, and use his false name, because nobody knew he was in Phoenix, except his parents. It goes right to the heart of his ability to escape this."

Still implacable, Wilkinson said, "I disagree."

Now, on returning to their places, McCormick kept a poker face so jurors couldn't know that he had lost this round.

He asked Kimberly, "Was David concerned about getting caught?"

Again, Bernays objected. The witness could not be allowed to speak for David's thoughts, he asserted. The judge said, "The objection is sustained." He added some advice about how the question may be formed.

McCormick restated it. "Did David express to you any concerns about getting caught?" No, said Kim.

"Did you ever discuss with him concerns about him getting caught?" Kimberly said they had talked about it on the ship and during the flight back to California. David had assured her that no one was going to catch him.

Did he say why? Yes, because he had been using another name. "I said to him, 'They are going to catch you,' and he said, 'That's not going to happen.'"

To be certain of no confusion in jurors' minds, McCormick asked Kimberly the false name David Legg had used. She said, "If I remember right, I think it was Daren Maloy."

"Did he talk to you about what to say if he did get caught?"

"Yes, he said that if they caught us, for me to say that we had found them already dead."

Anticipating that the defense would rely on David's excuse of finding his parents' murdered bodies, McCormick felt as if he had blocked a field goal.

Turning to Kimberly's interview with Detective Hansen after the arrest at LAX, McCormick asked, "Did you ever tell him you just found them like that?"

"No, never."

In the next half hour, McCormick inquired about numerous cards in Kimberly's possession at the time of the arrest. They included credit cards, Jeannie Legg's driver's license, and her Social Security card. Kimberly said that David had told her to keep them. He had also given her a substantial amount of cash. "I think approximately a thousand or fifteen hundred dollars." She hadn't spent any of it. They had used his parents' ATM cards to acquire more cash in Hawaii.

How did she know their personal identification numbers (PIN)? Kimberly said she didn't. She had only complied with orders to put the card into the ATM slot. "David was there. He was the one who would press the keys." When the cash came out, she would take it from the machine, but she could not recall whether she gave it to him or kept it in her own wallet.

In addition to plastic belonging to David's parents and found in Kimberly's day planner, she had also possessed an Arizona ID card in the name of Cecilia Maloy. She testified that David had taken her to get it, and filled out the form with that fake name.

* * *

After a welcome lunch break, McCormick showed a grainy black-and-white videotape, taken by a security camera, of four people shopping at a JCPenney store on June 9, 1996. Kimberly identified Brian, Jeannie, David, and herself. The prosecutor asked if she recognized the shirt David wore. She did. "Is that the shirt he was wearing the [night] he shot his parents?" Since the shirt had never been found by investigators, this would be the prosecutor's only chance to let jurors see it.

"I think so." She also agreed that a blue-checked blouse that could be seen on her in the video was the one she wore at the time of the murders, and that she had taken it to Hawaii with her.

McCormick showed a photograph on the television screen depicting blankets covering the bodies of the dead parents. "Did you involve yourself in putting those blankets over the couch?"

Kimberly denied it.

Producing several black-and-white still pictures, McCormick elicited from Kimberly her recognition of David and herself, as caught by ATM security photos, but she couldn't say exactly where they were taken. Nor could she recall how many ATMs they had used to acquire cash, but thought it might be more than five. She estimated each withdrawal to be about $200. Another security photo did click in her memory, depicting her and David in the Phoenix Bank of America, where they cashed the $7,000 check for Jeannie's diamond.

"Do you remember if you kissed him while you were in the bank?" Kimberly said she did, and acknowledged a photo that depicted her lips close to David's as they were about to kiss.

McCormick next entered a camcorder into evi-

dence, and through her testimony, he revealed that it had belonged to Brian Legg. Kimberly recalled seeing it among the things David had dumped out of a black trash bag onto the apartment floor after the murders. They had used it to record their trip in Hawaii, including the cruise. With the judge's permission, the prosecutor played the tape for jurors. They watched Kimberly frolicking, teasing, laughing, and flipping her skirt up. David's voice could be heard making comments. They both exchanged expressions of love.

While the show seemed to rivet everyone else in the courtroom, Kimberly kept her head down. In the gallery, reporter Doug Murphy fought a feeling of anger. How could these two act so happy, knowing what had happened? How could they be so jubilant while Mr. and Mrs. Legg's dead bodies might still be sitting on that love seat?

At McCormick's request, Judge Wilkinson ordered her to watch it. David's voice on the tape announced, "This is outside our hotel room"; at which point, McCormick paused it and asked Kimberly if they had stayed at the Hilton Turtle Bay. She said she didn't know, and couldn't remember the names of hotels.

When the amazing show ended, McCormick mentioned to Kimberly that she hadn't appeared to be interested in viewing the scenes David had recorded. Why? She uttered a single word of explanation: "Shame."

"What are you ashamed of?"

"Being there. I am sorry for being there."

The next exhibits—jewelry, clothing, and expensive watches—were accepted into evidence after Kimberly agreed she and David had bought them in Hawaii, using cards and cash belonging to his parents.

She also stated that David had bought a computer in Honolulu.

A personal planning calendar that belonged to Kimberly had been mentioned several times during her testimony. McCormick handed it to her and asked about entries in early June. She acknowledged they were in her handwriting. On June 1, they had driven to Juárez to take her mother home, and they returned on June 3. She also noted that her period had started on that day. McCormick referred her to June 8 and asked what she had recorded. She said, "Go shopping and go on a trip."

"You were going on a trip on June eighth?"

"Supposedly. According to David, he was going to take me to see my mom."

"Hadn't you just dropped your mom off?"

"Yes."

"You were going to see her again?"

"Yes, because of the problems I was having with David." McCormick asked if the entry might have meant a trip to Hawaii. "No, he never mentioned to me that we were going there."

Spectators and perhaps jurors felt a little skeptical of her comments. Also, they had been wondering about something very personal Kimberly had mentioned earlier, and McCormick voiced it. "You had indicated that on the evening of June ninth, you were going out to the car to get a sanitary hygiene item?" She agreed. "While you were at the house, or before leaving, did you get a chance to use that?"

No, she said, nor had she taken care of the matter anywhere else.

Kimberly's replies to the prosecutor in the last few

questions could have raised some doubts in jurors' minds about her veracity. A trip back to Juárez the very next day after returning from there! Did that make sense? David had never told her they were going to Hawaii? And she went out to the car to retrieve a sanitary napkin within a few minutes of the shooting, but had never used it? She claimed to be listening to music in the car, but she didn't know if it came from the radio or a CD. Her tale seemed flimsy and full of holes. Had she actually been present during the murders, and now felt the need to lie about it? Even though the judge had ruled her testimony immune from future prosecution, she probably would prefer not to reveal it *if* she had been complicit in the killings.

Observers familiar with murder trials could recognize McCormick's strategy of bringing these inconsistencies out first because he knew the defense would do it. It would be much better for the jury to hear it during the prosecution's direct examination.

Perhaps for those reasons, he next asked Kimberly about a telephone call she made from the cruise ship in Hawaii while David taped her. The video showed her speaking in Spanish. "Who were you calling?"

Kimberly said she had called her mother, but had spoken very briefly because David was there. Why would that matter? "Because maybe he thought that I was going to say something to my mom."

"Was it your intention to do that?"

Speaking almost in a whisper, Kimberly said she had tried to tell her mother to make calls to Brian and Jeannie's house. Eyebrows in the gallery shot up. Why would she do that? But no answer would clear it up.

Prosecutor Glenn McCormick announced, "No further questions, Your Honor."

With about an hour remaining for the day's session, Judge Wilkinson turned to the defense table and said, "Mr. Bernays."

Michael Bernays asked permission to reposition the "podium" before beginning his cross-examination. He, like countless other lawyers, erroneously called the upright stand, from which they often spoke, a podium. It is actually, by definition, a lectern. (A podium is a small raised platform upon which a musical conductor or speaker stands. A lectern is a desk or stand with a slanted top to hold a book or speaking notes.)

With the stand placed to his satisfaction, Bernays faced Kimberly in the witness chair, addressed her as Ms. Pierce, and courteously asked if that was how she liked to be called. She concurred, and acknowledged speaking to him several times before the trial. With the pleasantries covered, Bernays hit hard with his next question.

"Ms. Pierce, my contention is that you are a liar! You admit that?"

In the gallery, reporter Doug Murphy underlined a note that Bernays had spoken his accusation *in a loud voice.*

Before she could answer, Glenn McCormick objected, and the judge sustained it "as to the phraseology."

Bernays immediately shot back, "My contention, Ms. Pierce, is that you lie. Do you admit that?"

With her face clouding and tears forming in her eyes, Kimberly choked out, "No."

"Do you mean to tell me you can sit here for two

days and testify about David killing his parents without a tear, and when I call you a liar, you start crying?"

McCormick, his voice incredulous, barked, "Objection, badgering the witness already."

"Sustained. Argumentative." Bernays started to speak, but the judge warned, "Next question. Don't argue with the witness."

The defender clung to his subject. "Do you admit that you lie?"

"When?" Kimberly asked, almost inaudible.

"Whenever it suits you."

"No."

"You had a conversation with Detective Hansen from the Phoenix Police Department, did you not?" Kimberly said yes. "You lied to him, didn't you?"

"Yes."

"You told him you were telling the truth, didn't you?" Another objection came from the prosecutor, but was overruled.

Kimberly reverted to her frequently used answers to McCormick: "I don't remember."

Reminding her of the time at LAX when Hansen interviewed her, Bernays asked, "He questioned you about your activities with David Legg in the preceding two weeks, and you told him a complete fabrication at the outset, did you not?"

"Objection," McCormick said, "Too vague, Your Honor." Sustained.

Bernays reworded it more specifically. "You told him that you had been home all day on Sunday, June ninth, didn't you?"

Kimberly's little-girl voice matured somewhat. "I believe so. But I don't remember what I told him."

After suggesting, in interrogative form, that she was

using the "I don't remember" answer as a defense mechanism, and hearing her deny it, Bernays asked, "It's something you say when you don't know how to adequately protect yourself in answering a question, is it not?"

"No," she protested. "Two years have gone by, and I don't remember a lot of things."

"You told the detective a complete fabrication at the outset of your interview with him, didn't you?"

Clasping her hands tightly in her lap, Kimberly replied, "I lied to him at the beginning. Yes, it's true."

"So you lied at the beginning, but you are not sure whether you lied later?" Kimberly started to answer, but Bernays cut her off. "You told him that you had not seen Brian and Palma on the day before you left on the trip to Hawaii?"

"I don't know. I don't remember."

Bernays opened a thick packet of transcripts and read aloud. Referring to events of June 10, 1996, he said, "'Question—did you see them that day? Answer—no. Question—did you see them the day before? Answer—no.' Do you remember saying that to Detective Hansen?"

"Yes."

"And you told him that you weren't there the day they died, didn't you?"

"I believe so."

Looking again at the transcript, Bernays said, "In fact, he asked you if you were there when he did it. You answered, 'No, I was not there. I was not there.' That was a lie, too, wasn't it?"

"Well, yes, I was scared."

"You lie when you are scared, don't you?"

"No."

"In fact, you prefer lying when you are scared, don't you?"

"No."

Bringing up her deposition, taken September 20, 1996, and reminding Kimberly that she had sworn to tell the truth, Bernays read a question put to her by McCormick: "'When you first started talking to Detective Hansen, did you tell him what you knew? Answer— no. Question—why not? Answer—I don't know. I was scared. I preferred to lie.'"

Panic seemed to grip Kimberly's voice as she protested having said that. "Because I was afraid, I lied. I don't remember what I said. But I don't believe I said I prefer to lie."

Bernays reminded her that not only had a court reporter taken down every word, but the deposition had also been videotaped. He kept up the barrage for a few more minutes, and then asked if she recalled an interview with him, over a period of several days, in September 1996. Kimberly said she did. She had not been under oath at the time, but she had committed to Bernays she would be truthful. "And you weren't, were you?"

Hedging, Kimberly replied, "I told the truth, but I lied maybe two times."

The defender dropped his earlier formal addressing of Ms. Pierce and asked, "What two times, Kimberly?"

In the longest response she had yet given, the witness said, "I didn't mention that I had gone to buy the gun with David, and that we went to fire it at one of those places where you shoot."

Challenging her assessment of lying only two times, Bernays asked, "You told me in the interview that you didn't remember any wounds or blood. Isn't that correct?"

To observers, Kimberly appeared to squirm in the chair. "I didn't remember a lot of things, and I have read a lot of things now."

"So now, two years later, you remember a lot more about this case?"

"Well, yes, because I was in shock when that happened."

"You were in shock in September?" At that time, a full two months had passed since the murders. To her affirmative answer, Bernays said, "That's your defense for everything, isn't it, Kimmie? That you don't remember because you were in shock. But when it suits your purpose to come into court and tell lies, then you change your story?"

McCormick had sat patiently, but he could take no more. He rose and strenuously objected to the argumentative nature of the cross-examination. Judge Wilkinson sustained it.

The ruling didn't slow Bernays down. "How many times do you think you have said, 'I don't remember' over the last two days of testimony?"

"I don't know."

"Well, do you just not remember?"

Obviously exhausted, Kimberly droned, "I don't know."

Perhaps mercifully, Bernays turned away from the witness and said, "Judge, this might be a decent time to stop."

Judge Wilkinson quickly agreed. "All right, we'll take the evening recess." He alerted the jurors to avoid discussing the case with anyone and not to watch television or read news accounts about the case. They would have a three-day break, as he ordered them to return on Monday morning at ten thirty.

31

David Ruined My Life

In one of Doug Murphy's articles covering the David Legg case, he reflected an interesting viewpoint: the defendant actually faced two trials. The first and more serious charge, of course, involved the murder of his parents. Second, the state sought to convict him for stealing his mother's ring and his parents' financial resources for the purpose of paying some bills and taking an extravagant trip to Hawaii.

So far in the trial, said Murphy, a guilty verdict for the theft and fraud charges appeared to be a certain outcome: *But the question of who pulled the trigger and shot Palma and Brian Legg at close range while they sat in their family room that Sunday night, is far from clear.* Kimberly Pierce-Taylor's testimony, to this point, Murphy noted, had been *riddled with significant inconsistencies.*

Glenn McCormick understood the problems with Kimberly's statements, and would seek to reinforce them

with redirect questions when the defense completed their cross-examination, which might take quite a while.

A bailiff called the crowd to order in Judge Wilkinson's courtroom on Monday morning, September 28, and Michael Bernays stood at the lectern, again facing Kimberly Pierce-Taylor.

If the casserole of her lies had cooled over the weekend, he slipped it into a microwave and turned up the heat.

Reading from a transcript of his own interview with her in 1996, he reminded the witness that she had described David Legg's relationship with his parents as normal, warm, and loving. She had never mentioned hearing arguments. Kimberly defensively replied that a few family disputes didn't mean there was no love between David and his parents. So she didn't regard her failure to remember those incidents as lies.

"Do you know how many times you have testified you don't remember?"

"No, but I prefer to say I don't know [rather] than to tell a lie."

To observers, Kimberly might have won that small skirmish, but how it would register in jurors' minds remained to be seen. Bernays moved on to establish that no arguments or disagreements had occurred between David and his parents on that Sunday before they died. Kimberly agreed. Nor had she and David discussed, in advance of the murder, any desire to see them killed, or getting rid of them and taking their money.

Building more bulwarks in defense of his client, Bernays elicited from Kimberly that she had not seen

David carry a gun into his parents' house, and that when he came out to the car, where she sat listening to music, he did not seem angry or upset.

Suddenly shifting the spotlight from David and focusing it on Kimberly, the defender asked, "Now, the fact of the matter is, Kim, you didn't care much for the Leggs, did you?"

Indignant, Kimberly raised her voice to snap, "That is a lie."

"It's true—is it not—that you didn't like spending so much time with them?"

Several times during her testimony, Kimberly had been admonished to answer questions "yes" or "no" if possible. To this one, she said, "I can't answer that with a 'yes' or 'no.' Can I explain?" Bernays ignored her and repeated the questions. She again asked for permission to explain.

As if he hadn't heard her, Bernays reworded it. She held her ground. He asked it a fourth time. Kimberly replied, "Would you give me permission to explain?"

With a single, sharp "no," the defender opened his folder to Kim's sworn deposition. In it, she had agreed to a suggestion that she hadn't been "particularly thrilled" with frequent visits to David's parents. Bernays asked if she recalled saying that.

"Yes," she said, "but not because I didn't like the couple."

"You and David would argue about that, wouldn't you?"

"You are not giving me a chance to explain why."

"You didn't need a chance to explain it in the deposition, did you, Ms. Pierce?"

"It's because I never said that I didn't like his parents. I liked them very well."

Bernays returned to the "not particularly thrilled" comment and asked if that had been true. Kimberly said that was correct. "And it was your idea to move out of the Leggs' house they opened to you and David when you moved from Juárez?"

"No, that was not my idea."

Again, Bernays read aloud from the deposition and cited a passage in which Kimberly had said the idea to move could have been mutual, and had answered that it "might" have been hers.

Before Bernays could ask, she volunteered, "But I am not saying in that deposition that it was my idea." She maintained her position on that issue, despite several more inquiries from the defender.

Still working to show jurors that some friction could have existed between Kimberly and David's parents, Bernays asked, "You believed that Mr. Legg did not like you?"

"No. I never said that."

This time he had her. From the deposition and from two interviews, Bernays produced a trio of statements in which Kimberly had said she thought Brian Legg had not liked her. "So three different times you said you believed that David's father didn't like you, correct?"

The witness had no escape route. "Yes, that's right."

"And yet now, five minutes ago, to this jury, you testified, while under oath, that you never said that—correct?"

"Yes."

"So five minutes ago you lied to this jury?"

"Yes."

"You sat there, looking sweet, innocent as you can imagine, and you lied to this jury."

No doubt, Michael Bernays knew he had gone slightly over the line, and that Glenn McCormick would vigorously object. If so, he guessed correctly. The prosecutor lodged his objection, and Judge Wilkinson sustained it. In McCormick's football years, he had seen teams deliberately incur a penalty for strategic purposes. And that's exactly what Bernays had done.

Moving steadily toward a score against the witness, Bernays asked, "You believed that Mr. and Mrs. Legg were responsible for your church wedding not going forward. Isn't that true?" Kimberly denied it. Flipping to a marker in his transcripts and police reports, he introduced her previous statements affirming this belief and saying that she had been "very upset" over being left at the altar. Again, he accused her of lying to this jury.

"No," Kimberly disagreed. "No, I never said they were guilty of that, never."

If Bernays believed he could build a powerful defense of his client by using Kimberly's lies as concrete, destroying her credibility, he kept pouring more cement into the mixer. "Isn't it true, Kim," he lectured to her, "that your method of handling your testimony here today is that you will lie about something, as long as you think you are getting away with it, and then when you are caught in the lie, you will tell another lie, unless you think that you are getting caught with that one, at which point you will either say you don't know or you don't remember?"

She answered his seventy-word question with one syllable: "No."

In rejoinder, Bernays continued the inquisition and managed to repeat most points several times. His

attack had the effect of summarizing to the jury her multiple examples of mendacity. They included lies about the gun, having seen the bullets, and practicing at the firing range, as well as denial to Detective Ken Hansen that she knew anything about the death of David's parents and the use of their credit cards, and lies about withdrawing money from ATMs. Kimberly made a few feeble attempts to avoid answering and invoke loss of memory, but eventually she agreed that she had lied.

Bernays narrowed his focus, "The truth of the matter is, you bought that gun, didn't you?"

"No, that's not true."

"David bought the gun for you?"

Kimberly answered with her own question. "For me? Why would I want a gun?"

"That's a very interesting question," said Bernays, and reconstructed the visit she and David had made to the seller's house. He voiced suggestions that she had handled the guns, feeling "the heft and balance in your hand because the gun was being purchased for you?" Kimberly disagreed with the inference. The defender continued to create a picture of her lying about the gun sale until she had been faced with facts revealing her participation.

Steering in a different direction, Bernays turned toward Hawaii. Kimberly had testified in direct examination that David had never told her they were going to the Islands, saying that it came as a surprise. Bernays queried, "Isn't it a fact that you told your mother on June sixth, four days before departing, that you were going to Hawaii?"

"No, I didn't say I was going to Hawaii." David, she

insisted, had wanted to surprise her with a trip. "I didn't know if it was Hawaii or where."

Referring again to his transcripts of previous conversations, he read a question to Kimberly asking, "Did you tell your mother, on June sixth, you were going to Hawaii in a few days?"

She had answered, "Probably." In addition, she had entered a note in her diary about telling her mother she was going on a trip.

"So," said Bernays, "when you testified here in trial that you had never discussed going to Hawaii prior to actually doing it, that was a lie, wasn't it?"

"No," Kimberly growled. She held firm in denying that she had told her mother any specific destination for the trip, even when Bernays read again her answer of "probably." She commented, "That doesn't mean I told her."

"Just that you probably did?"

"Yeah."

"Is that another little device to avoid the question?"

To her negative answer, Bernays jumped back to reiterating Kimberly's mendacity about the gun—her denials of being involved in the purchase, never having seen it, never firing it, and never having been at a firing range. She admitted the lies. This time, though, he added something new. Kimberly had mentioned in her deposition that police relatives in Mexico had sometimes shown her some films and pamphlets about firearms. To Detective Hansen, she had denied knowing anything about guns, and she repeated it in an interview with Bernays. The defense attorney wanted jurors to believe that Kimberly's current stance of unfamiliarity with guns, and how to use them, was just another lie.

Digging through his thick notebook of previous

transcripts, Bernays came up with more inconsistencies. In an interview, Kimberly had told the defense attorney that when she heard gunshots and went back into the house, she had not seen any blood on David at that time. But later, she had noticed a bloodstain on his shirtsleeve. "Yet, in your testimony under oath, here in this trial, is that he had on a sleeveless shirt?"

Kimberly offered an explanation. She hadn't really said "shirtsleeve" in the interview, but perhaps someone had misinterpreted her comment, which was made in Spanish.

Another inconsistency, perhaps attributable to the language barrier, came up. In the interview with Detective Hansen, she had mentioned David carrying "a box" out of the Leggs' home when they left that night. But in direct testimony, she had said it was a black plastic bag. To Bernays's challenge on this point, she fell back on memory failure.

Rolling his eyes upward, he said, "And so you want this jury to believe that despite all these lies and lack of memories, and these 'don't knows,' all of that is just washed clean because now you are sitting there in front of them telling the gospel truth. Is that correct?"

"Correct, I am telling the truth."

Bernays had not yet exhausted his ammunition. He reminded her of testifying that David had grabbed her arm to pull her out of the house. But in her previous deposition testimony, she said she had left first and he had followed. Under direct examination by McCormick, she had said that David hurriedly packed their things for the trip to Hawaii, but in her deposition she had done the packing and could not recall if David helped. Last week, she had testified about going to a hotel after they left the apartment, but in

the deposition, she couldn't remember a hotel at all. According to her trial testimony, she had lain down in the hotel, but couldn't sleep. In the deposition, she had spoken of falling asleep.

Kimberly acknowledged these discrepancies as correct. Bernays said, "So you are lying about even little things here, aren't you?"

She muttered, "I believe so."

"And you are doing everything you can to make yourself look innocent and upset and disturbed by the whole thing, to make David look like the guilty party, aren't you?"

The witness had a sharp retort: "He is the guilty one."

Bernays instantly spoke up. "Move to strike the answer. It is not responsive to my question." Judge Wilkinson agreed.

For the next hour, Bernays chipped away at whatever credibility Kimberly may still have had in the jurors' minds. At one point, he challenged her contention that David had been in complete control of her, saying, "In fact, you were controlling him, weren't you?" She adamantly denied it.

Replaying the tape of their Hawaiian cruise, Bernays suggested she was anything but an innocent teenage girl. He brought up their behavior in the bank while cashing the check for Jeannie's diamond, hugging and kissing, and portrayed it as contradicting her alleged fear of David Legg.

At last, Bernays reminded her of his statement at the beginning of cross-examination, when he stated, "My contention is that you are a liar," and asked if she admitted it. "You denied it, didn't you?"

Kimberly answered, "I don't think I denied it. I told you that I lied."

Sounding weary, Bernays said, "We have now spent the better part of two days going through each and every lie you told under oath when you had promised to tell the truth and didn't. I ask you again, Ms. Pierce, do you admit that you are a liar?"

McCormick objected. "It's argumentative." Judge Wilkinson sustained it.

Bernays rephrased the question, asking if she admitted to lying constantly throughout the case. Kimberly replied, "I lied at the beginning, two years ago, yes." But she claimed to have done her best to be truthful during the trial.

"That's all I have, Your Honor." Bernays sighed as he trudged toward his chair.

A full hour remained on the court's clock, so Glenn McCormick stepped up, intending to repair Kimberly's shattered image.

He began with questions about jobs David had held in Phoenix, and how much he had earned. Kimberly couldn't recall how long each short term of employment had lasted, and had never seen any of his paychecks. David had also kept their bank statements and bills away from her. Reporter Doug Murphy jotted a note asking if this showed how a controlling wife behaves.

If jurors had wondered why Kimberly would still go with David to Phoenix after he had left her at the altar with the help of his parents, McCormick worked to provide the answer. He elicited from her that she was already his wife, and in her culture, wives had no choice. "I had to follow my husband. That's the way I am raised."

Several times during the cross by Michael Bernays,

he had rejected her attempts to explain answers. McCormick sought to bridge those gaps, beginning with her stated affection for Brian and Jeannie Legg. Kimberly said she liked them very well. The prosecutor asked, "Did you want to spend less time with them?"

"Not really. What I referred to was that I wanted to have time with my husband alone, and I wanted them to have time alone also. . . . We would go to their house every day. They had no time alone, because we were always there."

Regarding the immunity she had been granted, Kimberly stated that she would have testified with or without it. McCormick made it clear that while anything she said in trial could not be used against her, no agreement had been received from the state *not* to prosecute her if they wished to. She also understood that her immunity could be withdrawn if she committed perjury.

Some of the lies she had told had been foolish. Kimberly acknowledged it and reasoned, "I was really scared. I don't know, because I am a fool, I guess."

Still attempting to patch her punctured reputation, McCormick asked if anyone had provided her with a copy of the transcripts to which Bernays had frequently referred. No, she said, never. She did have a copy of the statement she gave to the police, but claimed never to have read it, or even touched it.

"Was all your testimony before this jury based on your memory?"

"That's right."

Through the next set of questions, McCormick established that Kimberly had almost no time alone, away from David, after the shooting, never more than a few brief minutes out of his sight.

One issue would probably be impossible to smooth over. McCormick asked why she had kissed David in the bank. Kimberly could only mutter, "I don't know."

Frequently during cross-examination, she had rationalized behavior by saying she was "scared," especially when she was interviewed by Detective Hansen. McCormick gave her the opportunity to explain. She said, "I was afraid. I was really scared about everything that had happened, and so I didn't—I didn't know what to do. I had never been stopped by the police. I had never been arrested. I was afraid."

McCormick pointed out that she had relatives who were police officers in Juárez and asked, "Don't you trust the police?" Her monosyllabic answer of "no" caused a few chuckles in the gallery.

Kimberly had made numerous statements during the deposition and later contradicted many of them. Her testimony had been taken in a courtroom, but with no judge or jury present. Kimberly and her attorney were there, along with McCormick and Detective Ron Jones. Michael Bernays and Tonya McMath had also attended with their client, David Legg. Now Glenn McCormick wanted the jury to hear about it.

"Was David looking at you while you were testifying?"

"Yes."

"How did that make you feel?"

"Bad. Scared."

"Has he been looking at you the same way at trial in front of this jury?"

"Well, I sit back so I don't see him because of the same reason."

"Are you afraid of David Legg?"

Bernays objected, but he was overruled.

"Yes," Kimberly replied.

"Did that affect your testimony during the deposition?"

"Yes." It had also colored her statement to Detective Hansen, said Kimberly. She worried that some of her words had been incorrectly translated, because no interpreter had been present at the airport interview. Her command of English, she added, had improved in the two years since then "because I practice a lot."

Allowing Kimberly to read a portion of the police report of her statement taken by Detective Hansen, McCormick asked her if she intended to give him the impression that she had not gone inside the house after hearing gunshots. She said that was not her intent. About telling him that David had carried a box outside rather than a black plastic bag, Kimberly thought it a misunderstanding, due to the lack of an interpreter.

On the subject of whether Brian Legg liked her, Kimberly welcomed the opportunity to explain her thoughts. "He would joke with me, and I'm a very sensitive person, and sometimes his comments would hurt me, but that doesn't mean I didn't love him. He would play with me, and I would [play] with him."

"Why would you tell a story today that is different from what you told Detective Hansen or the attorneys during the deposition and the interview?"

"Because I wanted to get this over with. I wanted to be happy again. David ruined my life and his family, and he needs to pay for this." Judge Wilkinson sustained the instant objection from Bernays regarding the last part of her comment.

McCormick stated that he had no further questions. Bernays, though, asked permission to start his recross. The judge said it could be taken up the next morning.

32

A Gaping Hole the Defense Could Have Exploited

Kimberly Pierce-Taylor scooted into the witness chair on Tuesday for a final round of battle with two men, Michael Bernays and Glenn McCormick, under the watchful eye of her former "husband." David Legg's close observation gave Bernays the idea for his initial questions of the day.

The first few queries established that Kim had lied repeatedly during the previous deposition. She rationalized the dishonesty by claiming that David's stare had frightened and intimidated her. Bernays asked if she had told lies during interviews at which David was not present. She admitted it. "And you still lied to me, even though you promised you were going to tell the truth?"

"Correct," Kimberly said.

Attempting to ravage her credibility even more,

Bernays recapped her immunity agreement. Her testimony could not be used against her, but she had not been shielded from possible future charges. "You understood that you were still subject to prosecution, both for the murder of Mr. and Mrs. Legg, and for perjury committed during the deposition. Isn't that correct?" With her agreement, he continued. "Do you anticipate that today, or by the latest tomorrow, you will be returning to Mexico on a ticket purchased by the state for you, and that you will be there safe from any charges filed against you and no realistic possibility that you will ever be charged in the murder and the perjury?"

McCormick objected, but Judge Wilkinson told Kimberly she could answer. Using her little-girl voice again, she replied, "I never thought that . . . I know I am going back to Mexico, [but] that doesn't mean they can't accuse me of anything."

References to lying or "failing to tell the truth" colored most of Bernays's recross for the next fifteen minutes, after which he announced, "That's all the questions I have."

Glenn McCormick declined the opportunity to conduct additional redirect examination. But their respite did not allow the witness to step down. Arizona trial procedures allow jurors to submit written questions to the judge, who generally holds a sidebar conference with the prosecutor and defense attorney to weigh the validity of each query. The judge decides whether to ask the acceptable questions of the witness, rule them out as inappropriate, or modify them for conformance to rules of evidence.

Judge Wilkinson would later comment on the procedure: "I think allowing jurors to make inquiries regarding a witness's testimony is very helpful to the attorneys. It gives them the opportunity to understand what the jury is thinking and how they grasp the testimony. It also aids the jurors, giving them a clearer picture of what the witness said and clearing up any misconceptions."

Turning to the panel, Wilkinson said, "Ladies and gentlemen of the jury, any questions? If so, please hand them to the clerk." Several slips of paper came forward, and the judge reviewed each at a whispered sidebar conference.

The first note inquired: *When David came out to the car to check on you, did he enter the car?*

Another asked: *Did Kimberly know how to drive or did David do all the driving?*

Does the court provide the interpreter?

Judge Wilkinson said he would personally handle that one.

A woman needed to know: *Kimberly said that in Hawaii David changed their plane tickets. It was changed from what to what?* Wilkinson commented, "I will ask about the plane tickets. That was very confusing yesterday."

Yet another wanted Kimberly to demonstrate something: *Can you please point out to me on your own body the location of the blood on David's shirt he was wearing?*

A final handwritten note asked, *How was the lighting in that living room? Could she see well?*

Addressing the jury once again, Wilkinson said, "As I told you, some of the questions will be asked, some won't. In some cases, I know that there are other witnesses who may be called to testify about

some of the issues. Other questions aren't legally permissible because of the rules." Dealing with the translation note, he said, "As far as who provides the interpreter, the court does."

Turning to the witness, Wilkinson asked, "Ms. Pierce, you indicated that in Hawaii, David changed the plane tickets. From what to what did he change them?"

Kimberly replied, "We were supposed to come back—I don't remember what day—and he suddenly said we are not going to leave, we are going to take a cruise, and we didn't come back."

Apparently satisfied with her explanation, Wilkinson asked her if David had entered the car when he came out from the house. No, she said. To the next juror question, she commented that David did all of the driving. Regarding the location on her body indicating where she could see the bloodstain on David's shirt, Kimberly pointed to an area slightly below her shoulder, but couldn't recall if it had been on his left arm or the right arm. The living-room lighting, she stated, had been adequate, but the source of it escaped her memory.

At last, the judge told Kimberly Pierce-Taylor she could step down. Obviously weary and relieved, she rose and walked quickly out of the room, avoiding eye contact with anyone.

Years later, Glenn McCormick would comment on Kimberly's impact as a witness. "I am not sure how much her testimony added to the case. Not having her as a witness would have left a gaping hole that the defense could have better exploited in their attempts to blame her. But her failure to clearly pin the shooting on David, her vague description of the time of the

shooting and the scene in the house after the shooting, made her testimony less powerful."

All morning, Doug Murphy had been jotting notes about Kimberly's inconsistent answers. He characterized the cross-examination by Bernays as "grueling" for the girl who was the *equivalent of a high school freshman at the time of the murders.* In Murphy's report, he would emphasize the focus on Kimberly's lies. He observed that Bernays took every opportunity to "trip up" the young witness, who could be a key to the prosecution's case.

Eager to see who would follow Kimberly on the witness stand, Murphy was pleased to see that it would be her mother.

As her daughter had a few days earlier, Cecilia Taylor-Castillo swore to tell the whole truth, before being seated. Glenn McCormick asked if he should refer to her as Miss Taylor and she assented to that name. Answers to his introductory questions established her relationship to Kimberly, her residence in Juárez, Mexico, and that she had been present at Kim's civil wedding in El Paso. It had been performed with Taylor's permission, due to Kim's age. David Legg, she said, had lived at her house about four months.

Just a few hours before the planned church wedding, Taylor recalled, David had told her he was going out to walk around the block. Nearly three weeks passed before he returned, and the church wedding never took place.

After Kim and David moved to Phoenix, Taylor told McCormick, the young couple had returned to Juárez several times to visit. She had also traveled to

Phoenix, where she spent about four weeks with them. They had taken her on a weekend excursion to the Grand Canyon during that period. Nearly every day, she had joined them in spending time at the home of David's parents. She thought they seemed quite affectionate with her and with Kim. "Mr. Legg would joke with her, tell her she was very small, and he would laugh and hug her."

"How did David treat Mr. and Mrs. Legg?"

"Well, I think he had a better relationship with his mom than with his dad." She mentioned seeing and hearing several disagreements between David and Brian. "David told his father not to get involved in his problems and to leave Kimmie alone and not joke with her. And two days before I went home, at the end of May, they argued about David's rent."

About ten days before her departure, the mother testified, she had been with David and Kim at the Leggs' home for a backyard barbecue. She had over-heard a conversation between David and his mother. "Jeannie said that this house was going to be for David and her grandchildren."

Taylor returned home, and on June 6, she received a call from Kimberly. "She told me that David wanted to surprise her with a honeymoon trip, but didn't know the exact date."

"Did she say where they might go?"

"She assumed to Hawaii, because David wanted to go back there."

Ears perked up in the gallery, and Doug Murphy dashed off entries for the story he would write. The words from Miss Taylor directly contradicted her daughter's testimony in which she knew nothing about David planning to take her to Hawaii. Instead,

Kimberly had said she thought they were going to Juárez, despite the fact they had just left there after taking her mother home. If the polarity in facts registered with the jury, would it further undermine Kimberly's credibility?

Taylor added to the issue by stating that David had talked to her in Juárez, back in April, about wishing to return to Hawaii. "He said it was very pretty there and he had some money hidden." Did this mean, in fact, that he was already planning on suddenly coming into some money and wanted to build an alibi in advance?

Another phone call came to Taylor from her daughter on June 11 or 12. "She called me from Hawaii. I think it was from a hotel." The witness hinted that Kim's call sounded serious and unhappy.

Michael Bernays, in his cross-examination, played the videotape made by David and asked, "Does she look unhappy or serious there?"

The mother's answer caught spectators off guard. "She's acting."

Seizing on that comment, Bernays queried, "So Kimmie is a little actress, is she?"

"If it's necessary."

A few more minutes of the tape ran, and Bernays asked, "Does she look serious or unhappy there as she holds up her little wallet full of cash that she got from the sale of Mrs. Legg's diamond?"

"Not apparently."

Observers wondered if Kim's profusion of lies were intended to cover up her own culpability in the murders. Would David Legg be found not guilty simply because Kimberly had destroyed her own image with obvious mendacity, thus creating a reasonable doubt

of his guilt by casting suspicion that she might have pulled the trigger?

On redirect, McCormick took the witness back to the telephone conversation with a detective, but she reverted to faulty memory. "I was way too nervous because they had just given me news of what happened. So it's not very clear in my mind."

"What did they tell you?"

Anticipating what she would probably say, Bernays fired a quick objection. At a sidebar, he whispered, "Your Honor, her answer is going to be the detective told her that David had killed his parents. They had already determined that in their investigation, and I don't think that's what is in the evidence, that has any business going to the jury."

It surprised both lawyers when Judge Wilkinson stated, "Objection overruled. She can state that the officer told her that David had killed his parents."

Dissatisfied, Bernays continued his objection. "I think it's very unfair for Glenn to redirect her on this—"

Judge Wilkinson intervened to direct traffic. "All right, let's go."

As expected, McCormick asked what the detective told her. The witness said, "That David had killed his parents." He directed her attention to a calendar of 1996 to establish that David and Kim had driven her back to Juárez on June 1 and stayed there three or four days.

When Glenn McCormick finished, the judge reviewed several questions from the jury. One of them

wanted to know more about the money the defendant
claimed to have hidden in Hawaii, but Judge Wilkinson
decided against asking it. He approved of three:

How long was your trip from Juárez to Phoenix? Approximately six hours.

*On what date did David and Kim leave Juárez and
return to Phoenix?* Around June 4.

*Did Kim tell you about the trip she and David might
take—while she was in Mexico between the 1st and the
4th?* No.

After a few perfunctory questions to Miss Taylor,
Bernays completed his recross. McCormick asked the
judge if Kimberly and her mother could be excused
to return home. Bernays wanted to know if that
meant they would go to Mexico. Judge Wilkinson mir-
rored the question to McCormick.

McCormick grinned and answered, "State certainly
doesn't intend to keep them in a hotel at taxpayer ex-
pense the entire time this trial takes place."

With no objection from the defense, Wilkinson excused Kimberly Pierce-Taylor and Cecilia Taylor-
Castillo to travel back to Ciudad Juárez. It would be
the first step in the long recovery from the most traumatic time of their lives.

33

She Held It
in the Firing Position

Kimberly Pierce-Taylor and her mother had spent a long time on the witness stand, and doubt had been cast on the veracity of their statements. Hints about acquisition of a handgun by David or Kim, and allegations of practicing with it, had been exposed. But like the moon on a cloudy night, these issues remained vague and undefined. Glenn McCormick needed to dispose of the murky atmosphere and bring the information into sharp, bright focus for the jury.

Ed Johnson, the elderly man who had reportedly sold the gun to the couple, had since passed away. His son, Ed, had been present during the entire transaction. As soon as Kimberly's mother walked out of the courtroom, McCormick summoned the younger Johnson to be sworn in.

The stocky man, with dark curly hair, sleepy eyes,

and a light mustache, settled into the chair and tugged the microphone closer to his face. Johnson acknowledged that his late father had collected guns and sold them out of his home, but he denied that he participated in the business. Asked if he recalled a transaction back in early June 1996 that took place with a young couple, the witness said, "Yes, I was there."

Johnson's answers to McCormick established that his father had sold a broad variety of handguns through newspaper ads. He recalled answering the door when the couple had knocked, looking around to see if his father was "decently dressed," and inviting them inside. Johnson had no trouble identifying the defendant as the male he had seen. He recalled staying close during the visit for the purpose of protecting his aging father.

According to Johnson, David Legg had done almost all of the talking. The defendant had carefully examined two pistols in which he showed interest, selected a rare 1912 pistol, but changed his mind when the senior Ed quoted a price of $500. After more conversation, the defendant had bought a Ruger semiautomatic and paid $225 in cash. David had made the decision, said Johnson and handed over the money. The young woman, whom he described as Hispanic, said very little during their forty-five minutes in the Johnson home.

"Did you see the female handle the .22?"

"Yes." Johnson said she seemed "somewhat uncomfortable" with the handgun. "It appeared that she was not too familiar with weapons. . . ." The witness said his impression had been that the pistol was for "home protection."

To prepare the jury for evidence that no bullet cas-

ings had been found at the crime scene, McCormick asked, "What happens to the casings when you shoot this gun?"

"They are ejected out of the top." This fact laid the foundation for an inference that David had systematically picked up the spent shells.

On cross-examination, Michael Bernays made it clear that he and Ed Johnson had met previously, and their conversation had been tape-recorded. He asked, "Isn't it true that it was your impression that the purchase of this gun was for the female who was there?"

"That was an impression, yes."

"And they said to you that the gun was being purchased not just for home protection . . . but for her protection. Isn't that correct?"

"As I recall, that's a possibility." Johnson hedged that his memory wasn't perfectly clear on that point.

Bernays quoted from the taped interview in which the witness said: "If I recall correctly, it was a personal weapon for her." Just to be certain that the jury understood who the "her" was, Bernays played the cruise video again, and Johnson said the female resembled the woman who had accompanied David Legg.

To further solidify his point, Bernays elicited from Johnson his recollection that Kimberly had handled both the Ruger and perhaps the Steyr-Hahn 9mm handgun. The defender asked, "She was feeling the heft of it and trying to work the safety, right?"

"Yes."

"When I say 'feel the heft of a weapon,' what does that mean to you?"

"Heft means feeling how the hand wraps around

the grip, where the finger placement is on the trigger, and the weight of it when your arm is extended."

"She handled and she felt that .22. She held it in the firing position?"

"Yes."

Bernays, seeming delighted with the mental pictures he had implanted in jurors' minds, added one more snapshot. To his question, Johnson stated that his father had expressed the opinion that the decision to buy the Ruger had been not just David's, but a joint agreement by the couple.

Glenn McCormick needed to do some damage control. "Did the male feel the heft of the weapon, too?"

"Yes." David and the girl, he said, had handled the guns "an equal" amount of time.

To observers watching Ed Johnson depart the courtroom, Michael Bernays had scored heavily in this round.

A woman replaced him on the stand. Sheila Lee had been the business manager for the 48th Street apartment complex where David and Kimberly had rented a unit under their fake names, Daren and Kimberly Maloy. Examining a document handed to her by McCormick, the witness said it was the application that had been filled out by the defendant. In her recollection, at some point in time David Legg had marched into her office while she had been on the telephone and laid a stack of cash on the desk. "His rent was very past due and had already been turned over to our attorney for collection."

Lee testified that "Maloy" had turned around as if in a big hurry to leave when she asked if the dollar

amount was correct for his overdue payment. Instead of answering, he had told her that he was going to be out of town for about a week.

McCormick asked if she could see anyone in the courtroom who might be the person she had known as "Daren Maloy." No, Lee said, she could not.

The apartment manager's testimony lasted less than five minutes.

Jeff Meeker, a branch manager for Terminix, came next. He recalled interviewing and hiring "Daren Maloy" in May 1996. To the witness, "Maloy" had looked like a good prospective employee due to his appearance, personality, and energy level, combined with what appeared to be high motivation. He "definitely" was looking to make as much money as he could. The new employee had lasted only about one week, working for supervisor Lance McMahon. "After that, I believe, he didn't come to work, and I went to find his whereabouts and his truck."

Meeker readily identified the defendant, David Legg, as the person he thought was Maloy. "He is the gentleman in the gray jacket and the maroon tie."

A few days after "Daren" had abandoned his work vehicle, said Meeker, a package had arrived at the manager's office. It contained keys to the truck and a short note of apology. "Daren said that he had to leave town. I believe he had some family business and here were the keys."

Tonya McMath conducted the cross-exam. Her short inquiries ascertained that "Daren Maloy" was

enthusiastic, energetic, polite, and had a pleasant
personality.

When she finished, the judge screened a few questions from jurors and asked, "Did Mr. Maloy talk
about any upcoming vacations he planned?" The witness said no. "Do you recall where the package containing the truck keys was mailed from?"

Jeff Meeker replied, "I don't know if it was Honolulu, but it was definitely from the state of Hawaii."

"What identification did you require from Maloy?"

"He gave us a driver's license and a Social Security
card."

Time had expired for Tuesday's session, and the
judge ordered the evening recess. The prosecution
and defense geared up for Wednesday to question six
employees of stores in Hawaii, plus David's half
brother, George Price.

34

They're Getting to Be
Perry Mason

On the final day of September 1998, with Judge Michael Wilkinson's court reassembled at ten in the morning, a woman who had been born in Hawaii and lived there her whole life took the witness chair. Kathleen "Kit" Hansen told jurors of her job as a cruise coordinator with a travel agency in the Ala Moana shopping mall. She remembered booking a four-island, seven-day cruise for honeymooners "Daren" and "Cecilia Maloy." On that Friday, June 14, 1996, he had paid her $2,325 in cash.

Of course, Kit Hansen had no way of knowing at the time that the swollen bodies of "Daren's" parents were sitting in deathly stillness on a love seat inside their home, waiting to be discovered the next day.

The whole transaction, she said, had been quite pleasant, even though "Cecilia Maloy" had been noticeably

quiet and didn't participate in the booking. "She looked a little nervous and just smiled."

McCormick's co-counsel, Steve Lynch, asked Hansen if she could see "Daren Maloy" in the courtroom. She stood up to get a better view, looked directly at David Legg, and said, "I see someone, I think, that looks like the person I sold the cruise to. He's wearing a beige suit and has brown hair." To confirm her identification, Lynch showed Hansen the six-pack photo lineups she had viewed in Hawaii. She quickly picked out pictures of David Legg and Kimberly Pierce-Taylor.

On cross, Michael Bernays wanted to know if public telephones were conveniently available near her office. Yes, she said. And are police officers accessible in the city? Yes. It soon became evident that he wanted jurors to understand that Kimberly could have made a call for help if she wanted to get away from David, but she chose not to do so.

"Did she look frightened?"

"She looked nervous. She looked young, and she didn't say anything. She didn't look frightened."

When the lawyers were finished, a few jurors had questions for the witness. Judge Wilkinson read them to the prosecution and defense at sidebar. "'Would the public telephones located on the same floor of your offices have been visible from where [Kim] sat in the reception area? Would they have been visible to someone as they came into your office?'"

Bernays quipped, "Inquiring minds want to know."

Grinning, the judge said, "They're getting to be Perry Mason."

"'Was a security guard there while the Maloys were purchasing their cruise?'"

"'Did Mr. and Mrs. Maloy show any affection towards one another, hugging, kissing, when they walked in or left your office?'"

Neither side objected to the jurors' inquisitiveness. Judge Wilkinson ruled out a few he believed redundant or inappropriate and asked the one about a security guard being there.

Kit Hansen said she could not recall. "There is a security desk right outside our office, but it is not manned all the time during business hours." Regarding the demonstration of affection between the couple, she said no. And no public telephone would have been visible by anyone entering the agency.

Kit Hansen answered a few more repetitive questions before Judge Wilkinson asked counsel if she could be excused. Bernays answered with a good-natured order, "Go back to Hawaii." Kit Hansen took his advice.

The affable internal investigator for Liberty House department store in the Ala Moana Center, Matthew Souza, took the oath and the witness chair. Steve Lynch greeted him and asked for a description of his job.

"Well, at that time, I concentrated on white-collar crime—generally credit card fraud, bad checks, the stuff that we consider high-dollar cases." Speaking of his background, Souza said he had been involved in department store security since 1985. "I went to

JCPenney first, basically to meet my wife, because, you know, she walked into the store and I fell in love. I went in and got a job." His bride had been from Hawaii, so when the chance came, they both moved to the Islands and he hooked up with Liberty House.

Steve Lynch and Glenn McCormick wondered if the jury would appreciate the irony of Souza's link with JCPenney. Brian and Jeannie had spent the last afternoon of their lives shopping with David and Kim at a JCPenney store. Now a former security employee of the chain might help bring about justice in the case.

The witness, answering questions from Lynch, told of two American Express credit card receipts drawing his attention on Saturday, June 15, 1996, at the Ala Moana Liberty House store. Imprints from the card had been in the name "B. E. Legg," and the buyer had signed that name, and then headed for the exit. But the bank had transmitted a message about the card, and two salesclerks in the fine-jewelry department, Diane Tagoshi and Soomie Choi, who had assisted the customers, had immediately summoned Souza. He had responded, but the couple who made the purchases had already reached the exit. Because the bank message had been nothing more than a "code 4," which requests the seller to take possession of the credit card, there was really nothing Souza could have done at that point. Security video cameras had caught images of the couple, but only of their backs, and the tapes had not been preserved. The witness explained that it had not been a high priority, like an armed robbery or an injury. "Fraudulent use of credit cards is a pretty standard thing in our day-to-day operations, I'm sorry to say."

* * *

Cross-examination by Tonya McMath followed the
same refrain as it had with travel agent Kit Hansen.
Were store detectives available for anyone in trouble,
and did those officers have means for quick contact
with Honolulu police? Were pay phones easily accessible in the Liberty House or the immediate sur-
roundings? Without explicitly saying it, the defender
wanted jurors to know that if Kimberly had wished to
escape David, seek help, or report him to authorities,
she had ample opportunities.

A juror's question dulled the thrust to some
degree: *Are there any people walking around Liberty House
with marked security uniforms?*

Souza answered, "No, not by Liberty House. The
mall itself has an extensive security staff, but our employees are all undercover." Another juror wanted to
know if the store's security office was clearly marked
and visible to customers. "The public can be directed
to it down on the first floor," said Souza. "Usually, a
manager will escort people down to it."

Another inquiry by a juror helped clear up a point
which had confused observers: *Does a code 4 prevent a
sales person from completing a transaction?*

"No," said Souza. "Actually, we encourage the
salesperson to complete the transaction and not to
immediately give the merchandise to the person
using the card. When the card is swiped through the
reader, we want the clerk to keep it until a signature
is completed, then compare the signature to that on
the card. In a perfect world, that would happen every
time. But sometimes our people give it back too
soon, get upset when they see a code 4, and then stop

to pick up a phone and call security. The customer figures something is up, picks up the bags, is gone, and we have no information. We like to question the buyer and find out what we can about the card. We generally treat it low-key. We are sensitive about that, since we are a high-tourist destination, which is the industry of our state. We don't broadcast the crime rate . . . just keep the whole thing low-key."

The loquacious witness gave up the chair to one of the salesclerks he had mentioned. In a trembling voice, the diminutive Diane Tagoshi said she still worked in the fine-jewelry department of Liberty House at the Ala Moana Center. Steve Lynch smiled and asked if she was a little nervous, and she replied in the affirmative. He suggested, "Well, why don't you take a couple of deep breaths and just relax, okay?" It seemed to help.

Tagoshi said she recalled selling a pair of Gucci wristwatches to a young couple, and it had been imprinted in her mind because the security manager had requested her to make a written report afterward. She still recalled the man as being tall, slim, and nice. No conversation had taken place with the young woman at his side.

Lynch showed Tagoshi the two watches seized from David and Kimberly when they were arrested, along with green boxes in which the watches had been packaged. Tagoshi said they were exactly like the ones she had sold. She also extracted a card from one of the boxes, and identified a stamped signature and date block she had personally signed. In addition, she con-

firmed the sale from receipts bearing her employee number and handwriting describing the watches.

The witness recalled identifying photos of the customers from a group of pictures shown to her by a detective, but she couldn't positively say the defendant in the courtroom had been the person to whom she had sold the watches.

Tonya McMath, on cross-exam, asked if the female customer had pointed to a watch in the showcase and extended her arm to try it on. Tagoshi said yes. The defender inquired, "Did she show any resistance?" No. "Did she cooperate in taking out some links from the band?" Yes. "Did she act happy?" Yes.

In Lynch's redirect, he asked, "Was it your impression the male was in charge?"

The witness answered affirmatively. For this tiny woman, the jury had no questions, and she seemed quite pleased to be excused so soon.

After the lunch break, the third Liberty House witness came forward. Soomie Choi had also made a written report at the request of Matthew Souza, and she had no trouble remembering the transaction she had made with a young couple over two years ago. In her recollection, the male had wanted a gold bracelet for his companion. The girl, she said, had been silent for the most part, but she made her choice of jewelry clear. Choi also recalled observing noticeable affection between the couple, after which she found out they were newlyweds, and she thought the male was totally in charge.

Steve Lynch unsealed a bag, lifted out a delicate bracelet, and asked Choi if she recognized it. She said, "This is lightweight fourteen-karat hug-and-kisses bracelet for ladies." It was the one she had sold to the couple. She also identified a diamond-cut rope chain they had bought "the gentleman."

When Steve Lynch announced he had no more questions, Tonya McMath rose and drew from the witness her opinion that while the female had not communicated directly, she had been involved in expressing her preferences. "She would tell him she wants to see the next one, instead of asking me. That's why I had impression of she very shy."

"Did she appear to be nervous or uncomfortable at all?" No. On the contrary, she seemed quite happy.

McMath read aloud from a police report: "'Soomie said she had helped a couple for about twenty minutes showing them items of jewelry for males and females. She said that all three of them were involved in conversations during that time.'" The defender asked, "Do you remember telling that to the detective from the Phoenix Police Department?"

The witness replied, "Yes." It appeared to be a direct contradiction of her earlier testimony.

McMath attempted to nail down the polarized answers. "And by saying that to the detective, did you mean to indicate that the female was also involved in communication directly with you?"

Soomie Choi cleared it up. "What I meant was, she wasn't paying attention what we're talking about. She didn't speak to me, but she was involved in the conversation . . . through the young man, not directly to

me. But she will pay attention what we are talking about. When I see they both have wedding bands, I asked if they are newlyweds. She listened, but gentleman say yes."

Still hoping to establish a modicum of contradiction, McMath referred again to the police report and asked Choi if she had said that both the man and the girl had responded with a yes, they had just gotten married.

"She did not speak, but she nodded her head."

McMath turned to the display of affection, asking if they had been "physically affectionate."

"I don't recall they were touching each other or kissing, but they stand close enough and I felt very much love between them."

"Okay," said McMath. "Thank you. That's all I have."

Steve Lynch had nothing else, either, but a juror wanted to know the date and time of the transaction. It had been printed on the sales slip: *July 15, 1996, 10:52 A.M.*

The court excused Soomie Choi.

The Liberty House team had completed their turn onstage.

Steve Lynch next called an employee from a Guess store in Hawaii. Shaleen Mosher, in her midtwenties, said she had since been transferred to Seattle with a promotion to manager. Recalling the day in June 1996 when a young couple had been her customers, Mosher told how the man had gone upstairs while the female had gathered armloads of clothing from the "young contemporary women's section" on the ground floor.

"She was picking out merchandise and didn't want to try anything on. And she didn't want anyone to help her." Mosher mentioned that salespeople at the store worked on commission, so there had been some competition between them to ring up the rich sale. Purchases by the couple had been paid with an American Express card.

Lynch introduced several exhibits of clothing, for both men and women, which had been seized from the luggage of David and Kimberly. All of it bore Guess labels. The witness verified each item as a product from the company, and thought nearly all of them could be the items purchased by the defendant.

Mosher had been able to pick out photos of the two customers when visited by detectives in Hawaii. Now Lynch asked, "Do you see the gentleman here today who made the purchases at your store?"

"Yes." Pointing her forefinger at David Legg, she said, "He has the khaki suit on—the man with brown hair."

Michael Bernays's first few questions drew descriptions of the store layout and confirmation that the defendant had spent most of his time upstairs, while the female had been on the ground floor.

After establishing that public telephones were easily available near the store, and that Shaleen Mosher would probably have allowed a good customer to use the store phone, Bernays inquired, "If a customer said, 'I'm here against my will and I'm only waiting for an opportunity to alert the authorities because the person I'm with has killed his parents,' would you let them use the phone?"

Wrinkling her smooth forehead, the witness nodded and said, "Yes."

"This girl didn't do anything like that, did she?" No. "If she had really wanted to, would she have had the time or the opportunity to talk to you or one of the other salespeople about that when her husband, boyfriend, whatever, was upstairs and out of sight?" Yes. "And she didn't take any opportunity to engage you in any such conversation, did she?"

"No," replied the witness.

With his point solidly made, Bernays sat down.

After a few questions from jurors, Judge Wilkinson thanked Mosher and said, "You may step down. You are excused."

Following a midafternoon break, Melanie Silva, another Guess employee, seated herself in the witness chair. Answering Steve Lynch, she said she had been an assistant manager in June 1996 at a Guess outlet store in Waikele, about a twenty-minute drive from the Ala Moana mall. Silva recalled the prosecutor's visit to the store, accompanied by a Phoenix Police Department detective, and telling them of a young couple who had exchanged some Guess clothing near closing time on June 14. In addition, they had bought four more items. The male had filled out an exchange slip and signed the name "Brian Legg." The small, slender girl, she said, had been dressed in a miniskirt and a stomach-baring blouse. During their time in the store, they had seemed happy, while hugging and kissing.

Lynch showed Silva the merchandise exchange form and she verified it was the one prepared by Legg.

At his request, she looked around the courtroom to see if anyone resembled the male customer. Silva identified the defendant, David Legg.

Tonya McMath for the defense asked if the female was the one doing most of the shopping and pretty much picking out whatever she wanted.

"I believe so," said the witness. She also agreed that most of the items exchanged were for a woman. At McMath's request, Silva estimated the girl's age. "Maybe fourteen," she guessed, but said her behavior seemed more mature and provocative.

Again, the defense played the videotape and asked the witness if she recognized the girl. "She looks a little familiar," replied Silva, but couldn't be sure it was the customer. "I thought the girl in the store had lighter hair."

Undeterred, McMath asked, "Putting the hair shade aside, does she look like her?"

"Yes."

"Were the actions of the girl in the tape consistent with the kind of provocative behavior you observed of the young lady in the store?"

"Yes."

On redirect, Steve Lynch flipped the coin over. "Did the man appear to be uncomfortable with the woman?" No. "So they appeared to be mutually affectionate?"

"Yes."

For this witness, the jurors had no questions and she was excused.

Observers had been wondering if anyone from the victims' family would testify. The next witness answered their question.

35

Ten Thousand Dollars
in Five Days

George Price, Palma Jean Legg's son and David's half brother, passed through the gallery, stood with his right hand raised, and swore to tell the truth. Slim, with left-parted full black hair, light blue eyes, and full lips, he wore fashionably casual clothing and moved with an air of confidence.

Glenn McCormick asked, "How old were you when your mother and Mr. Legg got together?"

"I was probably seven or eight." That had been thirty years ago.

Through the prosecutor's questions, Price transported the jury back to the traumatic time when he tried to contact his mother and Brian for the upcoming Father's Day, drove to Phoenix, and, with his cousin Joe Matise, eventually made a stunning discovery. Joe had gone in and found the gruesome sight.

Price said, "As soon as he opened the door, I knew what was wrong and—I mean, I was crying and I knew what had happened, and I just wasn't looking at anything."

"Did you see him come out of the house?"

"Yes. He seemed very agitated and said, 'Don't go in. Your parents are dead.'"

"Before that, when was the last time you saw your half brother, David?"

"I believe we celebrated Thanksgiving of 1995. We were also celebrating his birthday at that time. My wife, mother, father, David, and Kimmie were there." It took place in Phoenix at his parents' home.

"How did your father and David seem to be getting along?"

"As they always got along. They were with each other most of the time. Dad was the type of person that made jokes with people. It was nothing out of the ordinary."

"Is he the Don Rickles of the family?"

"He liked to make light of everything he could."

"How was he toward Kimberly?"

"Very cordial. My parents were the type of people that treated every guest well, and this was no different."

"How did she seem toward him?"

"Comfortable. She certainly seemed to like them, and my parents treated her well. Kimmie seemed to be fairly shy, reserved, quiet, but certainly not unhappy."

Referring to the videotape, McCormick said, "You've seen it over and over and over and over, right?" Yes. "Did she seem, on that family occasion, like she seemed in this little brief segment that has been shown so many times?" Price opined that she was

usually more reserved. He added that she always seemed to be close to David. "They seemed like two people having fun with each other and liking each other."

"Shortly after that time frame, were you aware of David living in Phoenix?"

"No." Price expressed ignorance of David ever visiting his parents after that 1995 Thanksgiving.

"In phone calls, would your parents typically talk to you about what was going on in their life and what they were doing?"

"There were many occasions they were talking about what was happening in their life."

"Did he ever talk about David and his girlfriend living with them?"

"No, never." Even though he had frequently visited Brian and Jeannie Legg during the first half of 1996, Price hadn't seen or heard any evidence of David living there or nearby.

"Did you talk with them about David?"

"Early in that year, we talked about him. As time wore on, we talked to them less and less about David, and finally not at all."

Price was aware of his parents driving to Juárez in February, and he considered going with them, but he decided not to. "David was in the army and was AWOL, I believe, or deserted. And they had told me that they recently found him and that he was in Mexico. They wanted to go down there, try to find him, and bring him back to the fort where he was stationed."

McCormick consumed several minutes with questions about the house's floor plan, his parents' occupations, and other related matters. He asked, "Did

you listen to the telephone answering machine to see who might have tried to call them?" Price replied that he had heard only part of it, mostly his own voice desperately trying to reach them.

With that settled, McCormick asked, "Did your parents have a camcorder?"

Yes, Price replied. It was a Sony, which used eight-millimeter tapes. "I remember them using it for David's first wedding, in 1992. My mother gave it to Dad for the previous Christmas. She had bought it at a JCPenney's." The witness said he had cooperated with police at the crime scene in determining what might have been stolen, including the camcorder.

Something else was missing, too. Price told of his mother's diamond ring, an anniversary gift from Brian, which she wore on her "wedding finger."

"Do you know how your mother felt about that ring?" The question brought a vociferous objection from Mike Bernays, and a sidebar discussion.

Bernays complained, "Judge, I would urge the court that the way the mother felt about property, even if that property is the subject of theft, is in no way relevant to the question of who did the theft or what motives they might have had. . . . The state's theory is the murder [occurred] to get the ring. It's just purely calculated to plead to the emotions and the passions of the jury."

Judge Wilkinson didn't agree. "I think it is relevant." He explained that the jury might be considering the possibility that Palma Jean Legg could have made a gift of the ring "to one or the other" to do what they want with it.

Michael Bernays stated that he had not raised the issue of it being a gift, and even Glenn McCormick

seemed a little puzzled. He said, "For the record, where I'm headed is the fact that she never took it off."

Wilkinson had heard enough. "Overruled. Let's go." To the witness, he said, "You may answer the last question."

Price uttered, "She revered that ring. I never saw her without it on her finger."

Another series of questions and answers informed jurors of Brian's military background and his pride that three stepchildren had served in the air force, while his own son chose the U.S. Army.

Judge Wilkinson took a look at the clock, saw the final day of September had run its course, and declared the evening recess. He ordered witness George Price to return the following morning.

On Thursday, October 1, Price resumed his place in the witness chair, expecting a long, arduous session of grilling by both sides. It surprised him when the prosecution said they had no further questions, and the defense declined the opportunity for cross-examination. The jury, though, needed a few points cleared up. The judge ruled most of their queries irrelevant, but he agreed to ask three of them.

Addressing Price, Judge Wilkinson said, "The first is a yes or no question. 'When you were searching for your parents to try and find out where they were, did you call your brother, David?'" Price said no. "'In your parents' home, were you aware if they had any firearms in the house, particularly a twenty-two-caliber?'"

"No," said the witness. "They had no weapons in the home."

"'When you listened to a part of the phone answer-

ing tape, did you hear any messages from David or Kimmie?'"

No, said Price, and with that, he was excused.

Diana Price, George's wife, came next. She told McCormick they had been married nineteen years and had known Brian and Jeannie twenty-one years. The last time they had spoken by telephone was on Saturday, June 8, 1996, when they had asked Brian if he knew how to do the cha-cha so they could teach a seventy-five-year-old neighbor, then talked about getting together on Father's Day, June 16. Repeated efforts to reach them, beginning on Tuesday, June 11, had failed.

"Why did you need to talk to them?"

"We had planned to be there on the Friday evening before Father's Day, but had to delay it. We decided to wait until Saturday afternoon, and we wanted to let them know of the change in plans."

The next question from McCormick brought a startling revelation: "Did you know where David was at that time frame in early June?"

"Yes." Ears perked up in the gallery. How could Diana know this? The prosecutor asked her. Diana answered, "Through Mom. I had spoken to her. We were there for Easter weekend and I took her aside. We were in the kitchen by ourselves and she told me."

Dead quiet loomed in the courtroom. Had Jeannie revealed the secret to her daughter-in-law? Diana explained that she had noticed some of David's personal possessions in the Leggs' guest bedroom during the Easter visit, and that's what prompted her to take Jeannie aside. "I asked her where David was, or what

was going on with his life. She told me that he was still being held at Fort Bliss awaiting court-martial."

A collective breath exhaled in the room. Apparently, Jeannie had lied to keep from spilling the beans about David's presence in Phoenix from early March. McCormick sought verification that the mother had not confessed. "Were you aware of David and Kim staying with his parents in the March-April time frame?" No. "Were you aware of him having an apartment in Phoenix in the May to June time frame?" No.

Wishing to hear Diana's point of view about their arrival at the Leggs' home on the day of discovering the dead bodies, McCormick took her, step-by-step, through that day. She mentioned the burning light on the garage exterior and explained that she had never seen it on before, not even at night. Spectators wondered if David had needed the light and failed to switch it off before leaving the crime scene.

Diana described their fearful exploration of the backyard and trying to see inside the house. "I looked through a French door pane and I could see the couch and love seat. There was a gray-and-white comforter they had, and I told George that it looked like someone might be sleeping there."

Showing Diana photos of the home's interior, McCormick asked about blinds covering a large window in the breakfast nook. She said, "It has pull-down blinds that were never down, because Mom liked the sun coming in." Blinds unusually obscuring all of the other windows had alarmed the couple. Diana told McCormick, "I said to George, 'Let's just go around in front, call Joe, and have him come over to see if this is exactly what he saw when he came over Thursday.'"

Joe had arrived shortly, she said, and used a spare

key to unlock the entry. "As soon as the door was opened, there was cold air that came out and there was this smell . . . like a dead animal, only ten times worse. Joe said, 'Just stay outside, something's wrong.' When he came out, his face was pale, and he told us that Mom and Dad were dead."

They were so shocked, Diana said, even the call to 911 was a problem. "We had our cell phone from Tucson, and we reached their police department." With emergency services help, local authorities were notified.

Stepping back in time, McCormick asked about the time they had met Kimberly Pierce-Taylor at Thanksgiving, 1995. Diana said that the young girl and David seemed happy together. She also thought that David and his father interacted well. Regarding Jeannie's diamond ring, Diana had never seen her take it off.

Earlier in the trial, implications had been made that Kimberly took offense at Brian's teasing her with comments about being small, which angered her so much she might have wanted revenge. McCormick asked Diana if Brian had also teased her.

"Sometimes," she said.

"Did you understand that just to be his way?"

She replied, "After a few years, yes."

Mike Bernays stood to cross-examine. Not having asked George Price any questions, he deadpanned a tongue-in-cheek apology to Diana. "Sorry, I'm not going to give you the free pass I gave your husband."

In a more serious tone, he inquired, "You just said that Brian Legg would joke with you about your size and other stuff. You said, 'After so many years.' Do I

understand you to be saying that when you first met him and he was doing that, it didn't feel so funny to you?"

Perhaps not wishing to sound critical of Brian, Diana said, "It was funny, but I was very sensitive and didn't know the family that well yet. As I got to know them, it didn't matter anymore." It had taken about a year to understand him, Diana explained. In the gallery, some thought Bernays had scored an important point. Kim might very well have disliked Brian over the teasing.

On redirect, McCormick asked, "Did you all of a sudden come to understand Brian Legg's way of joking with you after a year, or was it a gradual process?"

"No, I understood it."

Diana Price coped with a few questions from the jury before exhaling a sigh of relief when the judge allowed her to step down.

The next witness provided evidence of extensive charges to the Leggs' American Express cards by David and Kimberly in Phoenix and in Hawaii. Craig Piro had been a regional director of security for the firm in 1996. From documents shown on the big television screen, he read aloud a list that included:

Factory Outlet, Waipahu	*$ 85.34*
House of Music, Honolulu	*$ 40.57*
Kinney Store, Oahu	*$ 112.78*
Guess Retail Store, Honolulu	*$ 232.29*
J. Riggings, Oahu	*$ 184.80*
Red Lobster, Honolulu	*$ 70.00*
Guess Store, Honolulu	*$ 303.13*

Guess Retail, Honolulu	$ 589.58
Guess Outlet, Waipahu	$ 129.17
Computer City, Waipahu	$3,161.40
Red Lobster	$ 71.71
Liberty House, Honolulu	$1,145.63
Liberty House, Aiea	$ 250.00

Steve Lynch asked, "Could you please tell the members of the jury what the total is for that card?"

The total was $6,376.40, in the month of June.

A second American Express card had also been plundered. The witness voiced charges to it:

Delta Airlines	$ 964.00
Dollar Rent A Car, Honolulu	$ 488.00
Turtle Bay Hotel Resort	$ 712.00
Shop in Turtle Bay Hotel	$ 211.00
Warner Bros Store, Hawaii	$ 512.00
Liberty House, Honolulu	$ 184.00
Office Max, Honolulu	$ 132.00
Guess Store, Honolulu	$ 112.00
Bass Company, Honolulu	$ 83.00
Liberty House, Honolulu	$ 98.00
Liberty House, Honolulu	$ 418.00
Computer City, Honolulu	$ 171.00
K-Mart, Honolulu	$ 18.00
Total	$4,103.00
Grand Total	$10,479.40

Piro added a comment that made the total even more staggering. The first charge had been made on June 10 for the Delta Airline tickets in Phoenix. The final charge had been made on June 15! More than ten thousand dollars in five days!

The charges on the AmEx card would have been

even more, considering that David originally had charged $1,948 to buy the round-trip Delta Airline tickets, but had canceled the return flight from Hawaii and taken ATA Charter Airlines, instead.

Perhaps the jurors were too stunned to ask any questions after both attorneys agreed to excuse the witness. The judge declared a welcome noon recess.

After lunch, prosecutor Steve Lynch summoned Teresa Fields, an investigative consultant for Bank of America. Having shown the extravagant purchases made against the victims' credit, Lynch sought to demonstrate even further greed by the defendant and his female companion. The prosecutor questioned Fields about a pair of ATM cards issued to Brian and Palma Legg. Between June 10 and June 15, 1996, cash withdrawals had been made in the amount of $2,300, all in Phoenix and in Hawaii. Both cards had been drained down to balances of less than $20.

Financial gains from the crime had started with pawning Jeannie's diamond ring, and Lynch needed to provide hard evidence of how the defendant turned it into cash.

The witness looked at a scroll of photographs handed to her by the prosecutor. She verified the pictures had been taken by an ATM security camera at a Bank of America on 44th Street in Phoenix, only a short drive from an apartment complex on 48th Street, where David and Kimberly had lived as Daren and Cecilia Maloy. The photos portrayed a young man and woman at a counter inside the bank. Supplemental records proved the male cashed a check in the amount of $7,000 written by the jewelry store owner,

and then purchased a cashier's check of $2,000. He had used a driver's license as identification, and bank records showed the transactions had been made by Daren Maloy with an address on 48th Street. Time stamps on the photos indicated the bank visit covered a span of twenty-six minutes during which the couple exhibited affection for one another and could be seen kissing in one of the frames.

The testimony of Teresa Fields lasted no more than twenty minutes before she was excused.

A forged driver's license signed by "Daren Maloy" had been used as identification by David Legg. The defendant had also signed that name to several applications, registrations, and other documents. To provide the jury with proof that the signatures had actually been written by David Legg, Steve Lynch put a forensic document examiner on the stand. John S. Gorajczyk, a member of the Phoenix Police Department had been specializing in "handwriting, altered writing, trace writing, counterfeit currency, paper, ink, printers, photocopiers, typewriters, and things of that nature" for more than eighteen years.

Handing the driver's license to Gorajczyk, Lynch asked him if he had compared the signature on it to a series of handwriting examples by David Legg, including a hotel guest registry and various signed receipts. In complex terms, the witness gave a thorough explanation of the processes he used, and eventually concluded "with a high probability" that Legg had been the forger.

More comparative analysis from Gorajczyk, using handwriting examples of Brian Legg's signature,

showed that David had probably signed his father's name on several documents.

A few of the signatures the expert examined could not be conclusively attributed to David Legg, and Michael Bernays zeroed in on those with his cross-examination. The defender also asked if any requests had been made of John Gorajczyk to compare known exemplars from a woman named Kimberly Pierce-Taylor. No, said the witness.

Observers and jurors learned an interesting fact from an inquiry by Bernays. "You'd agree with me—would you not—that handwriting examination is somewhat different from, for example, fingerprint identification, in that there are some people who can write exactly like another person?"

"No," Gorajczyk stated. "That's proven wrong. But it is more subjective than objective." He would not agree that forgers can produce a document that is virtually impossible to distinguish from an original, nor that identical twins write exactly alike.

Bernays switched gears. "None of the documents you examined in this case were direct evidence of homicide—isn't that correct?"

"Not that I know of."

"There was no, for example, confession, correct?"

"Correct."

Of several questions submitted by jurors, one provoked considerable interest: *Can the expert tell if the handwriting was done by a right-handed or left-handed person?*

Gorajczyk answered, "I can't tell left-handed or

right-handed. There are people who write with their right hand with a back slant, and people who write with their left hand with a forward slant. You can't tell handedness, sex, age, education, or race."

The half hour John Gorajczyk spent on the stand had been an education to several people. They would have a whole weekend to think about it. Judge Michael Wilkinson ordered the court to reconvene on Monday morning.

36

Parade of Detectives

A cooling breeze swept through downtown Phoenix on Monday, October 5. People entering the East Court building on the southwest corner of Jefferson Street and 1st Avenue actually wore jackets and coats. Spectators and jurors for the David Legg trial took the elevator up to the fourth floor and entered Judge Wilkinson's domain through a door marked 411.

Observers in the gallery had been wondering when detectives from the Phoenix PD would be heard from. They weren't disappointed when Brian McIndoo took that stand that morning.

With Steve Lynch asking questions, McIndoo told of joining Detective Ron Jones's team and digging into credit card trails at first. A little later, he had been the lucky one to travel, with Lynch, to Hawaii and interview various store and hotel employees, including those who had already testified. The detective's testimony

corroborated statements the jury had heard from those merchandisers, plus their selections from six-pack photo lineups of David Legg and Kimberly Pierce-Taylor.

Tonya McMath, on cross-exam, focused on a few of the merchants who might have shown some doubt while trying to pick the defendant out in photographic six-pack lineups. She also questioned why exemplars of Kimberly's handwriting had not been collected and compared to signatures on credit card slips. McIndoo commented that some procedural matter involved in charges against Kimberly had kept them from doing that.

McMath inquired, "As a result of your investigation both in Hawaii and putting all those documents together, you ascertained that Kimberly Pierce-Taylor was actively involved in fraudulent activity, did you not?"

"She was there, present, participating in the things that were going on. Yes."

After a few wrap-up questions, McIndoo was excused.

Detective Ken Hansen stepped up from a seat in the gallery and replaced his colleague. Glenn McCormick gave him the opportunity to tell jurors of his extensive background in law enforcement. Following that, the detective spoke of his activities at the crime scene, the autopsy, searching the 48th Street apartment, various investigative steps, and the arrest in Los Angeles. His interview with Kimberly at LAX reconfirmed that she peppered her statement with lies.

The apartment search had yielded numerous items that would be introduced into evidence through Hansen's testimony, including checkbook boxes, a plastic container full of .22-caliber bullets, and various documents. The detective had also collected evidence from the Ford Escort, such as the blue plastic case for CDs, a parking-lot ticket, some receipts, a torn sheet from a Yellow Pages book, and a gold wedding band.

McCormick asked, "At some point during the investigation, did you find another band that was similar to that one?"

"Yes. It was on the finger of the victim Mr. Legg."

The prosecutor handed Hansen a sealed bag, instructed him to open it and to extract the contents. He asked, "What are we looking at here?"

"This is a pair of Bermuda-style shorts that were taken off of Mr. Legg. We are looking at the back pockets. Obviously, the white-colored things are the pockets pulled outward. The pockets were empty."

With that horrible image, and its implications, in the minds of everyone, Judge Wilkinson called for the evening recess.

On Tuesday, October 6, Michael Bernays fell ill, making him unavailable for court that day. He recovered rapidly, and showed up ready for action on Wednesday.

Detective Ken Hansen, still under oath, resumed his place in the witness chair. Certification of evidence seized inside the apartment consumed the first hour. Glenn McCormick also introduced jewelry, cash, credit cards, and clothing that had turned up during

the arrest in Los Angeles. They also revisited the crime scene to inform jurors about additional details.

Back in perfect form, Bernays used cross-examination to build a picture of how thoroughly Ken Hansen, Ron Jones, and others had examined the Leggs' home interior for clues. With that established, he asked, "It would be fair to say—wouldn't it, Detective—that despite your valiant efforts in this regard, and all the details you did at the crime scene, you didn't find anything in your investigation of the family room or master bedroom that helped you identify who had committed the murder?"

Hansen tried to dodge it by firing back, "As a personal identification?"

"Yes."

"In terms of what you refer to as trace evidence, like fingerprints?"

Bernays nodded his assent, saying, "Fingerprints and blood and hair or fibers."

Resigned to it, Hansen replied, "No. No personal identity, just bits of evidence that were found."

"All right," Bernays acquiesced. "Now, I don't mean to sound ridiculous, but sometimes the victims manage to scrawl something as they are dying, leaving some note or some evidence that tries to point back at something somebody did. Nothing like that in this case?"

"No, sir."

Reviewing efforts by fingerprint and serological experts, Bernays repeated the same query. Hansen had to agree. The defender brought up the main theme of his case. "There was nothing in your physical examination of the crime scene [that] excludes Kimberly

Pierce-Taylor as being the person who fired the shots, was there?"

"No, there wasn't."

"And there was nothing in your physical examination of the crime scene that absolutely identified David Legg as the person firing the shots?"

"Not absolutely, no."

Still aiming at Kimberly, Bernays got agreement that she liked and collected Mickey Mouse memorabilia. He then fired a surprising question. "Isn't it true that certain Mexican Mafia gangs adopt Mickey Mouse as their symbol because of the same initials?"

Hansen said he had never heard of that. Bernays left that subject to ferment, and concentrated again on Kimberly's pattern of lying. That topic burned away most of the morning.

On redirect, McCormick slashed away at the suggested Mickey Mouse/Mexican Mafia association. His experience in the Gangs Unit prepared him well for this battle. Several questions were loaded with his knowledge, and he finally elicited from Hansen that he had never known Mickey Mouse to be associated in any way with Mexican gangs.

A few questions from jurors revealed nothing of major importance, and Ken Hansen was allowed to step down, completing his final duty in the case of David Legg.

Serological evidence, consisting usually of bloodstains or other body fluids, often plays a crucial part in solving crimes. In the Legg case, though, it took a backseat. A pair of tan shorts found in the apartment bore small stains, which appeared to be blood, which

had raised Detective Ken Hansen's hopes for a direct lead to the killer. He had bagged the garment for testing.

Thomas Boylan, a serology expert who had examined the stain, accepted Glenn McCormick's invitation to the witness stand. He verified that the brownish stains were indeed made by blood. In the lab, he had compared these to samples from Brian and Jeannie Legg, taken from one of the blankets on their bodies. He ruled out either of the victims as the source of stains on the shorts. Nor did they match a sample from David Legg. One more test produced positive results, proving the stains came from Kimberly Pierce-Taylor.

The finding regarding Kim did not provide a link to the killer. Any number of scenarios could be conjured to explain why her blood would be on shorts found in the apartment where she lived.

Boylan had also examined the latex kitchen gloves found in a clothes hamper at the crime scene and found a tiny dot of blood, which could have been made by either Brian or Jeannie.

Cross-examination of the witness reconfirmed his findings that nothing in his tests had cast any light on a possible killer.

Another day ended for the trial. Judge Wilkinson ordered the jurors and lawyers to return on October 8.

Two employees from the Guess store at Ala Moana testified on Thursday morning. Yung Ju Lim and Tri Ley described the shopping spree by Kimberly and David, confirming previous statements from other employees.

After lunch, Dr. Philip Keen, the chief medical examiner for Maricopa County, took jurors through gruesome details of the autopsies conducted on the bodies of Jeannie and Brian Legg. He had not conducted the procedures, so he spoke from reports prepared by Dr. Udelle Zivot, the examiner. Through Keen's testimony, jurors learned the cause of death for both victims, the number of bullet wounds they had sustained, and the approximate angles from which the gun was fired. He also described injuries to Brian's head caused by blunt-force trauma consistent with blows from a handgun shortly before his death.

Faces in the gallery reflected sympathetic pain as Dr. Keen described an indented pale encirclement on the third finger of Jeannie's left hand, indicating where she had regularly worn a ring. McCormick asked, "Would you expect somebody who had taken their ring off, and left it off for a period of time, for that mark on the hand to go away somewhat, or maybe even completely?"

Keen answered, "It will disappear over time, if you take it off long enough. If the marks are rather pronounced, they may persist for days."

"Would you consider this a more pronounced or a slight mark on the finger?"

"I think it's a rather pronounced mark."

McCormick inquired if the doctor had an opinion as to when the ring had been removed in relation to the victim's death. Mike Bernays objected, but after some discussion, he withdrew it. The witness replied, "The absence of other injuries, pattern to the skin— the skin doesn't appear to be torn—it does not appear to be scuffed or slipping from those areas. It would be

my opinion that the ring was taken off while [she was] alive, or very shortly after death."

Several photographs of the decomposed victims made a few observers queasy.

As expected, Michael Bernays concentrated his cross-examination on establishing that nothing in the autopsy could suggest who had caused the victims' deaths. He added, "And you would agree with me—would you not—that it is equally feasible for an adolescent female to have caused these deaths as an adult male?"

"Yes, sir."

The blunt-force injuries to Brian's head next occupied Bernays. After getting agreement that instruments other than a handgun could possibly have been used to inflict the blows, he asked, "And such an instrument, wielded by a healthy adolescent female, could cause that injury as readily as if wielded by a healthy adult male?"

"I would think so."

Taking it one step further, the defender established that, according to sites of bullet wounds in the victims, and estimated angles at which the gun was held, Kimberly's height of about five-four would not preclude her from being the shooter.

Glenn McCormick, in redirect, tried to attack the theory that Kimberly could have done the shooting, as opposed to taller David, but made no headway. When he asked David to stand so the jury could have a look at his height, Bernays quipped, "No objection. I don't care, Judge. He is wearing my suit, so we are about the same size."

Both sides gave way to a few jurors' questions before letting Dr. Keen be excused.

Keith Maki, a jeweler who worked in the store where David had sold his mother's diamond, complied with Steve Lynch's request to take the stand. He verified that his boss, Warren Williams, advertised in Yellow Pages books. Maki also remembered receiving a telephone call in June 1996 in which a male voice had asked if they buy "larger" diamonds. Maki had said yes, but no monetary offer could be made over the phone. He also recalled seeing the young couple when they came into the store and had observed the male's conversation with Mr. Williams while the girl looked at showcases. Both parties had seemed relaxed and at ease, said Maki. His testimony concluded after no more than twenty minutes. If insiders wondered why Warren Williams had not testified, their curiosity would soon be satisfied. Only two more full days and one partial day of trial remained, and he would be one of the final witnesses.

One more person took the stand on Thursday. Lance McMahon had been the supervisor for "Daren Maloy" at Terminix, starting on May 28, 1996. He said Daren had last worked on Friday, June 7, and had been scheduled for the weekend, but he hadn't shown up. "I think it was the next Tuesday we started looking for his truck."

The court's day had wound down, and the trial would not resume until Tuesday, October 13. Judge Wilkinson explained to the jury, "Ladies and gentlemen, we are

going to recess and you get a number of days away from us. Monday is a court holiday because of Columbus Day, and, as we know, not for discovering America but discovering that he was lost." Laughter rippled through the courtroom. One of the jurors, seeing bleak prospects for the trial to end soon, asked the judge if he should cancel a previously arranged dentist appointment for Thursday, October 15. Wilkinson gave him a definite no, but he would not predict exactly when he expected the jury to begin deliberating.

37

Monitoring the Mail

Glenn McCormick opened Tuesday morning with a criminologist from the Phoenix PD crime lab, Randy Leister, who specialized in firearms and ammunition. He testified about examining bullet fragments found at the crime scene and in the heads of the victims. After analyzing and categorizing the damaged pieces of the projectiles, Leister concluded some of them were consistent with .22-caliber long-rifle bullets. He also had test-fired a few rounds of the .22-caliber bullets found inside a plastic container in the apartment. Leister told jurors that the bullets used by the killer had probably been fired from a Ruger .22-caliber pistol, but it could also have been from two other brands.

Showing the witness a catalog of Ruger weapons, McCormick established that one of the photographs in it would be like the weapon used. And the bullet

fragments were consistent with having been shot from that type of handgun.

In his cross-exam, Michael Bernays steered back toward his goal of convincing jurors that Kimberly could have been the killer. He asked if a Ruger .22-caliber pistol, being lightweight and compact, is a popular ladies' gun.

Randy Leister replied, "Sure, men or women."

Bernays asked, "It fits in a purse?"

With a smile teasing his lips, the witness said, "Large purse."

"Comes with color-coordinating handgrips?"

"I guess, looking at it that way."

The defender chuckled and admitted, "I am not serious." But he wanted to make his point. "You would agree that this weapon could as easily be wielded by a woman or a man, even a teenage girl?"

"Sure."

"And there is nothing in your examination [that] lends any light to who handled the weapon?"

"Right," said Leister. He acknowledged that no actual murder weapon had been brought to him for testing.

After grilling Leister in detail about possible variations in bullets and handguns, and getting his agreement, Bernays sat down. A short redirect by McCormick and a few technical questions from the jury wound up Leister's testimony.

Fingerprint expert Joseph Silva came next. Steve Lynch opened the door for Silva to tell jurors about the

EDPL process used at the crime scene, which produced
nothing of importance. Also, no usable latent prints
had been extracted from the latex rubber glove. But
other fingerprint techniques had matched David
Legg's thumbprint to a Yellow Pages leaf advertising
pawnshops, plus a few credit card receipts. Also, Kimberly Pierce-Taylor's right ring finger and right thumb
matched prints on a checkbook box that belonged to
the victims.

Tonya McMath handled the cross-exam and challenged some of the technical aspects of fingerprint
identification. She also led the witness in reaffirming
prints left by Kimberly, while minimizing any attributed to David. Before stepping down, Silva admitted
that none of his work had cast any light on who killed
Brian and Jeannie Legg.

Reporter Doug Murphy noticed that David Legg
couldn't seem to keep his eyes off Tonya McMath and
speculated that the defendant had developed a crush
on his attractive defender.

To wind up the day, McCormick put John Campbell on the stand. He had worked at the shooting
range where David and Kimberly had practiced with
a pistol. He apologized for having a scratchy voice. "I
have a sore throat and have a lozenge in my mouth,
trying to keep from coughing my head off."

The witness recalled a detective visiting in 1996,
showing him some photographs and asking if he
could identify a couple who had recently used the
range. Campbell was able to pick out a young man
and woman whom he had signed in and taken their

payment when they finished. But he had not actually seen them shooting.

A receipt from the range showed that two hours had been purchased that day, and Campbell verified the document's accuracy. Records also showed they brought their own gun, but they purchased ammunition, .22-caliber long-rifle bullets. Campbell withstood a few more questions without coughing, and then stepped down.

Another day had come to its end. Before excusing the jury, Judge Wilkinson advised them the trial was nearing an end. They would hear evidence all day on Wednesday. "Thursday morning is going to be very flexible. We are not going to start until all dental appointments are over with. That's my estimate, but we are keeping the schedule loose. Don't worry about it." He excused them until the next morning.

The first witness on Wednesday took only ten minutes. Captain David Alster, with the Maricopa County Sheriff's Office, told jurors of his position as commander of the Madison Street jail. David Legg had been an inmate there for over two years. Alster described the policy of informing all inmates, during processing, of rules regarding incoming and outgoing mail. It is all subject to being opened and inspected without a warrant for the purpose of controlling contraband materials. The written contents of outgoing mail are often read to determine if an escape plot or other criminal activity is mentioned or described.

If jurors wondered exactly why this testimony was necessary, they would get answers with the next witness. That witness was Ellen Upton, a detention officer

in the Madison Street jail. Out of the jury's presence, she stated that her duties included reading outgoing mail from inmates.

Glenn McCormick asked her, "In the course of your work, did you come in contact with mail from inmate David Legg?"

"Yes, sir." She explained it took place after a complaint had been received from an individual in Texas whom David had telephoned. "He had received calls from Mr. Legg and was highly upset. He didn't want him calling anymore. So I was asked by a lieutenant to look into the matter." As a result, they had activated a control to block Legg from calling that number. "And then the lieutenant asked if I would start scanning Legg's mail for a few days, just to make sure that no written threats were going out after the calls were stopped." This had taken place just two months earlier, in August.

"What did you find in Mr. Legg's mail?"

"That he received mail from a woman named Lynette from a Texas prison." There is no rule against that, said Upton, unless the correspondence is from someone in the county system. "They are not allowed to correspond with anyone in a county lockup."

"Did you find anything subsequently that caused alarm?"

"Yes. Within the next week or so, Mr. Legg booked a cruise for himself and Lynette—and she was calling herself 'Lynette Legg'—out of the country and through the Panama Canal. I was concerned that the cruise was booked for around the time this trial was supposed to start, and it might signal a plan to escape. I was curious as to how he was going to go on a cruise when he was just starting trial." Upton had continued

the monitoring process and learned that Lynette was getting out on parole.

Lynette had, indeed, been paroled, and she subsequently visited David in jail, said the witness. A few days later, David had written a long letter to her, and Upton read it. A subpoena had been issued at her request, after which she gave the letter to Detective Ron Jones, who passed it on to McCormick.

Mike Bernays's cross-exam disputed Upton's legal reasoning for reading and confiscating David's outgoing mail. His questions also prompted the witness to reveal that David had corresponded with a travel agency by mail, and had set up the cruise through letters. The prisoner had recently received a bill from the agency showing a balance due of $6,125. Observers stifled a chuckle. David's habits of spending money he didn't have had certainly not changed. He had even booked a separate cruise, at about the same cost, for Lynette's parents.

After Upton left, both sides argued exhaustively about the admissibility of David's letter to Lynette, as evidence in the murder case. The judge said he would make a ruling as soon as he could read case law on the subject.

With an apology to the jury for the long delay, Judge Wilkinson signaled McCormick to summon the next witness. It turned out to be a return engagement for David's half brother, George Price.

McCormick began by showing Price a pair of gold wedding bands. The first one had been found in the Ford Escort. Price identified it as his mother's. The second band had been removed from Brian's finger

during the autopsy, and Price recognized it as belonging to his stepfather. The two wedding rings matched.

With that completed, McCormick reminded Price of his previous testimony that his father had owned a camcorder, and then handed him the one confiscated from David's baggage in Los Angeles. Price identified it as the one that belonged to Brian Legg.

Judge Wilkinson called for the lunch break.

Before allowing the jury back in, the judge huddled with both attorneys and announced that he had read up on the issue regarding the letter from David to Lynette. He ruled against allowing it into evidence, citing an abundance of caution to assure that, in case of a guilty verdict, appeals courts would not overturn it based on a violation of constitutional rights.

At last, it came time for a key player in the investigation to testify. Detective Ron Jones took the witness chair.

38

Closing the Curtain

Wearing a medium gray suit, white shirt, and a blue-gray-red necktie, Detective Ron Jones settled confidently into the chair like he had been there before. And he had, many times over a long career in law enforcement.

He answered Glenn McCormick's questions in crisp, articulate terms with a pleasant, well-modulated voice. Jones took the jurors on a tour of the crime scene and told of his initial contacts with George and Diana Price, along with the cousin Joe Matise. Early on, he explained, he had been curious about David Legg's strange absence from the army. Jones commented that he, Ken Hansen, and Bob Mills had stayed in the Legg home until three o'clock the next morning.

The initial stages of investigation, said Jones, relied heavily on a paper and electronic trail of credit card usage. Step-by-step, McCormick and Jones re-created

the first leads: Dollar Rent A Car, Delta Airlines, and the profligate use of financial resources belonging to Jeannie and Brian Legg. Little by little, they uncovered the diamond ring sale, discovery of the apartment, and the huge red herring of Daren Maloy's name. That issue wouldn't be satisfactorily resolved until the long-distance depositions of the victimized soldier, which took place from Saudi Arabia. The various names used by Kimberly Pierce-Taylor also created confusion.

Locating the Ford Escort at Sky Harbor Airport, and a few items of evidence inside it, had kept hopes alive for a solution, said the detective.

Not until the arrest of Kimberly and David at the Los Angeles International Airport did some of the fog clear away and establish support for bringing fraud charges against the couple.

Jurors listened intently as Jones piled up all the circumstantial evidence. Spectators kept hoping Jones would be able to cap it with something more concrete, but the absence of a murder weapon, blood evidence, DNA, fibers, or any other irrefutable material kept a big question mark hanging overhead.

Testimony from Ron Jones consumed the remainder of that Wednesday and resumed again on Thursday morning, October 15.

Working in tandem, McCormick and Jones continued the chronology of an intensive investigation that kept encountering potholes and dead ends. Jurors heard of the hard work by detectives trying to build a stronger case against the defendant.

Telephone records, said Jones, helped a great deal. David Legg had made prolific use of the phone before the murders, which led detectives to the jewelry store

where the ring was sold, to the gun purchase, to the firing range, and to other contacts.

In Arizona criminal trial procedures, the defense is allowed to interrupt the prosecution and, through a process known as a "voir dire examination," interrogate the witness. Mike Bernays and his co-counsel Tonya McMath made prolific use of the privilege in attempts to dull points made by statements from Detective Jones. Their effectiveness could only be measured by twelve jurors.

Another interruption occurred in Ron Jones's testimony. Warren Williams, owner of the jewelry store where David Legg sold his mother's diamond, had been scheduled to testify a few days earlier, but delays had kept him waiting in the hall. Since then, he had been on a trip, and he had just returned. Now he came to court once more to tell his story.

Steve Lynch did the questioning, and Williams informed jurors in detail about the arrival of a young couple in his place of business, the $7,000 transaction for the diamond, and the male identifying himself with an Arizona driver's license in the name of "Daren Maloy."

Just before the couple left his store, said Williams, the girl had expressed an interest in some displayed jewelry, but "Daren" had said they would get something in Hawaii. If jurors were paying attention, the comment would suggest that Kimberly had been caught in another lie. She repeatedly had claimed she didn't know they were going to the Islands until they went to the airport.

McCormick asked Williams if he could see anyone

in the room resembling the man. With no reluctance, Williams pointed to David Legg and said, "The gentleman right over there—young man, in the blue suit."

Cross-examination by Tonya McMath lasered in on Kimberly Pierce-Taylor, directing attention to her alleged concurrence to accept the $7,000.

Warren Williams completed his turn in front of the court, and was excused.

Detective Ron Jones stepped back up for the final act involving trial testimony. He described more telephone records of calls by David Legg, with emphasis on his search for a pistol to buy, followed by details of the transaction with gun seller Ed Johnson, and the pawning of a computer to fund the purchase. Winding down, he testified about contacts with the U.S. Army to find out all he could about David Legg and Daren Maloy.

Detective Jones spent more than eight hours on the witness stand as he told the story of a meticulous, challenging murder investigation.

When he stepped down, the curtain closed on the evidentiary segment of the trial.

Now it would be up to Glenn McCormick and Michael Bernays to assemble hundreds of information bytes jurors had heard over the past month, and form them into understandable and convincing scenarios.

39

She Told Some Whoppers

Veteran court watchers and more than a few litigating attorneys believe that final arguments in a criminal trial carry a great deal of weight. But technically, jurors cannot consider them during deliberations.

Judge Wilkinson made that point clear. "Remember," he warned, "final arguments are not evidence. You have heard all the evidence, but these are attempts by the lawyers to explain and convince you of their positions."

The major purpose of this phase is to allow the prosecution and the defense to put all the puzzle pieces together in a sequential, logical order so the jury can have a comprehensible picture in their minds. If someone had given them a book with all the unnumbered pages torn out and stacked up in disarray, they would need something to reassemble and bind them in sequential order. Final arguments provide this opportunity. The

process also may be compared to a film editor putting miles of footage, shot in no recognizable sequence, into a gripping and easily understood story.

With this in mind, Glenn McCormick and Michael Bernays worked long hours to organize exactly how to present elements of the trial that supported their respective positions, and forge them into persuasive arguments.

Because the burden of proof is on the prosecution's shoulders, McCormick inherited the first turn. Bernays would then present his side of the story. And lastly, McCormick would make a final pitch to the jury. It was scheduled to start on Wednesday, October 21.

Shortly after the morning break, Glenn McCormick stood near the lectern, gave a pleasant nod to jurors, and began by thanking them for their rapt attention during four and a half weeks of an intense trial.

"At the beginning of this case, the state gave you an idea of what the evidence would show. The evidence is that the defendant took a Ruger twenty-two pistol . . . pointed it at his mother's head, and at his father. He shot his mother three times in the head, and shot his father twice from close range. How close? Across the room? Arm's length? No."

McCormick raised his arm and revealed a pistol gripped in his right hand. "Dr. Keen told you that the gun, very similar to this one I am holding . . . may have actually been touching their heads when he pulled the trigger. That is up close and personal. That is up close and *very* personal," the prosecutor said.

"The defense told you in their opening that this was a case about assumption." He explained that, instead,

it involved logical inferences. "There is a difference. Logical inferences are based on evidence, not just what someone thinks." The judge, he reminded, had given an example of logical inference. "A guy comes through the door shaking out an umbrella. You can infer what from that? Somebody hits a fire hydrant and water is high up in the air outside? No. The logical inference is that it's raining outside."

Because McCormick's case rested almost entirely on circumstantial evidence, he knew the importance of having jurors understand that it could be even more important than direct evidence. Eyewitness testimony is regarded as direct evidence. McCormick gave an example of how an inference could be drawn that would outweigh the statement of a witness. In his scenario, two people are in a room. One of them is looking out through a window at the wet, snowy weather and sees a man walk into a building. Moments later, two individuals enter the room. The person who saw a man come in from the cold identifies one of the two newcomers as that individual. "You say okay and you look at their feet. The one who was pointed out has dry shoes and dry pants. The other man has snow in the cuff of his pants and his shoes are wet." Circumstantial evidence, McCormick explained, made it clear the witness was wrong, and equally clear that the other man was the one who had been outside in the snow. Jurors need to use their powers of inference.

The defendant, David Legg, said McCormick, was charged with first-degree murder. Taking a few moments, he explained the prerequisites of first-degree murder include causing the death of another person, knowing that your actions would cause death, and premeditation. Instead of delivering a long definition,

McCormick reminded jurors that the judge would clarify it in his instructions before they would begin deliberations. Voicing his expectation that the defense would try to introduce reasonable doubt about their client's guilt, McCormick asked the jurors to pay close attention to the judge's explanation of that term as well.

Prosecutors in murder cases are not required to prove or explain a motive by the defendant. But McCormick knew that most jurors wonder about it. He said, "Let's talk for a moment about why this happened. Why is not a factor for you to determine. Still, inquiring minds, which we know you have from your questions, want to know why. Well, let's look at the evidence that's been presented to you. The defendant is a desperate man. He is on the run from the army. His desperation is so deep—he needs to make a plan. Before he left Fort Bliss, he took the identity of Daren Maloy, his roommate."

Using that identity, said McCormick, the defendant forged pay records in Maloy's name, a birth certificate, and an Arizona driver's license so the army couldn't catch him. The phony birth certificate for "Daren David Maloy," McCormick scoffed, even changed the names of his parents to Brian Edward Maloy and Palma Jean Maloy. In case jurors had any doubt that it was a forgery, the prosecutor asked, "How many Palmas do you know married to a Brian?

"What else do we know about the defendant? Well, you know logically that the army wasn't sending him any checks in Phoenix to live on. You know that he had no savings. You know from the detective that he didn't really have any job to speak of, either." Ticking off on his fingers the short-term employment David

held in Phoenix, McCormick named brief jobs. "So we know that he has serious money problems. He is on the run from the army."

With no source of income, McCormick said, David Legg still treated himself to generous expenditures. "What do you do to get the money to pay for these things?" Taking the apartment rental as an example, he enumerated the costs, totaling $2,000, which would cover it, up until the end of June 1996.

"We know that he liked acquiring things. You have seen the pictures from his apartment. He had a TV, probably bigger than most of you have. He had a VCR, nice stereo system, a stack of CDs, all nice stuff. He had no money, is on the run, and is a desperate man."

Turning to a key issue that could be a matter of major importance to the jury, McCormick said, "What did Kimberly Pierce-Taylor talk to you about when she testified? Did she lie? Oh, she told some whoppers, didn't she? Yeah, she lied. But you know what it comes down to in putting on criminal trials, the state doesn't get to choose witnesses. . . . Absolutely, she lied. Nobody is hiding that from you."

With that admitted, McCormick wanted to underline truthful elements of Kimberly's testimony. She had repeatedly told of frequent arguments with David and of wanting to leave him. These things could be corroborated by entries in her day planner, which she had used as a diary. She had written her personal thoughts in Spanish, probably to keep David from reading them. Translations, said McCormick, would be available for jurors to examine.

David Legg had no doubt realized Kim's unhappiness, said McCormick. The defendant's obsession with Kimberly, plus his need for her to keep her mouth

shut about his desertion from the army, and later the killings, drove him to do whatever he could to please his young mate. "He asks himself how he could make her feel good and stay with him. 'I will give her material things. I will give her a trip to Hawaii. I'll lavish her with bracelets and a beautiful watch. I will take her to the most beautiful place in the world.' Remember, he was stationed in Hawaii at one point."

To show David's mendacity, and to connect it with testimony from another witness, McCormick pointed to the defendant's application for the apartment he and Kim occupied. David had listed his employer as Physician Placement Service, at his parents' address. He gave his boss's name as Jeannie Grasso, his mother's maiden name, which she used in the business. As the responsible person in case of accident, he listed Brian Maloy at the home on 14th Street, instead of Brian Legg. When the apartment rent became overdue, said McCormick, "who do you suppose the collection agency called? You heard Cecilia Taylor-Castillo, Kimberly's mother, testify that just before they left to take her back to Juárez, David had an argument with his father, over the phone, with extremely rude comments. David told his dad not to worry about his problems.

"So we've got a desperate man on the run—a desperate man who needs money, who has none . . . now arguing with his father about money.

"What other pressure might come from his father?" McCormick brought up Brian Legg's pride in being a military retiree. He stressed the fact that Brian's stepchildren and David had emulated him by joining the military. But David had deserted, disappointing his father. This had undoubtedly created even more stress

for the defendant. "Why? Because he is irresponsible and makes dumb choices."

Telephone records had played a major part in the investigation, and McCormick recapped them. Thirty-nine calls had been made to gun vendors and a couple specifically to the Ed Johnson home, where David bought a pistol.

Five calls to travel agents on June 5 and two calls to hotels in Hawaii revealed something else. "Now I am going to jump forward to the defendant's statement made to Detective Jones on June twenty-second. He says he came into the house, found his parents dead, and didn't know what to do. He just didn't know what to do. He had to get out of there. So he went to Hawaii. He's calling travel agents about Hawaii on June fifth! He knew exactly what he wanted to do. This was a plan, and [he] wants to fool you."

A strange pattern of calls to David's parents' home became apparent on telephone records, said Mc-Cormick. It included several calls each day, despite the regular visits there.

The word "obsessed" kept popping up in McCormick's monologue. "So we have an obsessed person. Now he has another obsession—to get money from his parents. Now he has a plan. He's got a gun. He's going to target practice, takes his wife—or girlfriend—whatever you want to call her. She shoots the gun, too, which she finally admits in court, not before." They call the victims' house at least twice on June 8. Then, on June 9, they make no calls at all, which was an odd deviation from the pattern. McCormick said, "They were very busy that day." He paused before delivering his next sentence. "June ninth was their D-day."

David and Kim went shopping with the targeted

victims on that afternoon. "We have it on video, the last known pictures of the victims alive at JC Penney's. 'Isn't that nice, Mom and Dad? You know, I bought a gun the other day, I did target shooting. Could you take me shopping before I kill you?' They took him shopping.

"They came home, and they had dinner, according to Kim. The defendant told investigators that he didn't even call his parents that day until after midnight, which would be the tenth. But what did detectives find in the dishwasher? They found four plates, consistent with four people having dinner at the house that night."

More telephone usage on June 10 told a story of frenzied activity. "We have the rapid-fire calls to three veterinary establishments, including one for which a business card turned up in his luggage, suggesting that he loved his cats more than his parents. Isn't that sick? He made calls to Delta Airlines, the carrier that took them to Hawaii."

For some reason, David had tried to contact his most recent employer, too. "Two calls to Terminix came at three seventeen and three nineteen that afternoon, but he had not spoken to anyone. Why would he call Terminix? You know from the manager who testified, Mr. Meeker, that the person he thought to be 'Daren Maloy' had actually sent the truck keys to him, along with an apologetic note saying he had to leave town. Why do you suppose he did those things? Isn't it kind of strange? Well, if you take a Terminix vehicle and you don't turn it in to them, what might happen? You might get police snooping around." Such an investigation, said McCormick, could lead to complications for David that he wanted to avoid at all costs.

David had also used $2,000 of the cash he obtained by selling his mother's diamond to pay back rent before flying to Hawaii. "Why pay that rent? Same thing—he's got his stuff there. He needs to get out of town for a while. He wants to take his wife on this trip, so he needs to maintain that residence and not have the police come snooping around."

Back to Kimberly's lies, McCormick acknowledged again that she had been untruthful in the deposition and in police interviews. And she had been "inconsistent" in her court testimony. "What do we know about her? We know she likes Mickey Mouse. We know she likes toys. She has quite a few of them in the apartment on shelves and in her closet. She was fifteen years old—a young girl. In some ways, she seemed ever younger than her chronological age."

Retracing Kim's story about the evening of June 9, McCormick itemized the shopping trip, dinner afterward, watching a television movie, falling asleep, and her need to go out to the car. "She listened to a song, which may have been on the radio or on a CD. She couldn't remember. So, is that a big deal? No. The question is, why was she listening to a song? Why didn't she just go retrieve what she needed and come back inside? There is no real answer, other than she says she likes music. You can come up with your own conclusion as to whether or not she knew what was about to go on inside that house. She very well may have. She may have known what was going to happen."

More important, said McCormick, Kimberly willingly came back from Mexico to testify. "The state had no way to get her here from Mexico without some complicated arrangement with the Mexican government. She didn't have to come, but she did. Why? She said she wanted to

get this over with. And why did she lie? She lied because
she was ashamed. Rightly, she should have been more
than ashamed."

Picking up Kim's account of what happened on the
night of the murders, McCormick said, "She goes out
to the car. She is there when the defendant comes out
and says, 'Hey, Dad is wondering where you were.'
Then he goes back inside. She wants to finish listening to the song. Very well could have been. You say,
'When did he take the gun in the house?' Quite likely,
it happened right then. Quite likely, she knew he took
it right then. We don't know. That's not an issue we
have to determine in this case. It's not one of the elements of the offense.

"You have evidence that he came out to the car.
Who knows? Hey, just assume she is as innocent as she
wants you to think she is. He may have grabbed that
gun out of the car without her seeing him do it. We
don't know. But he goes back in the house and she
hears shots. She hears four shots. Now, then, if you are
a liar, you are going to lie about what happened.
There you are, thinking of lies to tell about how many
shots you heard.

"Well, let's count the shots. We have three that entered the head of Jeannie Legg. They don't exit, so
those bullets are accounted for. We have two shots
that entered the head of Mr. Brian Legg. One went
through and through. So we know we've got five bullets right there. Okay, then we have a bullet hitting a
magazine on the glass end table, right next to Mr.
Legg, piercing a potted plant and going through a
wall into a bedroom. So there were at least six shots.
She said she heard four.

"Remember, the criminalist talked about this gun

not being overly loud—makes a good crack. I asked him, 'If this was a room at the back of the house, door closed, out in the driveway, would you hear it?' You might hear it. You might not."

From the time of his arrest, David Legg had adhered to the tale of finding his parents already dead. McCormick reminded jurors of Kim's testimony revealing that David had ordered her to tell that story if anyone ever questioned them about the Leggs' deaths. Despite her other lies, she had been consistent with this detail.

The shirt David wore that night had never been found. "What else wasn't recovered?" McCormick asked rhetorically. "At least, six bullet casings. Remember, this type of weapon ejected the casings. *Pop, pop, pop,* they came out. They land in the house somewhere. They were picked up by someone trying to conceal the evidence. No gun, no casings, no shirt with a blood spot on it, were ever recovered."

The defense had worked hard to suggest that Kimberly could have been the shooter. McCormick found one small deflection to that argument. "They found her shirt. Remember, it was in the video. I guess it had no blood on it. I wonder why?"

Taking on a quizzical expression as he paced slowly back and forth in front of the jury box, McCormick tackled David's story to investigators. "He didn't know what to do. 'Gee, I don't know what to do. So let me just rob Mom and Dad blind, since they don't need it anymore.' He didn't know what to do, but he had been calling travel agencies on the fifth of June. He didn't know what to do, but he knows how to call regarding guns for sale on the sixth and seventh. Remember when he came to the door of the Johnson

house, the discussion that occurred, according to Ed Johnson's testimony? He said the male was doing all the talking and transacting the business. He was the one who said, 'Hey, we called about the gun.'"

Poking another pin into the balloon of the defense theory that Kim did it all, McCormick said, "In every bit of evidence, you see he is orchestrating it. Even if you look to the bank video, or the ATM photos, he is right there with her when she is part of the money transaction. In one of them, you saw that he actually takes the card from her planning calendar, goes up to the machine, and uses it. Who is in control here?"

If Kim had been a consummate liar, McCormick set out to show that David kept pace with her. David had told investigators about calling his parents from the apartment shortly after midnight on the fatal night. But telephone records for the twenty-four hours of June 10 showed no calls to the Legg residence. David had denied seeing his parents until dinner on June 9, but the video at JCPenney showed that to be a lie.

"The defendant, in his statements, seemed to know that his parents had been murdered. But the police, when they first came to the scene, thought it could have been a murder-suicide, until they found no gun. So, David Legg made an assumption. You know, that's something you've got to scratch your head about. He comes into the house and finds his parents dead." (There is no gun, and the house hasn't been ransacked.) "If you come into the house and find family members murdered, one of two things is going to happen. You are going to be outraged, racing around that house to find that person who did it. Or are you going to be scared to death, get out of there, and try to contact the police?

"You notice, he never said anything about looking around to find out who did this. Why? Because he knew who did it. He did it."

Reciting again David's theme, McCormick said, "He didn't know what to do, but he systematically went through the house, found his parents' valuables, and took them. . . . He took the checks, the credit cards, and Mom's ring. That is grisly."

Apologizing to jurors for showing crime scene photos depicting the dead bodies, McCormick said, "Not a pleasant photograph I will show next, but it's important. Mom's ring finger is absent a ring. What else do you see? If you look closely on the other hand, there is another rather large ring. She had a necklace on. She had her watch on, but she left her three-carat diamond sitting on the sink in the bathroom? That makes a lot of sense, doesn't it? That ring was taken off her finger by the defendant."

Before leaving the house that night, David had carefully turned off all the lights, except an exterior garage lamp. McCormick explained the reason for extinguishing the interior lights, saying that neighbors might take notice if they remained on night after night, twenty-four hours a day, and call the police. He added, "If nothing is suspected, it gives you more time to go frolicking in Hawaii."

The answer to David's covering their bodies, and closing all the blinds, was simple. "He did that so no one could see in, and if they did, they would only be able to make out some blankets on the couch. . . . Remember, Mrs. Price, Diana, testified that she could see in through that small rear window, and noticed only the blankets on the couch."

The blankets revealed another of David's lies, said

McCormick. If he had peeled away only enough to see their heads, as he told the detective, he could not have seen the lower blanket. But he described it. "That twine tied around them would have prevented him seeing it, unless he wants you to believe that he reset the twine afterward. He lied to Detective Jones."

What about the kitchen gloves in the clothes hamper? David had said he moved them from the sink to the hamper while trying to tidy up the place. "Not likely. He probably took them off by the hamper and threw them in. Why did he need gloves? Well, he was going to be opening the drawers in the master bedroom to take checks. He knew where they were. Who knows how long the little conniver had to look for those things?

"There has been zero evidence that anyone else was in that house. The evidence even suggests that whoever did it knew the victims and could maybe put a hand on their shoulders before sticking lead into their heads."

In meticulous detail, McCormick created a mental movie of what took place that night. He showed how David had confronted his parents, shot his mother, slugged his father in the head with the gun butt when he tried to rise, and then killed him. In gruesome word pictures complementing photos on a television screen, the prosecutor showed jurors the bloody blankets bound with twine. Autopsy photos of bullet holes in their skulls proved the method of death.

Speaking of the brutal injury inflicted by a blunt-force object to Brian's head, McCormick frowned and said, "Now the defense wants you to believe that a tiny fifteen-year-old girl did this. All of you held this gun without bullets in it. It's not especially light, but the

defense wants you to believe that a girl, perhaps one hundred pounds soaking wet, has the moxie and the strength to hit and control a two-hundred-twenty-five-pound man, and then shoot him in the head. It's pretty far-fetched.

"The defendant accuses Kim of doing this. Who pawned the ring? Who was in control of the circumstances? Who was in control at the stores? Who used the debit cards, all but two of the times? The defendant. Whose idea was it to go to Hawaii? The defendant's. He takes her to Hawaii, lavishes her with gifts, buys bracelets, buys her a watch, and takes her on a cruise for seven days. This is the girl that he is saying just killed his parents, and he is doing these things? The defense is quick to show you portions of the videotape to show her with her little day planner with the money. But I suppose they would like to redact what his statement was to her at that point. He asks her, what is wrong? Is it 'too much sex'?" McCormick's voice resonated with skeptical outrage. "'Too much sex' with the woman who just killed his parents? Give me a break. There is no way he would do that if she killed his parents, or was even involved in it."

More scathing doubt came from McCormick's lips about the torrent of love letters David had written to Kim from his jail cell. In none of them had he asked why she killed his parents, or had them killed by her gangster friends.

McCormick made a transition from the murder charge to discuss financial fraud and theft, other crimes on which the jury would be required to render verdicts.

Wishing to land a final blow against the defense tactics of blaming Kimberly for the murders, McCormick

said, "They want you to believe that her motive was being stood up by David and believing it was his parents' fault." No, that wouldn't work. It just didn't qualify as a motive to kill people she professed to love. "She had no motive. She didn't have the inner strength. She didn't have the power to knock a two-hundred-twenty-five-pound man down so he could be shot by battering him with a gun, causing injuries to his head. It takes a strong person to do that—a person with a lot of hate, a person who was obsessed, a person who needed money, a person who was on the run, a person who was in fear of losing his wife, a person who was in fear of financial problems from his misdealing with the apartment complex, a person who couldn't keep a job, a person who wanted material things—who wanted to go to Hawaii again.

"Kimberly Pierce-Taylor, she may be a lot of things, but she is not a murderer. She is not the one who pulled the trigger. That's the defendant, ladies and gentlemen of the jury. Convict him!

"Thank you, Your Honor."

40

Falsus in Uno,
Falsus in Omnibus

If Glenn McCormick's tactics of offense had driven Michael Bernays all the way back to the defensive team's one-yard line, the score still appeared to be a tie. But Bernays had the ball.

The jurors filed back into their box after lunch, and settled in to hear how the defense would tackle a series of powerful points McCormick had scored.

"Ladies and gentlemen," Bernays began in genial tones, "now comes the time for you to stop being by-standers, to stop being an audience, and to really begin the difficult and arduous task of being judges." He reminded them of their promises during jury selection to be fair, keep an open mind, and of their oath to follow the law. "Mr. McCormick's closing was very emotional and touched on a lot of hot buttons. Nobody's happy the Leggs are dead. Don't think for

one minute I stand here trying to justify their deaths. What I am going to say to you is that the state has not given you evidence. They have not proven facts beyond a reasonable doubt and placed the gun in David's hand that allows you to find beyond a reasonable doubt that David killed his parents."

Advising jurors they must not base a verdict on speculation, sympathy, or revulsion, he said their decision must be based on facts emanating from evidence supplied by exhibits and testimony.

Bernays's next comment surprised a few spectators. "Let me be right up front. We didn't spend too much time on the fraud and thefts. We have not wasted your time contesting those charges." The defender seemed to accept that David was guilty of the lesser crimes. Since he had been in jail two years, the sentence might be no more than time already served.

Plunging head-on into the murder charges, Bernays stated, "It's been proven to you that we do not know who shot Brian and Palma Legg." Detective Hansen, he said, had told them so.

"Under oath, from that witness stand right there, Ken Hansen told you that there was nothing in his investigation [that] identified who shot Brian and Palma Jean Legg. Nothing."

To reinforce the statement, Bernays cited the testimony by Dr. Philip Keen about the autopsy of both victims' bodies. Keen had not actually witnessed the autopsy and had testified by using facts contained in the written report from Dr. Zivot. "He told you there is no way to tell—from his aspect of the investigation—who shot Brian Legg and Palma Jean Legg." McCormick had mentioned wounds on Brian's head made from a blow with probable use of the

gun. Bernays disputed this, too. "Dr. Keen drew that conclusion from examination of photographs only."

Now, Bernays postulated, if wounds had been inflicted to Brian's temple and forehead, could they have been caused by an adolescent girl? Dr. Keen had said it was possible. So, said Bernays, "an adolescent girl is strong enough to cause the injuries that the witness claims to have divined from his examination of photographs." But nothing about the wounds could actually tell who caused them.

Testimony from a Phoenix Police Department criminalist, Randy Leister, had informed jurors all about the gun, Bernays said. Leister had talked about land and groove markings on bullet fragments. Still, "there was nothing in his examination [that] detailed an identity of who had fired those shots. Even Detective Jones testified there was nothing in the scene or in the scientific evidence that detailed who fired the shots."

Neither did testimony from Phoenix PD criminalist Tom Boylan point a finger at David Legg. The expert had determined that all the blood found at the crime scene had been from the victims. Said Bernays, "He is from the serology section. He did the blood analysis. And Mr. Boylan told us that there was nothing from his examination from which he could detail the identity of the person who had fired the shots."

Fingerprints came next under Bernays's observations. "Mr. Joe Silva testified that nothing in his examinations gave any light on who committed the homicides."

To some observers, Bernays appeared to be using a form of logic in which the absence of evidence proves a point. But an old axiom states that "absence of evidence is not evidence of absence." For example, a debater

might point out that no evidence exists of intelligent life on other planets, and cite countless experts' opinions. But does that really prove no such life exists? Jurors would have to decide how much weight these arguments from Bernays would carry.

Fingerprints identified during that investigation, Bernays reminded jurors, were those of Kimberly Pierce-Taylor, found on a box of checkbooks.

One of the most gut-wrenching aspects of the case revolved around the diamond ring taken from Jeannie's lifeless finger. Bernays addressed the emotional issue. "There is no evidence, despite Mr. McCormick's frequent assertions to the contrary, as to who took the ring off Palma Jean Legg, as to whether it was taken off before her death or after her death." The autopsy had been inconclusive regarding when the ring was removed. "There was nothing Dr. Keen could tell us about who took the ring off, or when it was taken off."

Telephone calls from the apartment had been an important factor of the investigation. They, too, came under Bernays's scalpel. "We don't know who made those calls. . . . The system that was in place at that apartment complex . . . by which they were able to capture the digital signals sent by the phone, when an outgoing call is made, captures only the signals made when you push the buttons on your telephone pad. There is nothing to tell us who made the calls."

Bernays offered a list of "we don't know" issues: who fired guns at the range, who held the gun at the Leggs' house, and whether the gun purchased from Ed Johnson was the murder weapon. "Absent the sort of hard evidence we are talking about, the scientific evidence, it is your duty as judges to critically analyze the state's case and to analyze with an eye toward

whether it convinces you beyond every reasonable doubt that David Legg committed the homicides."

Blasting the prosecution, Bernays said, "The state's theory is that David is guilty of murder because he committed financial crimes after his parents' death. Find him guilty because he stole his parents' money? Find him guilty because he went to Hawaii? So did Kim."

Having adopted a mantra of "find him guilty" or "convict David," Bernays used it repeatedly as a counterpoint.

"Find David guilty because his parents' property was in his possession? Kim had it, too.

"Find David guilty because he got the gun?" The seller's son, Ed Johnson, had stated that he thought it was being bought for the girl. He had described in detail how Kim picked it up, held it and felt the heft of it in her hand. Kim had lied about it, said the defender.

"Convict David because he went to a shooting range?" So did Kim. "And the evidence showed they purchased two targets—a clear inference that she fired the gun there.

"Convict David because he lied when arrested? Of course, we all know, so did Kim.

"Convict David because Kim says so? She is the only witness in this case to point her fingers, figuratively, at David Legg and say he shot his parents." The defender mockingly quoted her, "'He told me he shot his parents.'"

Another possibility existed and Bernays brought it up. If Kim had been the killer, was David her accomplice? If so, both of them could be convicted of murder. Bernays argued against the proposition. "I am saying to

you, he was not her accomplice. The evidence is
equally susceptible that Kim did it, with no foreknowledge by David, as it is the state's theory that David did
it, with no foreknowledge by Kim. . . . The evidence is
that Kim is an admitted perjurer. She sat up there on
the witness stand and admitted lying under oath. She
has lied about every important fact in this case. She has
demonstrated her willingness to fabricate on the
spot . . . and it has to do with the most critical piece of
evidence, the gun."

Replaying examples of Kim's dishonesty, Bernays
highlighted her denials about knowing anything
about the gun, helping to buy it, handling it, and failure to acknowledge bullets being stored at the apartment. "So now we are in a capital homicide trial, and
she gets on that stand and lies to you again about the
gun. It's not the same lies she told before, because we
see her method. We have caught her. . . . So once
again, we see Kimberly Pierce-Taylor lying about a
critical fact in a murder prosecution until she gets
caught at it.

"Why is Kim so intent on lying while under oath in
a murder prosecution against David Legg? Because
she wants it all to go away. And if David Legg is convicted, as far as she is concerned, it does all go away.
She struts back to Mexico, and that's the last we hear
of Kimberly Pierce-Taylor."

Emphasizing again the volume of lies from Kimberly, Bernays said, "The point is, there is an old Latin
phrase in the law—'*falsus in uno, falsus in omnibus.*' It
means 'false in one regard, false in all.' If you lie to
me on a critical point under oath, I'm entitled to
disregard every word that comes out of your perjury-
ridden mouth."

Not much had been made of Kimberly's claim to have been listening to the radio while the murders took place. Bernays wanted jurors to see its significance. "It's important because it's the lie Kim told in an effort to distance herself from having killed Brian and Palma Legg." The defender reminded jurors that Kim had said she listened to a song by Guns N' Roses, but Detective Ron Jones's testimony had cast doubt on it being played that night by a disc jockey.

To reiterate the entire focus of his argument, Bernays stated, "I don't have to prove to you that Kimberly Pierce-Taylor did this homicide. In order for you to find David not guilty, all you have to understand is that there is a real possibility that Kimberly Pierce-Taylor did the homicide."

Murder-mystery novels often use a cliché in which the case is solved because the suspect is right-handed and the real killer is left-handed. Bernays dealt this card, too, saying bullet wounds on the victims would more likely have been made by right-handed Kim than left-handed David.

The back pocket of Brian's clothing was found to be inside out from someone hastily removing his wallet. Bernays suggested that Kim could have done it after shooting both victims.

What motives might Kim have had for killing her in-laws? Bernays offered an explanation. "She believed the Leggs were responsible for fouling up her church wedding, which was a matter of some import for her. She believed that Mr. Legg had been cruel to her, had been nasty in his joking. She believed that she was married to David Legg, and a reasonable inference from that belief would be that any financial benefits flowing to David from his parents' death

would go to her. So for every motive that you can ascribe to David, you can ascribe to Kim."

David, said his attorney, had tried to protect Kim from any culpability in the murders, but Kim had accused him of doing it. This would indicate her avarice as opposed to his obsessive love for Kim, which made David unable to think clearly.

Once again, Bernays played the tape David had taken of them in Hawaii. This segment, obviously shot by Kim, showed David asleep in their room. Mockingly, Bernays quoted Kim: "'I never had the chance to get away from him.' Another lie. Another effort on her part to snow you. Balderdash, because she thinks it helps her escape responsibility."

Announcing his intention to respond to specific points in McCormick's argument, Bernays attacked. "He started off by saying to you that the evidence shows [David] took a Ruger at close range and shot his parents. What evidence? We don't know who took a Ruger—or whether it even was a Ruger—at close range and shot the Leggs. . . . Every bit of circumstantial evidence in this case points at Kimberly Pierce-Taylor as much as it points to David Legg. McCormick says that David's got a financial motive. But remember, David had taken a job with Terminix, and it was a good-paying job.

"Mr. McCormick says that Kim told some whoppers. They are not whoppers. They are lies in a court of law. They are perjury. Don't minimize them by calling them 'whoppers.'

"Mr. McCormick says that David is a desperate man who was being pressured by his father . . . having run away from the military. Sounds good, doesn't it? Where is the evidence of it? There isn't any.

"Mr. McCormick says David called about the guns. Maybe he was joking when he said it. There is no evidence that David called about the guns." (Kimberly might have done it.)

"Mr. McCormick says David's got an obsession to get money from his parents, and that he had a plan. There is no evidence of that."

"Mr. McCormick says David goes to pay back rent. You know, it appears that he did go and pay future rent. And what does that tell you? It tells you that David is planning on coming back to Phoenix, as do the round-trip tickets." To the defender, this exhibited a clear conscience, which a killer would not have.

For the next few minutes, Bernays lectured on the understanding of proof beyond a reasonable doubt. He also reminded jurors that the defendant is not obligated to testify. "You must not let this choice affect your deliberations in any way."

Winding down after nearly two hours of talking, Bernays said, "I want to try and give you a cogent understanding of what our theory of this case is. It is simply that the state has presented no compelling evidence that David actually killed his parents. Everything they point to reflects equally on Kim. There is no evidence before you [that] indicates that David acted as Kim's accomplice. There is no evidence either from Kim or anybody else that this was a planned-out thing that they worked on together, and then one of them did it.

"So we are not just saying, 'Hey, Kimmie was part of this, Kimmie did it, too.' You have got to let David go because she never got prosecuted for murder. She only got prosecuted for fraud. She is allowed to do a little time in detention and got to go home to Mexico.

"What we're saying is that when you critically analyze all the evidence in the case and understand what the state's theory is—to convict because of all of those other things that he did. That's what the state is asking you to follow—that he's guilty of the murders because he did Hawaii. He's guilty of murder because he sold the ring. That applies equally to Kim, and if you can't sort out which it applies more to, and not just fifty or fifty-one, 'I think fifty-one percent it was Dave.' 'No, I think it was fifty-one percent Kim.' It's not that. Are you convinced beyond every last conceivable doubt in your mind that it was David, and only David? Only then should you convict him.

"If you are not so convinced, you are duty-bound by your oaths . . . to find him not guilty of the homicides. . . . I am asking you to find reasonable doubt as to David Legg's guilt on the homicides of his parents. Return a not guilty verdict on those two counts. Thank you."

Plenty of time still remained on the court clock for Glenn McCormick to take one more turn in front of the jury. He needed to repair any holes Michael Bernays might have blasted in his earlier presentation.

41

Convict Him!

From the time Glenn McCormick had first inherited the Legg murder case, twenty-eight months ago, he had dropped over thirty pounds. During his professional football career, he had topped out at 275 pounds, and now he weighed a sleek, trim 230. A good portion of that loss had occurred in recent months and resulted from long hours, skipped meals, and no small element of stress.

For the final lap of the trial's guilt phase, McCormick addressed the jury to rebut arguments made by Michael Bernays. Without customary salutations or ingratiating greetings, he plunged directly forward. "The defense wants you to believe there is no direct evidence of the defendant having the gun in his hand, pulling the trigger. Therefore you must acquit. Why? Three words—'so did Kim. So did Kim.'

"That's like the playground. You catch one kid

doing something. 'Oh, he did it, too.' It doesn't take the guilt away. 'So did Kim.' You may think Kim did it, too, but Kim is not on trial today. David Legg is."

Evidence, he explained, must not be weighed in a vacuum. Any single exhibit or portion of testimony does not stand alone. It is all intertwined. In this case, "the evidence is substantial. You don't need Kim to convict this guy. You may very [well] believe some of, or a lot of, what she had to say. That's for you to decide. But when you take the various sources, put it all together, and analyze it, you used something the defense wants you to check at the door when you deliberate. You use your common sense."

He reminded the panel that they had been carefully selected from a large pool of prospective jurors because each of them had revealed life experiences that had developed their common sense. "Now put it to use. The human factor of the jury system in the United States of America is what . . . makes it the best in the world."

Perhaps self-conscious over extending his speech with a patriotic outburst, McCormick said, "I am trying to quit. I know you are tired of sitting and listening to me." Smiles on jurors' faces signaled no impatience.

Aiming now at specifics, McCormick said, "Let's do a commonsense test here. Have any of you ever tried to pick up an adult or move them around when they were asleep? Pardon this term, but 'deadweight' is hard to move. Now, are you going to believe that a one-hundred-pound no-ounce Kimberly Pierce-Taylor moved a two-hundred-twenty-five-pound man enough to reach in with her free hand and pull a wallet out of his back pocket? Use your common sense."

Kimberly's fingerprint had been found on checks and on the box that contained them. "How could that have happened? Remember, she testified seeing the stuff on the apartment floor?" It wouldn't take a great leap of inference to suppose she might have touched some of it. Furthermore, McCormick pointed out, no evidence had been presented to show those checks were ever used in any of the crimes—murder or financial.

"The defense told you that Detective Hansen said there was nothing from the crime scene that said who did it. No, the victims were not able to write in blood that 'David Legg shot me.' They lost consciousness immediately." Of course, McCormick explained, the autopsy didn't reveal who did the shooting. How could it? "The defense expects a lot for the medical examiner to come in here and tell you who did it."

Regarding the blunt-force wounds on Brian Legg's temple and forehead, McCormick countered an assertion by Bernays. "He argued that Dr. Keen had said a fifteen-year-old girl is capable of causing these injuries. See, Dr. Keen was just talking about the relative strength of an individual, the capability. He wasn't talking about essentially trying to control a full-grown, overweight man who was trying to get up off the couch. Certainly, a young girl, or anyone standing there, is going to be able to put a gun to the side of your head or forehead and cause an injury." The circumstances of the situation would have a huge influence, McCormick insisted, and in this particular case, the feasibility of Kimberly striking the blows appeared most unlikely.

The left-hand versus right-hand theory also needed clarification. To demonstrate, McCormick performed a short choreography in front of the jury box, showing

how a left-handed person could have delivered the mortal gunshots easily. "Look, isn't that a perfect angle? Two shots to the head, if you are coming at it like this, with your left hand. That was a red herring thrown your way to confuse you. You have your common sense—that's one thing they can't take away from you." Adding another matter for thought, McCormick commented, "There is really no evidence that the defendant would fire a pistol with his left hand, other than the fact he has been sitting there writing with his left hand during the trial. He may very well handle a gun with his right hand. You have never seen him throw a ball. He may be ambidextrous. There was nothing about the bullets or the wounds that determined if a left-handed or a right-handed person shot those victims in the head."

To McCormick, some of the defense's points had been taken out of context. "They argue that Detective Jones said there was nothing at the scene of a scientific nature to tell who did this. But that comment ignores the body of evidence you have." For example, the defense showed a portion of the video—the part shot by Kimberly showing David asleep on a bed—and inferred that it demonstrated an opportunity for her to get away from him. McCormick threw cold water on the theory. Perhaps she didn't want to get away, he theorized. And if so, did the video truly portray an opportunity? "Do you know where they were? They were on a ship, most likely out to sea. Where is she going to go? She could go find help from somebody else, maybe another passenger, but she can't get off the ship, and David Legg is still there."

The prosecutor hadn't thought Kim's testimony very helpful to his case and contradicted the character-

ization by Bernays that she was the star witness. Not true, said McCormick. "Kimberly Pierce-Taylor was a witness. She is only one of the people we put on the stand. She is not the star witness in this case. Really, the star of this case is not a witness, per se—it is the whole package of evidence."

Part of that package, McCormick reminded jurors, included David Legg's own words. "You have audio-tapes of the defendant being interviewed. Listen to the phony, trumped-up emotion when he is talking to the detective."

The defense's final argument relied heavily on Kimberly's lies, as exposed by intensive cross-examination. McCormick, though, suggested that little substance came from the questions and answers. He referred to a few of the queries as inconsequential. "They asked her, 'Weren't you there?' and 'Did you ever purchase a gun?' and those kinds of things. Where is the detail about what she did to kill Brian and Jeannie?"

Without repeating the Latin phrase used by Bernays ("*falsus in uno, falsus in omnibus*") to suggest that all of Kimberly's testimony should be regarded as un-truthful, McCormick told jurors, "It means 'false in one, false in all.' I suppose that applies to David Legg as well."

Efforts by the defense to blame Kimberly for the murders provided no reasonable doubt of David's guilt, said McCormick. Even if she did pull the trigger, or participate at all, the evidence against David clearly showed his culpability as at least an accomplice. He would still be guilty of first-degree murder. "Accomplice liability, even under their theory, he is still guilty."

In pointing at Kimberly, Bernays had suggested her

motive might be to inherit the Leggs' money, since she was married to David. McCormick scoffed: "So let's get this straight. Let's logically look at this with our common sense and say, 'Okay, she kills his parents.' He didn't know she is going to kill them, and then she's going to say, 'Honey, sorry I killed your folks. But look, we get to inherit all this stuff.' And he's going to say, 'That's too bad about them. You are right. We will inherit this stuff together.'" McCormick shook his head in disgust. "How ridiculous is that? That's not a motive. She had no motive."

On the contrary, said the prosecutor, David Legg was obsessed with Kimberly Pierce-Taylor and didn't want to lose her. He wanted to provide her with gifts he could not afford. That was his motive.

Bernays had brought up the matter of David paying the apartment rent. McCormick said, "Why pay the rent if you are trying to escape and flee? Well, you pay because you have the apartment in the name of Maloy. You believe nothing is going to tie you as Maloy to the Leggs—who are dead in their home—to get the police looking for you. So you go to Hawaii. You use their cards and money. You have your rent paid through the end of June. Why not longer? Because he wanted to come back long enough to get his stuff and then probably go to Mexico.

"The evidence is the star witness in this case. The defense claims the state's theory is that financial crimes were committed, therefore the defendant did it. That's not the case at all. Yes, the fraud is part of the evidence that suggests he killed his parents, but you look at all the other evidence, too.

"The defense's theory is that no compelling evidence proves the defendant did it, and no evidence

came out that he acted as an accomplice. Well, their presentation establishes otherwise—because if Kim did it, everything suggests that she had help and that was the defendant. So he is at least an accomplice.

"But who is the one obsessed? Who is the one that is desperate? Who is the one on the run? Who is the one who can't support his wife?

"He was frustrated and filled with obsession, need, greed, and murder.

"Ladies and gentlemen of the jury, evidence is clear in this case. Convict him!"

With those final words, Glenn McCormick returned to the defense table and eased into his chair.

Judge Wilkinson ordered his clerk to distribute copies of the jury instructions to each juror. He explained, "It is your duty to follow these instructions. It is also your duty to determine the facts. Facts mean what actually happened. You make that determination only from the evidence produced in this court." He spent the next twenty minutes reading aloud, while jurors followed every word on their copies.

Upon completion, he said, "I now ask you to take your notebooks, take the jury instructions that I have given you, go to the jury room and begin your deliberations. We will stand in recess."

Reporter Doug Murphy wrote in his article that the jury deliberations began Wednesday afternoon. Instructions read to them by the judge included the option of finding David Legg guilty of first-degree or second-degree murder. But, noted Murphy, considerable evidence had shown premeditation, including calls to travel agencies before the killings, the purchase

of a gun, and a visit to a target-shooting range. If jurors believed that David Legg had planned on shooting his parents, the premeditation would demand finding him guilty of first-degree murder, which could carry a possible death penalty.

The defendant, according to Murphy, showed little emotion but listened carefully during closing arguments: *As the jury filed out to begin deliberations, he stood, facing them as they walked past the defense table, and smiled.*

42

Please Spare My Life

It took three days of evidence examination, intense emotions, arguments, and occasional screaming at each other for the jury to arrive at a verdict. Several of them later told reporter Doug Murphy that the process had been rigorous.

Three days can seem like three weeks to those who anxiously await the decision. Mike Bernays later said the "long" deliberations gave him hope that the outcome would be favorable to his client. George and Diana Price felt exhausted by the entire process. Rather than speak about it, they prepared a written statement: *For more than two long years we have endured torment perpetuated by the unending delays in our judicial system.*

Part of the stress experienced by jurors developed over the issue of premeditation, an essential element of first-degree murder. A woman on the panel said, "It took three days because there were two people who

were holding out for second-degree murder. [They] thought there was not enough proof it was premeditated." She added, "It was extremely hard for me to think that I was responsible for someone else's life."

Another female juror spoke of her perfect, sheltered existence and how this experience had shattered it. "I am completely traumatized. It is the hardest thing I have ever done, sitting there and watching him."

All twelve had agreed on the first day that David Legg was guilty of financial crimes. But it took two full days of heated debates to find unity on murder charges. Another juror told Murphy, "This was a decision we have to live with for the rest of our lives."

Finally they settled the matter. "There was no doubt," said a third member, "there was absolutely no doubt."

On Tuesday, October 27, a signal came from the jury room that they had reached a verdict. The lawyers took their places and the gallery filled. One person didn't seem overly concerned. David Legg, two weeks short of his twenty-seventh birthday, appeared relaxed and confident as he smiled and chatted with Mike Bernays and Tonya McMath.

Twelve heavily burdened people filed into the jury box, some of them in tears. Shortly after four o'clock in the afternoon, the jury foreman, William Lee Creer, handed over a sheaf of forms, which were carried to Judge Michael Wilkinson. After reviewing them, he read aloud. The decision rendered:

Count I: First degree murder of Brian Legg: Guilty.

Count II: First degree murder of Palma Jean Legg: Guilty.

In nine additional counts, including theft of the diamond ring, trafficking in stolen property (the ring),

fraudulent schemes, and theft of credit cards, the jury delivered verdicts of guilty.

Doug Murphy watched from the gallery and noted that David Legg, after weeks of cocksure certainty evident in his posture and facial expressions, broke down and sobbed as the verdicts were read.

With the completion of the guilt phase, another enormous struggle still faced the attorneys and Judge Wilkinson. Glenn McCormick had sought the death penalty, and hearings would be held to make that decision. The complex process would be stretched out over a staggering eighteen months, ending in April 2000.

David Legg had always needed money, and a few weeks after the verdict, he thought he had found a way to obtain it. He contacted a local newspaper and requested copies of the articles about him and expressed interest in an interview. Doug Murphy drove to the Madison Street jail and met David, face-to-face. Before saying anything else, David asked, "What do I get out of this?"

Murphy asked what he meant. David said he thought his story would be a great book and he was willing to tell all for a 60-40 split of the profits from a publisher's advance and any movie or television deals. Murphy later said, "I will always remember that sociopath. When I interviewed him in jail, he wanted me to write the story about how his fifteen-year-old wife, or maybe her Mexican Mafia friends, had killed his parents." David told the reporter that Kimberly "had a mentality that something like this wouldn't be a big deal to her."

"Why didn't you tell the police about it?" Murphy

asked. David said he had feared for the life of the son he fathered while still in high school.

An Arizona law does not allow for convicted murderers to profit from their crimes, which includes book or movie deals. At Murphy's mention of this, David dismissed it with a rationale about the law being vague.

Murphy rejected the proposal and left the jail, feeling a deep revulsion.

In a series of court hearings preceding the sentence hearing, Glenn McCormick sought to prove aggravating factors, as required by Arizona law. He argued that the murders were carried out in an especially heinous and cruel manner, that the crime involved multiple murders, and that the defendant had expected receipt of money as a result of the murders.

Michael Bernays introduced mitigating factors, including the defendant's diminished capacity to appreciate the wrongfulness of his conduct and that "residual doubt" existed regarding his role in the planning and execution of the murders.

David Legg wrote two personal appeals to Judge Wilkinson. In the first one, dated March 17, 1999, he stated: *I am very scared about the possible sentence of death that I may receive. . . .* Complaining about the rapid "rate of speed" at which the sentencing approached, he noted that a "mitigation specialist" still had not been appointed for him. His attorneys, he stated, had handled his case in a "carefree" way. According to David, Michael Bernays and Tonya McMath consulted with him only a few times in thirty-three months. They never asked him to explain "the whole situation" regarding his side of the case. *This is the rest of my life in balance*

and I ask that you please don't punish me for my attorneys' lack of planning, he wrote. He closed by saying *I asked God to bless you.*

The second letter, dated exactly one year later, requested a chance to speak to the judge before the sentence hearing. Expressing sorrow "for all that has happened," David said he still didn't understand many things about the night of his parents' death and wished he could bring them back. Also acknowledging the pain he had caused his family, David poured out his regrets.

With compliments for Judge Wilkinson's fair handling of the trial, David wrote that he accepted the responsibility for his actions and could offer no excuse for the things he did: *I can only wish for the forgiveness of my family and pray that you will spare my life.* He had loved his parents, he said, and they had loved him.

Tossing in another plea for mercy, he promised to prove to his family, and to society, that he was not a horrible person and still had some value. The letter ended with apologies to the court, his mother, his father, his family, his new fiancée, Mary, his son, and to "God in Heaven."

Three other letters reached Judge Wilkinson. Brian Legg's brother stated his abhorrence for the brutal murders, and that David's actions probably warranted the death penalty, but he requested that David be sentenced to life in prison without parole.

George Price, David's half brother, commented that he had spent countless hours thinking about his sibling's fate. At first, Price said, he believed that David should receive the death penalty in view of a person who had such little regard for life—let alone the lives

of his own parents. But three years of philosophical pondering had altered George's opinions, even though he felt no love or compassion for David. It would take some time, he observed, to reconcile these conflicting feelings, and that could come about by a sentence of life in prison: *David has the obligation to take responsibility and realize the consequences of his actions, but this all takes time.*

George's wife, Diana, wrote of a firm belief in the death penalty, even though it went against what her religion asked of her. Noting her deep love for Brian and Jeannie, and a compassion for David, Diana expressed regret that he *continues to manipulate other innocent people.* In her belief that David should be sentenced to die, Diana wrote, *I do not see any genuine remorse in him.*

Judge Michael Wilkinson dealt with the matter of legal issues on April 21, 2000, in a lengthy written decision. In regard to the matters of aggravating circumstances, he stated: *The evidence proves beyond a reasonable doubt that the defendant committed these murders in expectation of the receipt of money.* Strike one against David Legg.

The judge wrote, *The Court finds that the State has proven the aggravating factor of the commission of two homicides at the same time.* Strike two.

In the third issue, Judge Wilkinson wrote, *The Court finds the State has failed to prove beyond a reasonable doubt that the murders of Brian Legg and Palma Jean Legg were committed in an especially heinous and cruel manner.*

Ball one! Wilkinson had studied Arizona Supreme Court rulings about this factor, and cited their view that it *must be limited to cases wherein the additional circumstances . . . set the crime apart from the usual or the norm.*

In dealing with mitigating factors, Wilkinson weighed

assertions from the defense that David Legg did not have the capacity to appreciate the wrongfulness of his crimes due to his suffering from bipolar affective disorder. The murders, Michael Bernays pointed out, took place while David was in a manic phase of that disorder. Two psychiatrists had offered expert opinions to support the assessment. In addition, records of David's treatment at Riveredge Hospital in 1990 further substantiated it.

The judge ruled, *The Court finds the defendant has established by a preponderance of the evidence the existence of a statutory mitigating factor.* Ball two.

Regarding the defense's assertion of "residual doubt" about David's role in planning and executing the murders, the judge stated: *All of the planning and preparation for the crimes was conducted by the defendant. Kimberly Pierce-Taylor, who was fifteen at the time of the homicides, initiated none of the necessary steps regarding the acquisition of the weapon or the making of travel plans. Nothing in the record points to her as the shooter.*

He ruled, *The Court finds the defense has failed to prove . . . any of the mitigating factors which have been alleged.* Strike three!

Had David Legg struck out in the game of "life in prison" versus "the death penalty"?

The umpire, Judge Michael Wilkinson, wrote, *The Court finds that the mitigating circumstances are sufficiently substantial to call for leniency.* Three strikes had not condemned David Legg to death.

The courtroom filled one final time on the afternoon of April 21, 2000. The defendant accepted the judge's offer of allowing a statement. David Legg

begged, "Please spare my life." Between sniffling sobs, he apologized profusely for everything he had done, expressed love for his late mother and father, and said he would give anything to have them back.

Judge Wilkinson then delivered the official sentence. He stated, "For Count One, it is ordered that the defendant is sentenced to a term of imprisonment and is committed to the Arizona Department of Corrections for the remainder of his natural life." He repeated the sentence for Count II. The judge tacked on fifty-nine years for the corollary crimes of theft and fraud, and assessed payment in restitution of $34,443.

Two bailiffs led David Legg out of the courtroom.

Doug Murphy had reported on the investigation and the trial. After the guilty verdicts, he had interviewed David Legg in jail. A few years later, Murphy made another visit for a second face-to-face encounter. It made Murphy sick to his stomach again.

He wrote: *I had never met a sociopath before, but when I interviewed David in jail, I knew instantly that this guy was cuckoo. He still creeps me out just thinking about him.* During the session, Murphy said, David smiled frequently and flashed friendly charm, but exhibited absolutely no remorse for killing his parents. Questions about hocking his mother's diamond ring or using their credit cards to acquire cash for a buying spree didn't bother him.

David mostly complained about prison conditions, and mentioned the cheap soap they provided. His biggest problem was how to get enough money to buy a television set for his cell.

Some things, and some people, never change.

Epilogue

Without the initiative of Alicia LaFlesh, a myriad of events told in this book might be lost in the shadows of time, known only to a few participants and local news readers.

Midway through 2009, I received an e-mail and nearly deleted it because I did not recognize the name. I read the subject line, "A story?" and it did little to jolt my imagination. For some reason, though, I opened it and read her words:

> My name is Alicia LaFlesh. I have always been told that I should write a book, but I'm not a writer. I wanted to know if you would be interested in talking with me regarding writing about the experiences with my ex-husband. I was married to him when he murdered my parents-in-law in Arizona. . . .
>
> Alicia LaFlesh

This type of proposal is not uncommon, and many of them are intriguing. Timing, though, is all-important. In this case, I just happened to be in the market for a new story and decided it might be interesting to see what Alicia had to say. We met at a restaurant.

After introductory chatter, I asked her reasons for doing this. Why did Alicia wish to reveal so many personal matters and to suffer the trauma of dragging herself through the horror once again? I knew that money had nothing to do with it. With tears in her eyes, she explained her deep overwhelming love for Brian and Jeannie Legg, and the incredible pain she had endured when David Legg killed them. The warmth and security of family affection had been absent through her own childhood, and she had been so grateful for finding it with the new in-laws. She even felt guilty, burdened by the improbable concept that David might not have shot them if she had never married him. Now Alicia hoped that putting the experience in a book might offer catharsis and healing.

We agreed to explore the matter further. Certainly, I needed a far more comprehensive understanding of the facts before committing to a book. Numerous telephone calls, Internet explorations, interviews, and stacks of documents acquired in a couple of trips to Phoenix provided the answers.

So Alicia LaFlesh tops the list of people to whom I want to express my gratitude for assistance in seeing this project through to completion.

And, as is the case with all authors of nonfiction books, the completed product is a result of teamwork.

As always, Michaela Hamilton, executive editor at Kensington, provided wise counsel, warm encouragement, and the green light.

Literary agent Susan Crawford never fails to inspire and nail down essential logistics for me.

In Arizona, Michael Jeanes, clerk of the Maricopa County Superior Court, came through with extraordi-

nary and courteous assistance, and the best staff
folks I have ever encountered in years of research.

His programs manager, Aaron Nash, was an absolute
delight in his correspondence and personal cooperation during my visits to Phoenix.

In the basement of the Central Court building, Lil-
lian Barnett patiently aided me in examining and
copying exhibits from the trial, twice. Connie Estrada
and Evelyn Lavorin expeditiously handled my questions and needs.

I had a tough time keeping on subject in corresponding with Glenn McCormick, the prosecutor. My
mind kept wandering to football and I had to exercise
extreme self-discipline to prevent driving him crazy
with questions about his former athletic career. His
thorough and witty responses about the case were extremely helpful.

Judge Michael Wilkinson generously spoke to me
about the trial, his background, Arizona law, and his
later years.

Doug Murphy reported the case for a local newspaper and shared his experiences with me by e-mail and
over lunch at a Phoenix restaurant.

Life has moved on for many of the people mentioned in this case.

David Legg is serving a life sentence in the Arizona Department of Corrections system, in a Yuma
facility, at the time of this writing. He has been assigned inmate jobs, including "house porter, duties
with Arizona corrections industries, inmate newspaper, and academic/scholastic clerical duties." Only

one disciplinary infraction is listed on his record. In January 2001, he was guilty of "disorderly conduct." David's need to romance young women apparently still burns brightly. In March 2000, Judge Wilkinson received a letter from a girl named Mary. She professed her love for David Legg "with all my heart and soul" and claimed to look into his eyes and see a special spirit within him. Mary rhapsodized for a full page and noted: *I am not complete without him and one day I would like to marrie* [sic] *and share the rest of my life with him.* Only David and Mary know how the relationship turned out.

Kimberly Pierce-Taylor returned to Mexico and lives in obscure privacy.

Glenn McCormick left the county attorney's office in 1998 for a position with the United States Attorney's Office in Phoenix. He took time out from the new role to complete the sentencing phase of David Legg's trial, in 2000. Currently McCormick works in the U.S. Organized Crime Drug Enforcement Task Force as a supervisor.

Steven Lynch, McCormick's co-counsel in the trial, is a superior court commissioner.

Michael Bernays remains in private law practice from his Phoenix office.

Judge Michael Wilkinson retired from the bench in 2007 to teach and work for the Supreme Court.

Doug Murphy continues his career as a reporter and editorial writer.

Detectives Ron Jones, Ken Hansen, and Brian McIndoo retired from the Phoenix Police Department.

Alicia LaFlesh, with her two young sons, is in a loving relationship, and works as an auditor in the

PINNACLE BOOKS are published by

Kensington Publishing Corp.
119 West 40th Street
New York, NY 10018

All Kensington Titles, Imprints, and Distributed Lines are available at special quantity discounts for bulk purchases for sales promotions, premiums, fund-raising, and educational or institutional use. Special book excerpts or customized printings can also be created to fit specific needs. For details, write or phone the office of the Kensington special sales manager: Kensington Publishing Corp., 119 West 40th Street, New York, NY 10018, attn: Special Sales Department, Phone: 1-800-221-2647.

Pinnacle and the P logo Reg. U.S. Pat. & TM Off.

ISBN-13: 978-0-7860-2034-8
ISBN-10: 0-7860-2034-2

First printing: April 2011

10 9 8 7 6 5 4 3 2 1

Printed in the United States of America

DEADLY
DECEIT

DON
LASSETER

PINNACLE BOOKS
Kensington Publishing Corp.
http://www.kensingtonbooks.com